Privatisation and re
A review of the issu

Privatisation and regulation: A review of the issues

Edited by Peter M. Jackson and Catherine M. Price

LONGMAN
London and New York

Longman Group Limited,
Longman House, Burnt Mill,
Harlow, Essex CM20 2JE, England
and Associated Companies throughout the world,

Published in the United States of America
by Longman Publishing, New York

© Longman Group Limited 1994

First published 1994

11 200 103

ISBN 0 582 00974 X PPR

British Library Cataloguing in Publication Data
A catalogue record for this book is available from the British Library

Library of Congress Cataloging-in-Publication Data
Privatisation and regulation: a review of the issues / edited by Peter Jackson and
Catherine Price.
     p. cm. —(Longman economics series)
   Includes bibliographical references and index.
   ISBN 0-582-00974-X (Ppr)
   1. Government ownership.   2. Privatization.   3. Trade regulation.
4. Deregulation.   I. Jackson, Peter, 1946-   . II. Price, Catherine, 1948–   . III. Title:
Privatisation and regulation.
IV. Series.
HD3850. P7455   1994
338.9—dc20   93–50163
CIP

Set by 13 in 10/11pt Palatino
Produced through Longman Malaysia, TCP

Contents

Preface

Privatisation in its variety of forms has been a predominant global ideology of the 1980s. The sale of public assets, the introduction of competitive tendering, deregulation and the establishment of surrogate markets within public sector organisations are examples of the generic policy referred to as *'privatisation'*. These policies have been implemented across a variety of economies; industrialised, developing and Eastern European.

This edited volume is addressed to those readers who seek to penetrate the ideology to analyse the process and objectively examine its success and limitations. The readership will include policy makers and those who implement policy at national and international levels (including those who work in privatised entities or their regulatory agencies). Researchers in political economy, political science, management and sociology in addition to undergraduate and postgraduate students should also find a wealth of information and ideas in this volume.

The authors, distinguished experts in their own fields, have written with a minimum of jargon, to make the volume accessible to those from a variety of disciplinary backgrounds, without losing the incisiveness of their analysis. The subject impinges on everyday life and is of sufficient general interest that we hope that the book will be of interest to the general reader who seeks clarification of these important issues.

The privatisation movement has been, in part, a reaffirmation of the role of markets as a social institution which allocates scarce resources efficiently and effectively. This immediately raises questions about the limitations of markets and the necessity for regulation. These issues are addressed in this book along with those of ownership and organisation. Alternative perspectives drawn from a variety of disciplines and applications are used to illuminate understanding of these issues.

The authors invited to contribute to this volume provide a balanced view of the issues in a number of different contexts including local authority services; health services; education; recently privatised industries such as gas and electricity; developing countries and East European economies. A dominant theme which emerges is that the organisation and *'sequencing'* of change are as significant in determining outcomes as ownership per se. The role of regulation is also particularly significant.

Much of the philosophy of the privatisation programme originated in a variety of think tanks in the UK during the 1970s. This philosophy was implemented in the UK in the 1980s and the lessons learned were shared with other countries. It is for this reason that most of the chapters relate to the UK experience.

By the early *'nineties'*, a new stage of the programme had been reached. The sale of assets was largely complete and attention shifted to the implications of organising and regulating markets. These issues arose both in natural monopolies as well as *'internal markets'* in public service organisations such as the National Health Service. A number of chapters deal specifically with issues in markets at an early stage of development – in less developed countries and Eastern Europe.

The editors are grateful to each other for encouragement and to the authors for providing a stimulating, varied, yet coherent study of the subject. In particular, we are grateful to Ian Bradley, Peter Fearon, Subrata Ghatak, Audax Rutabanzibwa, and Dean Garratt at Leicester University for their helpful comments on drafts of particular chapters. All errors, as tradition has it, reside with the authors.

P. M. Jackson
C.M. Price

University of Leicester
July 1993

Acknowledgements

The publishers are grateful to the following for permission to reproduce copyright material: Chapman and Hall Ltd for a Table (6.3) from the article 'Organisational status and performance: the effects on employment' by D. Parker and K. Hartley from *Applied Economics* vol. 23, no. 2, February 1991; the Controller of Her Majesty's Stationery Office for a Table (6.1) from *Economic Progress Report* no. 193, December 1987, Crown Copyright; the Institute for Fiscal Studies for a Table (6.4) from the article 'Organisational status, ownership and productivity' by K. Hartley, D. Parker and S. Martin from *Fiscal Studies* vol. 12, no. 2, May 1991; John Wiley and Sons Ltd for a Table (6.5) from the article 'Do changes in organisational status affect financial performance?' by D. Parker and K. Hartley from *Strategic Management Journal* vol. 12, no. 8, November 1991.

Notes on contributors

Peter M. Jackson is Professor of Economics and Director of the Public Sector Economics Research Centre at the University of Leicester, author of *Public Sector Economics* (with C.V. Brown), and *The Political Economy of Bureaucracy*. He has written articles on Public Sector Economics and Public Sector Management. His current research interests include public expenditure analysis, and performance measurement of public sector organisations. He has recently published (with B. Palmer) a book: *Developing Performance Monitoring in Public Sector Organisations.*

Catherine Price is Senior Lecturer in Economics and Dean of Social Sciences at the University of Leicester. She has a long-standing interest in the public sector, particularly natural monopolies and the energy industries, and has published widely on privatisation and regulation, especially in the gas industry. She has undertaken consultancy work for the (then) Department of Energy, Office of Gas Supply, Gas Consumers' Council and several private sector energy companies.

Julia O'Connell Davidson is Lecturer in Sociology at the University of Leicester. She was formerly a researcher in the Sociology Department at Bristol University where she was involved in a three year ESRC funded research project examining restructuring and changing employment in the privatised utilities.

Tom Weyman-Jones is Senior Lecturer in Economics at Loughborough University. A graduate of LSE and the University of Melbourne, he worked in the public sector as an economist before moving into academic life first at the University of Melbourne and subsequently at Loughborough University. His research interests are in the field of privatisation and regulation of the major UK and European public utilities.

Ray Robinson is Professor of Health Policy and Director of the Institute for Health Policy Studies at the University of Southampton. Prior to joining the Institute, he was Deputy Director of the King's Fund Institute in London. Earlier in his career he was a reader in economics at the University of Sussex and also worked as an economist in HM Treasury. He is author and co-author of numerous books and articles on health and social policy including *Health Check: The NHS Reforms in an International Context*, King's

Fund, 1990 and *The Economics of Social Problems, 3rd edition,* Macmillan, 1992.

Paul Hare was educated at Cambridge and Oxford Universities and has spent most of his subsequent academic career in Scotland, first at Stirling University and since 1985 as Professor of Economics and, since 1990, Director of the Centre for Economic Reform and Transformation (CERT) at Heriot-Watt University. His research interests have always focused on the economics of Central and Eastern Europe. Recently, his research has included studies of privatisation, industrial competitiveness and industrial policy in various countries both for the ESRC and for international organisations.

Anna Canning graduated in Interpreting Translating at Heriot-Watt University, then worked in Hungary for three years for the Ecumenical Youth Council in Europe. Since joining CERT in 1991, she has worked on privatisation in Hungary and prepared a variety of other reports on Hungarian economic policy, including contributions to reports for the Economist Intelligence Unit.

Timothy Ash studied Economics at Manchester and worked as a researcher in Agricultural Economics at Exeter University before joining the Centre for Economic Reform and Transformation at Heriot-Watt University in 1991. His current research interests include privatisation in Russia, agricultural and food industry reform in Russia, and other aspects of agrarian reform in Eastern Europe. He has recently prepared reports for the FAO and for the UK government on food and agricultural policy in Eastern Europe.

Mike Wright is Professor of Financial Studies and Director of the Centre for Management Buy-out Research at the University of Nottingham. Before entering academia he was employed by British Gas. He has written extensively on accounting and control in the public sector, privatisation, management buy-outs, mergers and divestment, competition policy and the transformation of Central and Eastern Europe. His more recent books include *Management Buy-outs; Divestment and Strategic Change; Internal Organisation, Efficiency and Profit;* and *Buy-outs: New Strategies in Corporate Management.*

Steve Thompson is Professor of Managerial Economics at the University of Nottingham. He previously taught at University College Cork, UMIST and Bentley College Massachusetts. Dr Thompson has published over 50 articles in the economics and business journals and co-written three books. His current research interests involve agency problems in financial mutuals and business franchising.

David Parker has lectured in a number of universities in the UK, has been a visiting senior research fellow at the University of York and a research consultant at the University of Naples. He currently lectures in the Business School at the University of Birmingham. He has researched and published widely in the area of public sector and private sector efficiency.

CHAPTER 1

Privatisation and regulation: a review of the issues

Peter M. Jackson and Catherine Price

Introduction

Significant changes were made to the economic structure of the State during the 1980s and 1990s in both Western and Eastern Europe. First, there was the privatisation or denationalisation of many parts of the public sector which had a commercial role. Second, there was the introduction of new forms of management practice into the social services of the public sector. Third, there was a greater emphasis upon market testing with the introduction of contracting and contracting out. Fourth, many activities which had previously been the subject of State intervention and regulation were deregulated. Finally, there was a massive transition in Eastern European countries from Socialist owned and managed means of production and distribution to a privatised capitalistic system.

These changes were not confined to Europe though the pace of change, especially in Britain and Eastern Europe, was greatest there during the 1980s and 1990s. Many of the changes started in the United States have been adopted by State and Federal governments in Scandinavia, Australasia and the newly industrialised countries of Africa, Latin American and South-East Asia. Privatisation, deregulation, the opening up of markets and the expansion of the contracting state is a worldwide phenomenon, which some would claim began in Chile in the 1980s.[1]

1.1 Fiscal crisis

The origins of these changes are multi-dimensional. During the 1970s there was a breakdown in the social democratic Keynesian consensus which had, during the 30 years following the publication of the Beveridge Report, ascribed a strong social and economic role to the state. The growth of the welfare state had not only resulted in a significant expansion in the relative size of the public sector (from 25 per cent of UK GDP in 1946 to 52 per cent in 1970), it had also created powerful professional interest groups which were a challenge to the traditional power bases of politics, religion and industry. Public expenditure reflected the activities of the welfare state and was also a budgetary instrument of Keynesian short-run demand management. In less developed countries it was also used to encourage the development process.

The 1970s were years in which the intellectual climate which governed views about the relative roles of the public sector and the market-place changed. Ideas of market failure, which had provided a role for government intervention, were challenged by notions of government failure. Policies, which had been designed to alleviate the problems associated with the failures of capitalist economies, such as the great depression of 1929–33, had not provided the expected pay-off. Moreover, the concept of rational government acting dispassionately in the public interest was to be more of an ideal than a reality. Vote-maximising politicians, as the public choice theorists have demonstrated (Buchanan and Tullock 1962), will produce policies that do not necessarily serve the public interest, while utility-maximising bureaucrats (Niskanen 1971; Jackson 1982), have their own private agenda for the production of public policies.

Government failure (or public sector failure) arises because of the problems of securing appropriate incentives to pursue the public interest and appropriate information to determine what it is. Markets, on the other hand, offer solutions to these problems. They can be used to produce incentives and are efficient in their use of information. If markets are by-passed and replaced by bureaucracy then the problems of incentives and information still have to be confronted. The history of the past 40–50 years is that public sector organisations failed to confront these issues adequately. The result was a public sector which failed. It failed to deliver public services efficiently and effectively. An ideological pronouncement to do the right thing and serve the public interest was simply not enough.

Britain's nationalisation programme failed to establish an adequate framework that would ensure efficiency. The incentives for serving customer interests and controlling costs were usually non-existent or at best weak. Management were given ill defined objectives and these frequently conflicted with political objectives. The accounting systems were not appropriate to the information needs required for efficient pricing, i.e. setting prices equal to long-run marginal costs (NEDO, 1976) and investment projects were often appraised against technical criteria rather than economic hurdle rates of return. Lack of clear objectives, ambiguous incentives, poor financial information, and inadequate cost control systems all coupled with political interference to produce one unsurprising result – inefficiency.

The charges which have just been laid at the doorstep of the nationalised industries apply with equal, if not greater, force to other public services including the NHS, the education system, the defence industries and so on. Public sector managers without doubt were dedicated to the public interest and did their best, but they had to manage within an environment which gave them no clear signals about whether or not they were efficient or effective in what they did.

The stagflationary years of the 1970s, with rising levels of unemployment and inflation, were years of crisis. There was a crisis of confidence in the foundations of Keynesian policies. A situation of rising unemployment and rising rates of inflation was not easily accommodated within the Keynesian models of the day and had not, therefore, been predicted by them. Public expenditure and the welfare state were seen to be part of the problem, not the solution.

Those economists, who subscribed to the libertarian minimalist theories of the state, argued that the welfare state destroyed incentives. Unemployment benefits destroyed the incentives to search for work. Housing subsidies had destroyed the housing market and had probably been more successful in doing so than the blitz. High levels and rates of taxation, which were necessary to finance growing public spending, it was claimed, created disincentive effects which had important consequences for the supply side of the economy. High rates of taxation reduced the supply of work effort, the supply of savings and the propensity to take risk. Thus, reductions in the supply of labour and capital, especially risk capital, constrained the growth of the economy and hence, its ability to finance the welfare state. Therein lay the inherent paradox or inconsistency of the Keynesian welfare state.

Additional arguments were used to draw attention to the need to control and to reduce public expenditure. Public sector deficits rose during the stagflation years. The public sector borrowing requirement in the UK reached a maximum of 10.75 per cent of GDP in 1975. There was a great fear at the time that this would challenge the political stability of Western democracies (see Friedman, 1976). Also, the problem of how these deficits were to be financed and the economic consequences of financing them caused anxiety and concern. There was a danger that if they were to be financed by the sale of bonds then this would force up interest rates which in turn would crowd out private sector investment thereby further constraining economic growth.[2] If, on the other hand, public sector deficits were to be funded through the banking sector, then this would cause an expansion in the money supply which would spill over into even higher rates of inflation. The use of Keynesian fiscal policy was discredited by these events. Alternative policy instruments were sought, especially monetary policies.

The growth of the welfare state had brought with it an army of professional groups who supplied the services. These were teachers, doctors, dentists, planners, etc. They existed in bureaucratic organisations which were sheltered from the winds and gales of competitive forces (Schumpeter 1961). Welfare services are provided free of charge at the point of consumption. This state of affairs creates a number of potential problems. First, because consumers of welfare services do not pay directly there will be an excess demand for these services. At the same time it is in the interests of monopolised professional providers to over-supply welfare services. The consequence is that public expenditure on welfare services, in the absence of market testing, exceeds its optimum. The problem, however, does not end there. Professional groups usually decide upon the level, mix and quality of services according to their definition and assessment of need. This is usually done without reference to users' perceptions or assessments of what is required. The result is that not only is public expenditure on welfare services too high, it is also of the wrong type (Niskanen, 1971).

The processes used to produce and deliver public welfare services and the outputs of state-owned nationalised industries can be highly inefficient. In the absence of the profit motive and the disciplinary powers of competitive markets, slack and wasteful practices can arise and usually do. Within bureaucracies, incentives seldom exist to ensure that budgets are spent efficiently and effectively. Often there is no clear sense of purpose or direction. Resources are absorbed by elaborate and often ineffective control mechanisms rather than being devoted to the service itself. There is scope to serve the interests of producers rather than consumers. Weak market forces give unfettered discretionary powers to producers. Resources are, therefore, allocated according to the interests and needs of producers rather than those of consumers.

The managers of state-owned enterprises have few incentives to improve their technical efficiency. Prices of final output and their capital inputs are often heavily subsidised. Moreover, any deviation from an agreed production and financial plan can be blamed upon ministerial interference. Because it is difficult to isolate the reasons for any variance between the plan and its outcomes, monitoring and control systems are weak and accountability becomes ineffective. These conditions are an ideal breeding ground for technical inefficiency.

Over-expanded public sector budgets, the delivery of public services according to professional suppliers' assessments of what is needed rather than consumers' assessments, technical waste and inefficiency in public sector production processes, all add up to a sense of public sector failure, a failure to deliver effective public services efficiently. In other words, a failure to deliver 'value for money' (these ideas are explored at greater length in Chapter 5).

The arguments supporting the claims that the public sector had failed are simple enough, but they are contestable and they have been contested. Nevertheless, they were sufficiently persuasive at the time to cause a sense of crisis and the need to search for an alternative model. The model which emerged and which is now a significant element of the hallmark of the radicalism of the Thatcher governments of the UK during the 1980s focused upon the return to the private sector of a number of state-owned businesses, the liberalisation of markets and the exposure of welfare services to a greater degree of competition and market discipline.

1.2 The new model

The emergence of the new model, which focuses upon privatisation, and its initial successes and failures is the subject matter of the remainder of this book. Privatisation can be defined in narrow terms reserving the concept for the sale of public sector assets. Alternatively, it can be widened to incorporate a number of associated policies. No single definition is right or wrong. Each must be judged in terms of its usefulness for a specific purpose. The menu of activities which could make up a definition of privatisation includes:

- the sale of public assets
- deregulation
- opening up state monopolies to greater competition
- contracting out
- the private provision of public services
- joint capital projects using public and private finance
- reducing subsidies and increasing or introducing user charges.

Trends in privatisation have been reviewed by Heald and Steel (1982), Le Grand and Robinson (1984), Young (1986), Savas (1987), Velanovski (1987), Wiltshire (1987), Abromeit (1988), Fraser (1988), Ramanadham (1988), Vickers and Yarrow (1988), Jackson (1989), Parry (1989), Mitchell (1990), Bos (1991), Ott and Hartley (1991), and Foster (1992).

Consider first the sale of public assets: privatisation of monopoly suppliers of public utilities such as telecommunications, water, gas and electricity and industries which had earlier been taken into public ownership because of commercial failure or because they were of strategic economic importance (i.e. the 'commanding heights'), e.g. British Steel, British Leyland, Jaguar, Rolls-Royce and British Airways. Another strand to privatisation policy was the sale of council houses under the 'right to buy' programme (Forrest, 1988).

The injection of new incentive structures into those public services which remained under public ownership and control is another element of the new model and its origin predates extensive asset sales. This took a variety of forms and varied from service to service. Devolved budgeting in central government departments through the Financial Management Initiative (FMI) introduced greater clarity of objectives, improved accountability, a more focused emphasis upon performance in terms of efficiency and effectiveness and a bringing together of the responsibilities of making spending decisions and accountability for the results. At the level of local government, emphasis was also placed on the benefits of decentralised budgeting and decision making, especially through the Local Management of Schools (LMS) initiative.

The FMI programme was developed further by the Efficiency Unit which reported directly to the Prime Minister (then Mrs Thatcher) indicating the importance of a high level commitment given to improvements in the efficiency of public services. Under the direction of Sir Robin Ibbs, who had been a deputy chairman at ICI, a report was published in 1988 entitled 'Improving Management in Government: The Next Steps'. The outcome of this report was the establishment of free-standing, self-contained Executive Agencies, at arm's length from government, with enhanced managerial freedom and responsibility and a contractual obligation to deliver specified services. These agencies are not totally free from government and are not wholly part of the private domain. They are non-elected and might, in a previous time, have been thought of as 'quangos' but are overseen by a government minister who in turn is responsible to Parliament for their activities.

Delegation of decision-making powers and the devolution of budgets was also a feature of higher education institutions. The Education Reform Act of 1988 obliged local authorities to establish schemes for allocating budgets and for delegating their management to the polytechnics and colleges of higher education. The director of a polytechnic then assumed the powers and responsibilities of a chief executive with the board of governors becoming equivalent to a company board of directors. Funding was shifted out of the control of the local authorities to an independent Polytechnic and Colleges Funding Council (PCFC). Along with the traditional universities, polytechnics and colleges were encouraged to compete for students.

With the change of status of the polytechnics, when they became 'new' universities, the funding councils merged into the Higher Education Funding Councils. Research assessment exercises, external regulation of teaching quality, and the student-based resource allocation formula, rather then a block grant, has changed the incentives faced by universities. The environment is now much more competitive and a greater proportion of a university's income is now dependent not only on how well it performs relative to a variety of criteria, but also upon private funding and how well it satisfies its private sector clients.

National Health Service Trusts were introduced by the NHS and Community Care Act, 1990. Trusts provide specialist health care services which are purchased by District Health Authorities. Management of the trust is devolved and trusts can retain operating surpluses and have freedom to develop their own employment terms and conditions of service. The creation of hospital trusts again represents an introduction of more acute forms of competition into those public services which had hitherto been protected from any aspect of market forces. Other health service reforms include the introduction of internal markets into the NHS. These 'quasi' markets separate out purchasing and providing decisions and, therefore, represent threats to the professional monopoly suppliers of public services. Rather than regulate directly professionals such as doctors, internal markets supplement direct regulation with the indirect forces coming from the market-place. The expectation of the reform is that the supply of health care services will be closer to those demanded by the users of the service. Whether or not these expectations have been realised is the subject of Chapters 6 and 8.

Competitive forces have also been introduced to local authority personal services through the removal of barriers to entry. The NHS and Community Care Act, 1990 empowers local authority social services departments to consider alternative sources of supply for services such as day centres for the elderly and residential care for young persons and elderly. A local authority's own social services department now competes against external suppliers from the private and the voluntary and charitable sectors.

Many of these changes can be viewed as an attempt to ensure that those who make supply decisions about the level and quality of public services get close to the customer or user of the service and seek to elicit the views and needs of public service clients. This new wave of 'consumerism' in public services is to be found in the many variants of the Citizen's Charter, introduced in 1991. Each public service now has its own charter, for example, the NHS has a Patients' Charter. These policy initiatives seek to introduce a greater amount of consumer choice either by giving powers directly to consumers or by giving them greater and more effective 'voice' through their agents or representatives. An increasing number of general practitioners (GPs) have become 'fund holders' and are now responsible for purchasing health care services on behalf of their patients. In order to get the best out of their budgets GP fund holders need to pay attention to, and make informed judgements about, the quality and cost effectiveness of the services on offer through a variety of suppliers including the NHS trusts.

1.3 Theoretical foundations

While privatisation can be judged purely on ideological grounds as a preference for private rather than public ownership, economists have sought to establish the superiority of resource allocations based upon market mechanisms rather than the administrative fiat of bureaucracy.

The competitive forces which are to be found in markets rather than bureaucracy produce a superior allocation of resources. Privatisation will, therefore, it is claimed, provide greater incentives for cost minimisation; encourage more effective managerial supervision; and stimulate greater employee effort. The performance of privatised enterprises will be judged in terms of profits and the return on capital and not according to other objectives such as employment levels. In other words, privatisation policies change the structure of incentives and the criteria used to judge success.

The propositions set out above are simplistic and therein is to be found their popular appeal. They are, however, not as innocuous as they appear at first reading. Once they are discarded as homilies and treated instead as contestable propositions, then the logical foundation of privatisation is an area of which policy-makers need to be aware if their policies are to succeed.

Central to the analysis of privatisation is the concept of 'efficiency'. This is a term which is frequently used without careful definition. The economist uses a formal definition of efficiency – 'Pareto efficiency' – which means that it is not possible to re-arrange the firms, the flows, the production decisions, the consumption decisions or anything else in the economy, and make someone better off without making someone else worse off. The achievement of such an outcome with competitive markets depends, crucially, upon a restrictive set of assumptions; that there are constant returns to scale, that firms and consumers make decisions completely on the basis of profit and utility without any intrinsic interests in co-ordination or other people's welfare, that there are no external effects or interactions among agents outside the market place. That is to say, in perfect competition with no externalities, competitively determined prices will settle down to marginal costs. One of the most important of these assumptions is that there should be no externalities which cause private and social costs to diverge. If there is imperfect competition or other forms of market failure then the basic propositions of Pareto efficiency will not be achieved.

There are at least two principal dimensions to efficiency. First, allocative efficiency, which requires that firms produce the level, mix and quality of output at a price where it is not possible to re-arrange the outputs of an economy and make one consumer better off without making another worse off. All possible gains from trade have been exhausted. Second, there is technical or productive efficiency. This requires that the firms produce the output demanded by consumers at the lowest possible cost subject to the technical constraints of production. Technical efficiency assumes that it is not possible to re-arrange the production inputs and obtain more output of one good or service without reducing the output of another. The input mix is, therefore, efficient.

It is important to distinguish these two types of efficiency because the popular literature on privatisation has tended to focus upon technical efficiency and ignore allocative efficiency. This results in policies directed at cost-cutting while policies that might result in price reflecting costs more closely are often ignored.

Improvements in efficiency are, however, only one dimension of the economic aspects of privatisation. Other factors to consider include distribution and stability. These are of importance when evaluating the privatisation programmes of transition economies, such as those in Eastern Europe (Isachsen *et al.* 1992). Efficiency focuses attention on questions of ownership. How should property rights be organised to ensure the most efficient short-run utilisation of productive resources and real estate? These are, however, issues of static efficiency and the short run. In the longer run dynamic efficiency raises questions about the effectiveness of investment in new productive capacity. In the privatisation literature static efficiency has been over-emphasised. Little discussion centres upon whether or not there are significant market failures in the capital market and whether investment decisions made by public enterprises are more dynamically efficient than decisions made by private firms. Given the risk-pooling advantages of the public sector and the public sector's access to future tax revenues to underwrite financial risks, then the case for private decision making need not be as clear cut as is often supposed if the argument is couched purely in terms of static efficiency (Arrow and Lind, 1970).

Dynamic efficiency requires that new investments are based on correct long-term prices. In an economy where major sectors have heavily subsidised producer prices and regulated foreign trade, then unprofitable investments may result in the long run, e.g. in Eastern European and public enterprise firms. Any reforms directed at reducing subsidies in an attempt to release the forces of dynamic efficiency are likely to be restricted by interest groups who have recently implemented investments at the subsidised prices. Improvements in dynamic and static efficiency usually require, therefore, price reforms which are often difficult to accept because of their distributional and political consequences.

Questions of distributive justice are, in economics, usually set alongside those of efficiency. Okun (1975) pointed out that efficiency and equity are part of a trade-off and that the implicit prices of the trade-off are highest especially in slow growth economies. Questions arise as to how the distribution of income in the short run is affected by privatisation. In the longer run privatisation can affect the distribution of wealth by changing the distribution of property rights and entitlements to income.

Finally, how are macroeconomic variables such as inflation and unemployment influenced in the short run by privatisation? To the extent that the revenues arising from a privatisation policy are used to repay debt, replace tax revenues, or are offset against new borrowing, then privatisation can have macroeconomic consequences over the short term. In the longer term, it is questions of structural adjustment that are of interest. Does privatisation help or hinder adjustment to internal and external shocks? These issues are summarised in Table 1.1.

Table 1.1   Economic effects of privatisation

	Short term	Long term
Efficiency	Static efficiency	Dynamic efficiency
Distribution	Distribution of income	Distribution of wealth
Stabilisation	Adjustments to cyclical fluctuations	Structural adjustments

Questions of the transition of socialist economies to capitalist modes of production and distribution through large-scale privatisation programmes are treated by Ash *et al.* in Chapter 9. In these cases price reforms, changes in the structure of ownership and changes to the structure of economic incentives are elements of a privatisation programme. The nature of local capital markets places severe constraints upon the speed at which the benefits of privatisation can be realised in formerly socialist economies. These countries lack the basic financial and legal infrastructure within which transactions take place in capitalistic economies. Purchasing new and existing businesses in Eastern European countries requires a well-defined set of enforceable property rights. Those who wish to purchase capital assets need to have access to finance (i.e. borrowing) and this in turn requires developed money and capital markets. In most Eastern European countries there is no market-orientated banking system. Bankers and financial analysts who can assess the worth of a business or evaluate investments do not exist in sufficiently large numbers. Business leaders are unable to access them. This situation can quickly leave a vacuum which can have uncomfortable political consequences. For example, should foreigners be allowed to purchase firms in the formerly socialist economies? They have the finance, the managerial know-how and the technological expertise. As in the case of direct foreign investment in developing countries, if too much of the capital base of an economy is owned by foreigners, then some economic control is lost, and the initial benefit from incoming foreign investment must be balanced against the drain of profits reunited overseas.

The benefits of privatisation are the potential improvements in efficiency which come from greater competition. How effective are the disciplinary forces of the market? In order to compete in price terms, private sector firms are assumed to have a greater incentive to reduce their costs of production and distribution, i.e. improve their technical efficiency. This depends, however, upon the degree of managerial discretion. Costs which lie above their technical minimum need not result in higher prices. They might instead cut into profits. Firms can be overstaffed and managerial budgets can be greater than necessary if shareholders do not pose a creditable threat. Privatisation often results in new business relationships and constraints; e.g. management may be answerable to shareholders and subject to explicit economic regulation rather than reporting to a government minister with vaguely defined objectives. The threat of shareholders depends upon the costs of monitoring managerial effort and whether or not shareholders' power is concentrated or diffuse (Stiglitz, 1985). One of the paradoxes is that privatisation could reduce the performance of private firms by reducing shareholder power and therefore promote the conditions for a reduction in efficiency. Wider share ownership can dilute shareholder power and weaken control over the management of newly privatised firms. The government as a single agency can have more power over managers if it uses such power properly. Managerial discretion is constrained by the threat of takeover. If the performance of a company, as measured by its profitability, is well below its potential, then that will be reflected in its share price and make it a target for a takeover. The result of a takeover is to replace the existing management by managers who can improve the firm's profitability. Fear of the threat of takeover is, therefore, frequently used to justify privatisation. But how effective is the market for corporate control as a discipline on managerial discretionary behaviour? Singh (1971, 1975), Meeks (1977), Firth (1979, 1980), Grossman and Hart (1982), Hughes and Singh (1987), and Hughes (1989), suggest that there is no evidence to support the claim that performance improves after a merger or takeover. These studies are, however, challenged by Halpern (1973), Mandelker (1974) and Asquith (1983). While a theoretical case can be erected to demonstrate that the market for corporate control is an important discipline on the management of a firm and will promote improvements in performance, the empirical evidence to support it is weak and contestable. This, therefore, weakens one of the strands of the pro-privatisation thesis. In developing countries and emergent capitalist economies, the threat of takeover is slight.

Even if firms are owned and managed by a single 'owner manager', there comes a critical size beyond which the owner manager is unable to monitor all the activities within the boundaries of the firm. In that case, efficiency can deteriorate. Empirical evidence suggests that it is not just low performance that is important in the market for corporate control – the size of the firm is also of significance. Thus, a large inefficient firm has a better chance of survival (i.e. freedom from takeover) than small inefficient firms.

The exit of shareholders is one potential discipline facing the management of a firm. Exit of customers is another. If costs, prices and quality are out of line compared to those of competitors, then consumers are likely to vote with their feet and take their custom elsewhere. Consumer exit is a disciplinary measure because the resulting decline in profits will probably cause an exit of shareholders. In the case of many newly privatised firms, consumers do not have the opportunity of exercising their exit vote because the privatised firms are effectively monopolies. It is not ownership which is crucial for efficiency; rather it is the degree of competition which exists in the final product market (Yarrow, 1989).

The 'voice' option (Hirschman, 1970) rather than the exit option is too often overlooked as a source of consumer power (Ahoroni, 1986). Even if private monopolies do exist efficiency need not deteriorate if the voice of consumers and shareholders can be heard and if management act upon consumers' demands. Clearly one of the principal roles of the 'regulator' and consumer representation groups is to give voice to consumers' interests and to ensure that this voice is treated seriously.

Allocative efficiency requires that the firm produces a socially appropriate level of output using a socially efficient input combination. Large private monopolies, which exhibit economies of scale and scope, usually end up using their market power to produce below the socially efficient level. The role of government must be to promote competition and privatisation does not absolve government of this responsibility. Privatisation is not the only solution to the problem of public enterprise performance. Empirical studies suggest that increased competition and organisational reforms have been more important than change of ownership (Bishop and Kay, 1989; Yotopolous, 1989; Vernon-Wortzel *et al.*, 1989; Newbery 1990; Rowthorn and Chang, 1991).

A puzzle which emerges from the experience of privatisation is that prior to the sale of a public enterprise to the private sector, it is frequently observed that governments make a drive to improve the performance of the enterprise: fattening the calf before taking it to market. This is often more than just a cosmetic exercise of fixing the accounts by writing off debt, etc. If efficiency can be improved through better management then why sell the public enterprises – can the private market improve upon it? In the UK an extensive programme of regulatory reform within the nationalised industries was initiated after the 1978 White Paper, introducing tighter financial controls with significant effects (Bishop and Thompson, 1992). Privatisation then ceases to be a simple argument about improving efficiency and is instead squarely in the area of ideology (Bienen and Waterbury, 1989; Heller and Schiller, 1989).

Newly privatised firms have generally been monopolies, natural or otherwise. This implies the need for establishing a regulator to ensure that consumers' interests and the public interest are safeguarded. The principal problem facing the regulator is information asymmetry. In particular the regulator does not have accurate information about the firm's production function or cost function. Because of this the regulator has a problem designing an appropriate regulatory regime which would prevent the firm using its monopoly power while maintaining incentives for the firm to produce efficiently. The design of regulatory mechanisms has been examined by Vogelsang and Finsinger (1979), Baron and Myerson (1982), Baron and Besanko (1984, 1987), and Laffont and Tirole (1986). Regulatory capture, i.e. when the regulated firm bribes or influences the decisions of the regulator to its advantage, is a problem that has featured predominantly in the literature (Posner 1971; Stigler, 1971). Bhaskar (1992) gives examples of regulatory capture in developing countries, especially India. It would be fair to say that regulatory capture has not yet been a problem in the UK. The regulators, probably aware of the issue of capture, have instead been a source of threat to the firm's decisions.

Governments don't want their privatisation programme to be resisted. This might cause governments to compromise when introducing a regulatory regime. It is the government which, in a weak sense, is captured and not the regulator itself. To be acceptable to the managers of the newly privatised firm, the regulations must not be too strict to constrain their freedom to manage. Also, regulation can reduce profits and, therefore, the value of the shares in the company thereby reducing revenues to the exchequer if the government retains shares in the company.

1.4   *Privatisation and regulation*

Regulation is crucially important in assessing the privatisation of monopolies. The theory of regulation has only comparatively recently been applied in the UK context, but has a long history in the United States. Experience of UK regulation is well documentated in Veljanovski (1991) and Cave (1991) and the theory in Sherman (1989) and Train (1991). The problem of regulation is to configure the economic system so that individual economic actors making decisions in their own best interest achieve allocative efficiency for the wider society. Much of the theory (and the practice) is thus concerned with designing incentives and anticipates the choice of individual units. Early experience in the UK suggests that firms have responded to incentives much as the theory would predict.

Experience of regulation is much longer in the United States, where utilities have been in private ownership for many years. The traditional regulatory constraint has been to limit the rate of return on capital. This led to just the type of over-capitalisation which Averch and Johnson (1962) predicted. It also proved very expensive to operate. Theoretical developments centred on the responses of firms to rate of return regulation, how it affected their choice of prices and outputs and possible alternatives to rate of return regulation.

The earliest explicit consideration of regulation in the UK was by Littlechild, writing in 1983 about options for regulating British Telecom. The problems with rate of return led him to reject this method and recommend a price cap, which reinforced the cost-minimising incentives of profit maximisation rather than distorting it as rate of return regulation did. At the same time regulation was seen as a temporary expedient while competition developed, and the level of the price cap was to be determined at privatisation.

The advantages of the price cap were accepted by the UK government which proceeded to apply it to all privatised industries with a natural monopoly component. United States regulators also showed considerable interest in the price cap as an alternative to rate of return regulation (Acton and Vogelsang, 1989). The design of the price cap, its extent and the method of weighting average is superior in certain circumstances to prevent strategic behaviour on the part of the firm (Bradley and Price, 1988). However as the initial period of privatisation for each industry concludes, it becomes clear that whatever the form of the price cap its subsequent level would be determined at least in part by endogenous factors, particularly the achieved rate of return. The drawbacks of rate of return regulation thus returned to haunt the newly privatised companies.

Meanwhile the debate about the relative merits of price cap and rate of return regulation continued. Beesley and Littlechild (1989) suggested that the criteria should be the rate of change of technology and the number of firms in the industry. However the industry structure is itself partially under government control and is crucial in both the privatisation of the industry and its subsequent regulation.

The appropriate form of regulation depends on the structure of the privatised industry. Some industries are privatised as vertically and horizontally integrated monoliths (telecoms and gas) while others are desegregated before divestiture (water and electricity). In the latter case the natural monopoly element can be more easily isolated and regulated, reducing the conflict which otherwise arises between encouraging entry to increase competition and controlling incumbent firms to reduce exploitative behaviour. The timing of any restructuring of firms to be privatised (before or after flotation) is a crucial factor in determining the distribution of proceeds from the divestiture. In particular, the government may be tempted to sell firms with monopoly power intact to maximise flotation proceeds, and restructure (reducing expected profits) afterwards (for a general framework within which to analyse this trade-off see Jones, Tandon and Vogelsang, 1990). Shareholders may see this as reneging on the original privatisation bargain where the price they offered was determined by a particular industry structure. Even more insidious are changes in the regulatory bargain, where regulation has been uniformly tightened at the first review following flotation. In part this is a response to unexpectedly high profitability (emphasising the significance of rate of return) and in part a recognition that the exchequer no longer has a vested interest in the share value which depends on potential profitability. Such apparent 're-negotiation' of the privatisation terms after the event may damage the government's credibility in the later phases of the programme.

These problems of regulation and 'sequencing', even with the privatisation programme, let alone the relation to other reforms, are even more acute in developing market economies, whether these are in formerly planned economies or in areas of low income. The problems for privatising and regulating natural monopolies in such circumstances are formidable, and underline the importance of achieving an appropriate structure for the industry. These issues are discussed further in the chapters by Ash, Hare and Canning, and Price, which underline the particular significance of distributive issues in these cases. All these factors make the political dimension both unique and peculiarly sensitive in such countries.

1.5 The political dimension

The UK Conservative Party's 1979 election manifesto made no reference to the term 'privatisation' (Jackson, 1985). Prior to coming to power they did, however, have a commitment to selling shares in the National Freight Corporation (NFC), deregulation of the bus industry, the sale of council houses, and the denationalisation of shipbuilding and aerospace (Young, 1986). This was not a consistent policy that added up to a privatisation programme (Mitchell, 1990). Early justifications for privatisation were founded on economic arguments that greater competition would result in improvements in efficiency. Privatisation it was also assumed, would take pressures off public expenditure and borrowing. These arguments were not specific to the first Thatcher government of 1979. The Labour government of 1974–79 had sold assets in British Petroleum (BP) to reduce the public sector borrowing requirement.

It was not until the Thatcher government's second term, 1983–88 that it was realised that the political benefits of privatisation might exceed the economic benefits. Raising revenue from the sale of public assets was less politically damaging than raising taxes or cutting public spending and was regarded as a more acceptable means of reducing the public sector borrowing requirement (Fraser, 1988; Abromeit, 1988).

Privatisation policy emerged and evolved incrementally rather than being planned rationally as an element of a political strategy. Bishop and Kay (1988) argue that privatisation was 'a policy which was adopted almost by accident but has become politically central; a policy which has no clear-cut objectives, but has become almost an end in itself'. It was ministers such as John Moore who made *post hoc ergo propter hoc* rationalisations for the policy.

Central to the policies of Thatcherism was the objective of curbing trades union power. The Heath government had been brought down as a result of the miners' dispute and it was generally argued that the power of the unions was at the roots of the British economic disease. Privatisation of nationalised industries would not only distance government ministers from politically damaging public sector industrial relations disputes, it would also reduce the bargaining power of public sector workers' unions and their influence over policy (Marsh, 1991, 1992).

As privatisation programmes took form, they came to be justified in terms of the benefits of wider share ownership. These were set out by John Moore to be an 'increase [in] personal independence and freedom, and by establishing a new breed of owners, have an important effect on attitudes. They tend to break down the divisions between owners and earners' (see Abromeit, 1988, p. 71).

Vickers and Yarrow (1988) claim that the government gained political advantage from the privatisation programme. The evidence does not, however, wholly support this view. Crewe (1988) found from Gallup poll data that 57 per cent of those surveyed regarded the privatisation of British Gas to be a bad idea; 56 per cent had similar views about British Telecom and Electricity and 72 per cent were against the privatisation of Water before the event (see also McCarthy, 1988, for similar results based on NOP data). Over time privatisation might have become more popular among voters. That is certainly what Veljanovski (1989) found using MORI opinion poll data. The sale of council houses was undoubtedly favoured by those who had bought their homes. When Crewe (1989) analysed the British Election Survey data, he found that between 1979 and 1983 those who had bought their council homes had swung significantly towards the Conservative Government. Between 1983 and 1989 there had been a smaller swing towards the Conservatives among those who had purchased shares in the newly privatised public utilities.

These results are open to a variety of interpretations. It can be argued that, in choosing to become shareholders and owner occupiers, voters were more evidently affirming their existing social and political wishes rather than re-organising them. In a carefully executed study which used British Election Survey data and which controlled for many other intervening variables, McAllister and Studlar (1989) conclude, 'Conservatives gained 10 per cent more of the vote among new shareholders compared with those who had never owned shares, while Labour lost 9 per cent of the vote, net of other things. Similarly, council tenants who had purchased their shares showed some 15 per cent greater levels of Conservative support compared to stable council tenants, net of other things' (pp. 172–3). Conservatives, according to McAllister and Studlar gained more from selling shares than they did from selling council houses because more people bought shares than purchased council houses and then had a vested interest in the success of the programme.

1.6   *The achievements*

As Marsh (1991) points out,

> the scale of privatisation is immense. In fact, by early 1991: over 50 per cent of the public sector had been transferred to the private sector; 650,000 workers had changed sectors, of whom 90 per cent had become shareholders; 9 million people were shareholders, which represented 20 per cent of the population as compared to 7 per cent in 1979; the nationalised sector accounted for less than 5 per cent of the UK output as compared with 9 per cent in 1979; about 1,250,000 council houses had been sold, most to sitting tenants under the 'right to buy' provisions, ... (p. 463)

Did privatisation result in improvements in efficiency? While economists have long argued the virtues of competition in terms of enhanced efficiency, this debate is usually carried out at the theoretical level. It is very difficult in practice to measure efficiency and, therefore, to identify efficiency gains. Given this proviso, what conclusions have the empirical studies arrived at?

The liberalisation and deregulation of markets does not appear to have resulted in substantial improvements in efficiency. Helm and Yarrow (1988) conclude that the legislation wasn't sufficiently focused and lacked credible penalties. The new regulatory framework set up for the UK telecommunications industry is not considered to be sufficiently strong (see Gist and Meadowcroft, 1986). Similar conclusions are found for electricity (Hammond et al., 1986). Small but positive effects were found by Kemp (1990) following the liberalisation of the housing market. Barriers to entry rather than relative efficiency allowed National Express to dominate the bus industry following deregulation (Jaffer and Thompson, 1986).

A number of studies have reported cost savings as a result of the contracting out of services: see Domberger et al., 1986, and Cubbin et al. 1987, for refuse collection; Hartley and Hubey, 1985; Ascher, 1987; and Domberger et al., 1987, for hospital and local authority services. These and other studies are reviewed in Chapter 5.

It has already been argued that it is difficult to identify efficiency gains. Equally it is difficult to attribute cost savings purely to greater competition. Costs can be cut if the quality of service is reduced. If the service user would prefer to pay for a higher quality but is given no choice then such cost cutting cannot be counted as an efficiency improvement (Gomley and Grahl, 1988). Also, as is argued and demonstrated clearly in Chapter 5 of this volume, the consequences of contracting out and other forms of privatisation have been a deterioration in the pay and conditions of employment of workers.

Economists are now generally agreed that simply changing the ownership of assets is not sufficient, and indeed is not even necessary, to improve efficiency. What is important is the threat of competition and, therefore, market conditions and perhaps the regulatory regime (Bishop and Thomson, 1992). The sale of assets did little for efficiency and must instead be judged in terms of the effects of change of ownership on the distribution of entitlements in the economy. Vickers and Yarrow (1988) argue that, 'By failing to introduce sufficiently effective frameworks of competition and regulation before privatising such industries as telecommunications and gas, the Government has lost a major opportunity to tackle fundamental problems experienced in the past under public ownership' (p. 425).

One explanation for the maintenance of the near or absolute monopoly position of the newly privatised industries and the weakness of the regulatory framework is that the chairman of the companies managed to 'capture' their sponsor departments prior to privatisation. 'The BT managers, for instance, succeeded – quite conspicuously – in inducing the Government to drop most of its original ideas about liberalisation in the telecommunications industry', Abromeit (1988) p. 75. The maintenance of a monopoly structure also made the sale of assets more attractive in terms of the share price at flotation (Baldwin, 1990; Thompson, 1990). To introduce a complex market infrastructure, which would have increased competition, would have delayed the privatisation programme notoriously in the case of BG. Both of these arguments suggest that the government probably had a closer eye on the revenue consequences of how privatisation should be implemented rather than on achieving the greatest improvement in economic efficiency.

Have the newly privatised companies improved their efficiency? Curwen (1986) shows that the picture is variable. Some have improved their performance while others have not. Moreover, many of the companies which were privatised, especially the early privatisations, were relatively efficient prior to privatisation. Veljanovski (1990) is much more bullish and claims substantial improvements in performance. Dunsire *et al.* (1991) found that if they used total factor productivity (TFP) as a measure of efficiency and compared the TFP of the newly privatised enterprises with the national trend, then only the National Freight Corporation was above trend. Using productivity as an alternative performance measure resulted in only the Royal Ordnance Factory showing an improvement: see Parker, Chapter 6 in this volume. Bishop and Kay (1988), and Thompson (1990), could not find any significant improvement in productivity following privatisation though the picture was patchy when a profitability measure was used. Foreman-Peck and Manning (1988) compared British Telecom with its European counterparts and could not conclude that it performed better than the state-owned monopolistic telecommunication firms elsewhere in Europe. That, however, is a different issue. It suggests that change of ownership is not sufficient for efficiency levels but how did the efficiency of the privatised BT compare to the previous state-owned monopoly? Pitt (1990) demonstrates that BT introduced managerial and organisational changes that improved performance, however these conclusions are disputed by Foreman-Peck (1990).

The lack of competition resulted in reliance being placed upon a new regulatory framework in which the regulator played a significant role in ensuring the protection of consumers' interests. These regulatory agencies OFTEL, OFGAS, OFFER, OFWAT have been the subject of critical evaluation (Helm and Yarrow, 1988). They are hampered by access to relevant information and by formal legislative powers and need to proceed through complex and time-consuming processes of consultation and negotiation with the privatised companies (see Graham and Prosser, 1988; Vickers and Yarrow, 1988; Pitt, 1990; Gilland, 1992; Spring, 1992).

The success of privatisation should not only be judged in terms of improvements in performance indicators such as productivity and profitability. Such measures focus upon the distribution of benefits primarily to shareholders. There are other stakeholders in the benefits of privatisation, especially consumers, who need to be considered. Consumers can benefit from privatisation by paying less for their service, by facing more stable prices, or by receiving an improvement in the quality of the service. Bunn and Vlahos (1989) suggest that privatisation of electricity will increase electricity prices in the long run. While quality of service is difficult to measure, Thompson (1990) suggests it has not improved. There is, however, now a general move within the public sector to get closer to the customer and to pay greater attention to public service users' perceptions of quality (Clarke and Stewart, 1991), a trend fostered by the government's emphasis on consumer charter and performance indicators. The threat of competitive tendering has probably been important in promoting changes in managerial practice which place much more emphasis upon ensuring that the standards of public services are in greater accord with users' requirements.

Any benefits of privatisation must be set against the cost of achieving them. It has already been mentioned that one possible source of efficiency gain is the redundancy of public sector workers and the changes in the wages and conditions of those who remain with the privatised firm (see Ascher, 1987; Milne, 1987; Chapter 6 (this volume). Another is an increase in the prices charged to consumers or a reduction in the quality of service. In a complex economic system, changes in the distribution of the rents paid to the different stakeholders will influence any assessment of whether or not privatisation is judged to be a good thing. If all of the efficiency gains end up with shareholders (capital) at the expense of customers and workers, then the last two groups of stakeholders are unlikely to vote in favour of more privatisation. The issues, however, are more complex than this. What is happening in this argument is that short-run gains and losses are being compared. The distribution of dynamic efficiency improvements in the long run might be of more significance. These benefits are, however, difficult to identify, difficult to assure, and, therefore, difficult to sell to the public. In any case, as Keynes pointed out, in the very long run we are all dead. The long run might be too far away; so let's discount it heavily and focus on the short run. Short-termism might not be economically optimal but it can be significant for the purposes of politics and short-term electoral cycles.

Privatisation is not costless. There are important transactions costs that need to be offset against any gains. First, there are the agency costs of floating new shares on the stock market. These costs in the UK have totalled about £3 billion. Second, there are the costs of discounting the new share prices at the time of flotation. This added about another £2 billion.

In developing countries there is a shortage of qualified accountants to value public enterprises and take them to market. This is a significant constraint on the privatisation programme. The same problems exist in the recently socialist economies of Eastern Europe. The costs of underwriting share issues and the costs of floating shares are additional constraints in such economies.

Did privatisation curb trade union power? Vickers and Yarrow (1988) argue that the privatised companies will have fewer resources than the government to resist union pressures and could not ride a year-long strike as the government managed to do with the miners in 1984–85. Pitt (1990) records major changes to industrial relations systems in British Telecom following privatisation but few changes were made at British Gas (Thomas, 1986). Marsh (1991) notes that,

> There seems little doubt that the situation for unions has worsened in many of these companies, but there is doubt both as to how much it has worsened and how far this change results from privatisation . . . Overall, it seems fair to

conclude that the change in ownership involved in privatisation has had a limited effect on trade unions. It is significant that while membership of public sector unions declined, there is no clear pattern in that decline . . . it was public sector industries largely unaffected by privatisation (the coal industry and the railways) and in the civil service where union membership fell most dramatically (pp. 473–4).

1.7 Privatisation and developing countries

Public enterprises are usually a large component of a developing country's economic activity. Poor performance in the public enterprise sector, which is reflected in high debt levels, low productivity and poor profitability can, therefore, constrain the rest of the economy and act as a brake on economic growth and development. Bhaskar (1992) found that 21 out of the 25 developing countries that he studied contributed significantly to public sector debt and to the countries' external debts: the median share was 48 per cent. Public enterprises absorb a large share of national savings and seldom have a higher than average capital productivity.

Privatisation is a policy which has been strongly advocated by the IMF and the World Bank to improve the performance of state run enterprises and for developing countries to reduce their levels of debt. Over 31 developing countries had some kind of privatisation programme when the World Bank surveyed them in 1990. In most developing countries, however, the amount of privatisation has been small scale: Bangladesh is the biggest privatiser in Asia; Chile the biggest in South America; Nigeria the biggest in Africa; and Malaysia the biggest in South-East Asia (Adams and Cavendish, 1991). Analysis is somewhat complicated by the encouragement of policies which can be labelled 'privatisation', even where their content is not clearly described.

The trends and outcomes of privatisation in developing countries are examined by Price in Chapter 10. One of the problems of assessing the outcome of a privatisation programme is that attention is often given to the short-term gains while changes over the long run are ignored. Privatisation in Chile in 1973, for example, was followed by government intervention in the longer term. Forestry privatisation resulted in a massive increase in forestry exports. Between 1971 and 1980 the US dollar value of exports rose 15-fold. Reafforestation, however, declined and the government had to intervene with a regulatory policy. The privatised sugar mills failed in 1983 because they had built up too much debt. Government intervention saved them.

Privatisation in Chile took place in the depths of a recession, so public companies were purchased at rock bottom prices. The government did not receive much revenue from the sale. Those who purchased the enterprises tended to be those who had access to capital markets (especially international finance). The result was a concentration of ownership (see Marshall, 1986; Yotopoulos, 1989).

Since 1982 over 500 industrial and commercial companies in Bangladesh have been transferred from public to private ownership. The ratio of government spending to GDP fell from 90 per cent (1982) to 40 per cent (1990). Bhaskar (1992) examined in detail a number of case studies of recently privatised companies in Bangladesh. In the case of cotton textiles, profitability fell and the output of yarn fell following privatisation.

Jute textiles are used in the production of hessians, sacking cloth and carpet backing cloth. Following privatisation, production was shifted away from hessian towards sacking cloth reflecting the relatively higher profit margins on sacking. While this might indicate that privatisation had been successful, it was a short-run gain. In the longer run, employment and total output in the jute textile industry fell.

Many of the studies of privatisation in developing countries suggest that privatisation has not produced the dynamic efficiency gains that had been hoped for. Why is this? First, in many cases firms were sold back to their former owners who were not necessarily the best people with the appropriate skills to manage them. Second, after privatisation managers seek subsidies, legal protection for the firms and licences to give them monopoly powers. This rent-seeking behaviour often has a bigger pay-off than putting energies into improving the efficiency and productivity of the firm.

Privatisation did, however, help the public finances of developing countries but not by as much as is often supposed. The burden of the losses of newly privatised industries are absorbed by the publicly owned financial institutions; 'Unless privatisation is accompanied by financial reform, which makes the private sector accountable for its decisions, the burden may only be concealed' (Bhaskar, 1992, p. 30). The government might also be forced, because of the under-development of capital markets, to sell assets to foreigners or to ethnic minorities against whom there might be resentment. This can result in social and political instability. Under-developed capital markets often result in direct sales of assets rather than floating shares on stock markets. Assets are, therefore, often underpriced resulting in a loss in revenue for the government.

Not all state owned enterprises are inefficient. The most efficient steel company in the world is the Korean Posco (Pohang Steel Company) which is state owned. Other examples of high-performance public enterprises include the Kenyan Tea Development Authority; the Ethiopian Telecommunications Authority; the Tanzanian Electric Supply Company and the Guma Valley Water Company of Sierra Leone. These observations give rise to a number of puzzles and questions which await answers. Why should some public enterprises be so successful? What makes them so and why are others so inefficient? Is it all down to establishing an appropriate system of incentives which privatisation promises but doesn't always deliver or is there another answer awaiting discovery?

1.8 Privatisation in centrally planned economies

Since the opening up of Eastern Europe and Russia, no-one can deny that the debilitating dominance of the state over economic activities resulted in an erosion, and eventually paralysis, of incentives to do anything about improving efficiency. Levels of pollution beyond tolerable limits, inadequate working and living conditions, the lack of variety and the suspension of consumer choice, all illustrate, often with poignant imagery, the failure to achieve reasonable social objectives. Provided the managers of state enterprises complied with the centrally determined plan, they were rewarded. Performance was not judged and, therefore, good performance was neither defined nor rewarded. Losses were constantly underwritten. The managers of state-owned enterprises faced what Kornai (1986) has termed 'soft budget' constraints.

The privatisation of centrally planned economies is a major task in social and economic engineering. It means creating markets and all the associated legal, commercial, and socio-political infrastructure that is necessary to enable markets to perform effectively.

Trading through markets requires well-defined property rights and a legal system which will design and enforce contracts. Exchange in a monetary economy needs a commercial and a banking system which will provide financial and commercial instruments to facilitate internal and external trade. Privatised trade in a monetary economy most of all requires 'trust', without which transactions costs will be high. Consider the legal and commercial infrastructure and the amount of trust which lies behind effecting a transaction when a cheque is written to pay for goods. Even more imagination is required when payment is made by means of a plastic credit card!

Change takes time and needs to be carefully managed. The sequence through which changes will be implemented needs to be carefully considered. Are all of the necessary pieces of the jigsaw of the infrastructure in place for trade to be effective? This cannot happen with a big bang. Not only design but also negotiating new systems into place is also time-consuming. Most important it will take time to re-orientate and train the population to accept the new system and to work, with confidence, within it. It takes time for trust to be built. Early demonstrations of the benefits of the new regime compared to the old will be essential. This has important implications.

The experience of privatisation in centrally planned economies is reviewed in Chapter 9 by Ash, Hare and Canning. Other contributions to this debate include Blanchard *et al.,* (1991), and Corbo *et al.,* (1991).

1.9   Decentralisation and the contract state

Privatisation is regarded by some as part of a more general trend in society towards post-Fordism (see Hoggett, 1991, and Jessop, 1991). While terms such as Fordism and post-Fordism, and the concepts which lie behind them, are ambiguous and not part of the generally accepted currency of social science, nevertheless, they are used to describe periods of socio-economic history. They are labels which some have adopted in an attempt to account for what is going on in society. Fordism refers to the age of large-scale mass production of standardised products for mass markets and large-scale private bureaucracies organised on hierarchical designs to service such manufacturing systems. At the macroeconomic level, Fordism acknowledges the Keynesian interventionist welfare state.

As such, Fordism is a *post hoc* generalisation of what has happened. Fordism has not disappeared but it is now challenged as being the unique best way of managing and organising. Post-Fordism attempts to describe and rationalise the changes that took place in the 1970s and to extrapolate and speculate about where the trends that started in the 1970s might be leading.

During the 1970s, new computer-based technologies introduced greater amounts of flexibility and information and challenged the inflexibility of routinised bureaucracies. Product markets also changed. Standardised products for mass markets gave way to greater variety and customisation of products, greater market segmentation and niche marketing, and products with a shorter life span. New and more flexible organisations were introduced that improved response times to market changes. Loose/tight organisations were designed in which the centre loosens control over production and decentralises more decision-making while retaining central control over the making of strategy. The post-Fordism model of organisation is one of a central core with the periphery of decentralised cost and profit centres serviced by ever more sophisticated management information systems. The post-Fordism state replaces the Keynesian welfare state by the Schumpeterian entrepreneurial state and gives the state a greater regulatory role. The role of the state is seen to encourage enterprise and economic growth and to regularise economic relationships. The state itself is also in need of regulation and so greater emphasis is placed upon the design of constitutions that will constrain state activity (see Brennan and Buchanan, 1980).

The decentralising tendencies which characterise the privatisation programmes are easily accommodated under the post-Fordism label. Whether or not privatisation is part of post-Fordism or whether privatisation gives substance to post-Fordism is an ontological debate that will continue. Privatisation does involve the decentralisation of decision-making through markets rather than bureaucracies and also creates a decentralised network of decision-making within public service organisations. In both cases, decentralisation is accompanied by demands for greater democratic accountability and community (customer) involvement in decision-making. Neither the right nor the left of the political spectrum wants a return to the inflexible centralised bureaucratic monopoly supply of public services. There does, however, remain the problem of how best to manage (regulate) the new system. A vacuum exists which remains to be filled. New systems of public administration involving regulatory control are being experimented with.

Decentralisation describes a number of tendencies not all of which need be present at the same time. Decentralisation is most readily understood as a pushing down within an organisation to those who deliver public services the right to make accountable decisions without continual referral to a higher authority for approval. Planning and control functions have increasingly been devolved to business units within public service organisations. The break-up of inflexible bureaucratic hierarchies and their replacement with leaner, flatter, more flexible and faster structures is another feature of decentralisation. Decentralisation involves a new structure of responsibilities and new forms of accountability. It requires information about the performance of devolved units (see Jackson and Palmer, 1993).

One strand of the government's privatisation programme in the UK has been to introduce greater amounts of decentralisation into public services organisations. The belief is that efficiency, and hence, value for money, will be improved through the creation of service units and business units that are closer to public service customers, that can respond quicker and more accurately to their needs, and which will, if appropriate to do so, engage in a greater degree of market testing. The introduction of surrogate competitive market systems, such as the internal market in the NHS and local authorities, the greater use of competitive tendering, and measurement of the performance of decision-making units are all reflections of greater decentralisation.

These changes have transformed the landscape of the public sector. Whereas in the past, central and local government departments were responsible for both the financing and production of public services, this is now, increasingly, giving way to the State purchasing (financing) services from a variety of alternative public and private sector producers. There is now emerging a clearer division (at the conceptual level) between the roles of purchaser and provider. Local authorities, for example, are becoming viewed as *'enabling councils'*, charged with the responsibility of ensuring that services are provided irrespective of the source of supply (Stewart 1986, Clarke and Stewart 1990; Osborne and Gaebler, 1992). It does not matter who produces the service, the public sector, the private sector or the voluntary sector, provided that the services are supplied and provided they are delivered in a way that gives value for money. Provision is different from production and while public sector economists have long recognised this (Musgrave, 1958), it has not been reflected in the institutions of public service supply. The split between purchaser and provider gives rise to the new notion of the 'contract state'. Providers of public services compete for contracts. Competition might take place in external markets, as in competitive tendering, or in internal or quasi markets. The requirements of value for money can be written into contracts and made explicit while performance measurement and monitoring systems can inform whether or not value for money has been delivered.

In the contract state, budgets and decision-making powers are devolved to purchasers who bid for resources on behalf of their client group. The purchaser then buys services from that supplier who, in competition, offers the best value for money. The performance of the contractor is then monitored through a set of well-chosen indicators. Recent experiences of the contract state, as it applies to the NHS and education, are discussed by Jackson in Chapter 5.

1.10 Privatisation and efficiency

Has privatisation resulted in improvements in efficiency as was hoped for by the advocates of the programme? The chapters in this volume represent a systematic attempt to answer this question. Efficiency or performance of a market-based organisation are usually evaluated in terms of the organisation's profitability but the concept of profitability is problematic because there are a number of alternative measures to choose from and it is incomplete since it does not include consumer welfare. Different measures of profitability will give different answers to questions about performance. Theory distinguishes between two broad classes or measures of profit, first, accounting rates of return which focus upon accounting definitions of profit which are essentially revenues minus recorded costs and second, economists' definitions of rates of return which attempt to measure 'normal' profit (Harcourt, 1965; Fisher and McGowan, 1983; Kay and Mayer, 1986; Edwards, *et al.*, 1987). Profit calculations are influenced by accounting conventions such as whether or not it is historic or current costs that are used and how depreciation is calculated. These issues were reviewed in the context of public enterprises in the Byatt Report (1986). Problems also arise if the share price is used as a measure of performance. The dividend growth model of share valuation should, if capital markets are efficient and investors have rational expectations, reflect future profits, but many factors, including sentiment, will affect share prices. Also, at the time of flotation, the shares of the newly privatised companies were undervalued (Chown, 1993). Measuring improvements in efficiency by reference to increases in the share price and then attributing them to the act of privatisation will bias the conclusions. Because the privatised companies are monopolies it is difficult to separate out any improvements in technical efficiency from the effects arising from the market power of monopoly.

Kay (1992) has reviewed the performance of privatised firms by reference to telecommunications, gas and steel. The rate of return on British Telecom operations rose dramatically after privatisation from 14.2 per cent to 25.6 per cent in 1988. However, performance with respect to customer satisfaction and the quality of service was severely criticised by the regulator, OFTEL, in 1987. British Telecom responded rapidly to these criticisms (evidence of the importance of the regulator) and by 1988, 83 per cent of customers were fairly satisfied. This rose to 87 per cent in 1989 and fell to 84 per cent in 1990. The Deloitte, Haskins and Sells (1983) study of the efficiency of the British Gas Corporation prior to privatisation in 1986, concluded that its performance during the 1970s was that of, 'which any commercial organisation could be proud'. (Why, therefore was it privatised?) There was, however, a wide variation in the efficiency of the different gas regions (confirmed by Price and Weyman-Jones, 1993). British Gas had always met the financial targets set by government but the Deloitte report questioned whether or not these were challenging enough and, therefore, whether there was not scope for improvements in efficiency. Privatisation clearly wasn't necessary to tighten financial targets and get British Gas management more focused. During 1988, British Gas was the subject of a Monopolies and Mergers Commission study of its pricing policy to industrial customers and in 1989–90 substantial changes were made to the structure of its industrial market. Decentralised business units were set up. This gave management greater freedom over day-to-day matters while establishing a centralised framework that gave clearer corporate objectives and measures of performance. Profits have increased during the post privatisation period but whether or not British Gas is more efficient than it would otherwise have been is a moot point (Price, 1991).

Aylens' (1988) study of the UK steel industry found that the performance of the British Steel Corporation improved dramatically as a result of privatisation. In 1980, British Steel was one of the lowest performing UK companies producing steel at prices significantly higher than its competitors. By the mid-1980s this had reversed and the privatised British Steel Corporation was among the world's leaders in the steel industry. This was not only achieved by changing ownership. Radical managerial and organisational reforms were introduced. Decentralised business units with clear commercial objectives which focused on outcomes, were established. Productivity bonuses were paid which in 1987 represented about 20 per cent of steel workers' total earnings. The improvement in performance reflects the changes that were made to the incentive structure facing both management and the work force.

What happened to the performance of the public enterprises that were not privatised? How did they compare? Over the period 1979–83, they did not perform well. That probably had much to do with the recession. Public enterprises such as British Coal, British Airports Authority, British Rail and the Post Office have business bases that are sensitive to what is happening more generally in the economy. After 1983, the performance of these industries improved significantly. The performance gains in British Coal and British Rail exceeded those in the privatised British Telecom and greatly exceeded the performance of British Gas (Bishop and Thompson, 1992).

It would be wrong to judge the success or the performance of the privatisation programme purely in terms of cost efficiency. Society has other goals and these were in large measure reflected in the objectives of the public enterprises. In addition to serving customer needs, public enterprises were used as instruments of government policy to assist with the achievement of employment generation, the development of under-developed regions, earning foreign exchange, and distributional equity. Where the market infrastructure is under-developed, as in developing countries, public enterprises play an important role in meeting these objectives. As has been pointed out already, however, the efficiency objective can come into conflict with these other objectives and that has been an age-old problem facing politicians and the managers of public enterprises. Not only do the objectives conflict but this can provide a point of friction that creates conflict between public enterprise managers and their political masters.

Transferring public enterprises into the private domain means that the trade-off between the efficiency objective and other objectives, such as distributional justice and macro-stabilisation, becomes heavily skewed in favour of efficiency and needs to be made explicit. In a post-privatised world, how are these other objectives to be achieved? The new classical economists will argue that liberalised markets will solve these problems, but it is because markets are imperfect or fail to exist that the problems arise in the first place. One way of obtaining social policy outcomes would be to contract directly with the privatised sector to deliver them. In practice, such a contract would be very complex, difficult to write and even more difficult to monitor and enforce. These problems, however, do not make it an uninteresting suggestion. But these difficulties are not different from the problems that have been faced to date by public enterprise managers who have had in effect a similar 'implicit' contract. Is there any reason to believe that private enterprise managers would find it any easier to deliver the contract?

Another way of proceeding would be to define 'social profits' using the differences between social benefits and social costs. Managers would be given 'social prices', which may differ from market prices, to be used in pricing, output, and investment decisions (see Vernon-Wortzel and Wortzel, 1989; Sen, 1982).

This discussion opens up the issue of which efficiency objective is being pursued. Is it the narrow notion of private efficiency or the wider concept of social efficiency? Capitalist systems produce significant externalities, few of which can themselves be adequately traded through markets. Unless a privatisation programme is accompanied by policies which will establish a full set of highly competitive markets and other means of achieving distributional and stabilisation objectives, then private efficiency will drive out social efficiency and active socio-economic policy will be set back decades.

Productivity growth and performance do not seem to be related to privatisation (a change in ownership) in any clear or unambiguous way. Privatisation seems to be neither necessary nor sufficient. What then is significant? The managerial 'culture' in both public and privatised organisations has changed. The value and the belief system has been revolutionised. There is now a greater emphasis upon establishing clear commercial objectives; measuring performance in terms of outputs rather than inputs; improving management information systems, especially financial systems; introducing effective cost control mechanisms; and ensuring that the incentive systems of rewards are compatible with the objectives. In the final analysis it is the design of incentive structures which is crucial for economic performance.

Competition rather than privatisation *per se* seems to be the main stimulus to efficiency improvements. It has been in industries such as steel where competition is strongest that the greatest improvements have been made. Those privatised industries, such as gas, which still enjoy the protection created by their monopoly power, have not shown dramatic improvements in performance.

An element of the 'folklore' of economic thought is that increased competition will yield welfare gains by reducing internal slack in organisations. These are regarded to be the dynamic effects of the market. The efficiency gains from some of the privatisations of public enterprises seem to bear this out. Nevertheless, it must be recognised that the nature of the discipline of the market and the mechanisms through which welfare gains are effected remains vague. The whole literature on the separation of ownership from control from Berle and Means (1933) to Williamson (1985) and the more recent analysis of principal/agent relationships is a testimony to this.

Privatisation is not a panacea. It creates new problems while solving old ones or recreates the difficulties which nationalisation and increased public activity sought to solve. It provides an attractive solution to governments who wish to reduce (or stabilise) fiscal deficits. But that is a one-shot solution. The family silver can only be sold once. The experiences and early lessons along with the analytical foundations of privatisation in its many forms (which is the subject matter of this book) are described in the following chapters.

Notes

1. See Berg and Shirley (1988); the military takeover in Chile in 1973 reversed the socialist policies introduced by the Allende government which had taken over 500 enterprises into state ownership and placed them under state control. In 1973 trade and capital markets were liberalised, prices were decontrolled and a rigorous monetary policy was introduced.
2. Presumption is that all private sector investment spending is more productive than public spending.

References

Abromeit, H. (1988) British privatisation policy, *Parliamentary Affairs*, vol. 41, no.1, pp. 68–85.

Acton, J. and **Vogelsang, I.** (1989) Introduction, Symposium on price cap regulation, *Rand Journal of Economics*, vol. 20, no. 3, pp. 369–72.

Adams, C. and **Cavendish, W.** (1991) Can privatisation succeed? Economic structure and programme design in eight commonwealth countries, *Working Paper No. 34*, Oxford: Centro Studi Luca D'Angliano, Queen Elizabeth House.

Aharoni, Y. (1986) *The Evolution and Management of State-Owned Enterprises*, Cambridge, Massachusetts: Balinger Publishing Company.

Arrow, K. J. and **Lind, R. C.** (1970) Uncertainty and the evaluation of public investment, *American Economic Review*, June.

Ascher, K. (1987) *The Politics of Privatisation: Contracting Out Public Services*, Basingstoke: Macmillian.

Asquith, P. (1983) Merger bids, uncertainty and stockholder returns *Journal of Financial Economics*, vol. 11, pp. 51–83.

Averch, H. and **Johnson, L.** (1962) Behaviour of the Firm Under Regulatory Constraint, *American Economic Review*, vol. 52, no. 5.

Aylen, J. (1988) Privatisation of the British Steel Corporation, *Fiscal Studies*, vol. 9, no. 3, pp. 1–26.

Baldwin, P. (1990) Privatisation and regulation: the case of British Airways, in J. Richardson (ed.), *Privatisation and Deregulation in Canada and Britain,* Aldershot: Dartmouth.

Baron, D. and **Besanko, D.** (1984) Regulation, asymmetric information and auditing, *Rand Journal of Economics,* vol. 15, pp. 447–70.

Baron, D. and **Besanko, D.** (1987) Commitment and fairness in a dynamic regulatory relationship, *Review of Economic Studies,* vol. 54, pp. 413–36.

Baron, D. and **Myerson, R.** (1982) Regulating a monopolist with unknown costs, *Econometrica,* vol. 50, pp. 911–30.

Beesley, M. and **Littlechild, S.** (1989) The regulation of privatised monopolies in the United Kingdom, *Rand Journal of Economics,* vol. 20, no. 3, pp. 454–72.

Berle, A. A. and **Means, G. C.** (1933) *The Modern Corporation and Private Property,* New York: Macmillan.

Bhaskar, V. (1992) Privatization and the developing countries: the issues and the evidence (mimeo) UNCTAD Geneva Discussion Paper 47, August.

Bienen, H. and **Waterbury, J.** (1989) The political economy of privatisation in developing countries, *World Development,* vol. 17, no. 5.

Bishop, M. R. and **Kay, J. A.** (1988) Does privatization work? Lessons from the UK, Centre for Business Strategy Report, London Business School.

Bishop, M. and **Kay, J.** (1989) Privatisation in the United Kingdom: lessons from Experience, *World Development* vol. 17, no. 5.

Bishop, M. and **Thompson, D.** (1992) Regulatory Reform and Productivity Growth in the UK's Public Utilities, *Applied Economics,* vol. 24, pp. 1181–90.

Blanchard, O., Dornbush, R., Krugman, P., Layard, R., and **Summers, L.** (1991) *Reform in Eastern Europe,* WIDER Macroeconomics Policy Group; MIT Press.

Bos, D. (1991) *Privatization,* Oxford: Clarendon Press.

Bradley, I. and **Price, C.** (1988) The economic regulation of private industries by price constraints, *Journal of Industrial Economics,* vol. xxxvii, no. 1, pp. 99–106.

Brennan, G. and **Buchanan, J. M.** (1980) *The Power to Tax: Analytical Foundations of a Fiscal Constitution,* Cambridge: Cambridge University Press.

Buchanan, J. M. and **Tullock, G.** (1962) *The Calculus of Consent,* Ann Arbor: University of Michigan Press.

Bunn, D. and **Vlahos, K.** (1989) Evaluation of the long term effects of UK electricity prices following privatisation, *Fiscal Studies,* pp. 104–16

Byatt Report (1986) *Accounting for Economic Costs and Changing Prices,* London: HMSO.

Carbo, V., Coricelli, J. and **Bossak, J.** (eds) (1992) *Reforming Central and Eastern European Economies,* World Bank, Washington DC.

Cave, M. (1991) Recent developments in the regulation of former nationalised industries, Government economic service working paper No. 114, HM Treasury.

Chown, J. F. (1993) The costs of privatization, *Economic Affairs,* April, pp. 22–4.

Clarke, M. and **Stewart, J.** (1990) *General Management in Local Government: Getting the Balance Right,* Longman, in association with the Local Government Training Board.

Clarke, M. and **Stewart, J.** (1991) *Choices for Local Government for the 1990s and Beyond,* London: Longman.

Crewe, I. (1988) Has the electorate become more Thatcherite? in R. Skidelsky (ed.) *Thatcherism,* London: Chatto and Windus.

Crewe, I. (1989) The decline of Labour and the decline of labour, *Essex Papers in Politics and Government,* no. 65.

Cubbin, J., Doinberger, S. and **Meadowcroft, S.** (1987) Competitive tendering and refuse collection, *Fiscal Studies,* pp. 49–58.

Curwen, P. (1986) *Public Enterprise: A Modern Approach,* London: Wheatsheaf.

Deloitte, Haskins and **Sells** (1983) *British Gas Efficiency Study,* London: Deloitte, Haskins, and Sells.

Domberger, S., Meadowcroft, S. and **Thompson, D.** (1986) Competitive tendering and efficiency: the case of refuse collection, *Fiscal Studies,* pp. 69–87.

Domberger, S., Meadowcroft, S. and **Thompson, D.** (1987) The Impact of Competitive tendering on the costs of hospital domestic services, *Fiscal Studies,* pp. 39–54.

Dunsire, A., Hartley, K. and **Parker, D.** (1991) Organisational status and performance: a summary of the findings, *Public Administration,* vol. 69, no. 1, pp. 21–40.

Edwards, J. E., Kay, J. A. and **Mayer, C.** (1987) *The economic analysis of profitability,* Oxford: Clarendon Press.

Firth, M. (1979) The profitability of takeovers and mergers, *Economic Journal,* vol. 89, pp. 316–28.

Firth, M. (1980) Takeovers, shareholder returns, and the theory of the firm, *Quarterly Journal of Economics,* vol. 94, pp. 235–60.

Fischer, S. and **McGowan G. E.** (1983) On the misuse of accounting rates of return to inter monopoly profits, *American Economic Review.*

Foreman-Peck, J. (1990) Ownership, competition and productivity growth: the impact of liberalisation and privatisation on BT, University of Warwick Economic Research Papers, no. 338.

Foreman-Peck, J. and **Manning, D.** (1988) How well is BT performing?: An international comparison of telecommunications total factor productivity, *Fiscal Studies,* pp. 54–67.

Forrest, R. (1988) *Selling the Welfare State: the Privatisation of Public Housing,* London: Routledge.

Foster, C. D. (1992) *Privatisation, Public Ownership and the Regulation of Natural Monopoly,* Blackwell: Oxford.

Fraser, R. (1988) *Privatisation: The UK Experience and International Trends,* London: Longman.

Friedman, M. (1976) The line we dare not cross, *Encounter.*

Gilland, T. (ed.) (1992) *Incentive Regulation,* Public Finance Foundation: Centre for the Study of Regulated Industries.

Gist, P. and **Meadowcroft, S.** (1986) Regulating for competition: the newly liberalised market for branch exchanges, *Fiscal Studies,* pp. 41–66.

Goodrich, J. (ed.) *Privatisation in Global Perspective,* London: Pinter. *Canada and Britain,* Aldershot: Dartmouth.

Gomley, J. and **Grahl, J.** (1988) Competition and efficiency in refuse collection: a critical comment, *Fiscal Studies,* pp. 80–5.

Graham, C. and **Prosser, T.** (1988) Rolling back the frontiers, in C. Graham and T. Prosser, *Waiving The Rules,* Milton Keynes: Open University Press.

Grossman, S. and **Hart D.** (1980) Takeover bids, the free-rider problem and the theory of the corporation, *The Bell Journal of Economics,* Spring.

Halpern, P. J. (1973) Empirical Estimates of The Amount and Distribution of Gains to Companies in Mergers, *Journal of Business,* October, vol. 46, pp. 554–75.

Hammond, E., Helm, D. and **Thompson, D.** (1986) Competition in electricity supply: has the Energy Act failed? *Fiscal Studies,* pp. 11–33.

Harcourt, G. (1965) The accountant in a golden age *Oxford Economic Papers.*

Hartley, K. and **Huby, M.** (1985) Contracting-out in health and local authorities: prospects, progress and pitfalls, *Public Money,* vol. 5, no. 2, pp. 23–6.

Heald, D. and **Steel, D.** (1982) Privatising public enterprises: an analysis of the government's case, *Political Quarterly,* vol. 53, no. 3, pp. 333–49.

Heller, P. and **Schiller, C.** (1989) The fiscal impact of privatisation, with some examples from Arab countries, *World Development,* vol. 17, no. 5.

Helm, D. and **Yarrow, G.** (1988) Assessment: the regulation of utilities, *Oxford Review of Economic Policy,* vol. 4, no. 2, pp. i-xxxi.

Hirschman, A. (1970) *Exit, Voice and Loyalty,* Cambridge, Mass.: Harvard University Press.

Hoggett, P. (1991) A new management in the public sector? *Policy and Politics,* vol. 19, no. 4, pp. 243–56.

Hughes, A. (1989) The impact of merger: a survey of empirical evidence for the UK, in J. Fairburn and J. Kay (eds) *Mergers and Merger Policy,* Oxford: Oxford University Press.

Hughes, A. and **Singh, A.** (1987) Takeovers and the stockmarket, *Contributions to Political Economy,* vol. 6.

Isachsen, A. J., Hamilton, C. B. and **Glyfasow, T.** (1992) Privatisation – Central and Eastern Europe, *Skandinaviska Enskilda Banken Quarterly Review,* 1/2.

Jackson, P. M. (1985) *Implementing Government Policy Initiatives: The Thatcher Administration 1979–83,* London: RIPA.

Jackson, P. M. and **Palmer, B.** (1993) *Developing Performance Monitoring in Public Sector Organisations,* Management Centre, University of Leicester.

Jaffer, S. and **Thompson, D.** (1986) Deregulating express coaches: a reassessment, *Fiscal Studies,* pp. 45–68.

Jessop, R. (1991) The Welfare State in the transition from Fordism to Post-Fordism, in R. Jessop, H. Kastendiek, K. Nielsen and O. K. Pederson, *The Politics of Flexibility,* Aldershot: Edward Elgar.

Jones, L., Tandon, P. and **Vogelsang, I.** (1990), *Selling Public Enterprises,* MIT Press.

Kay, J. A. (1992) Privatisation in Western economies – mimeo-paper presented to International Seminar in Public Economics, Tokyo, September.

Kay, J. A. and **Mayer, C.** (1986) On the application of accounting rates of return, *Oxford Economic Papers.*

Kemp, P. (1990) Deregulation, markets and the 1988 Housing Act, *Social Policy and Administration,* vol. 24, pp. 145–55.

Kornai, J. (1986) *Contradictions and Dilemmas,* Cambridge, Mass: MIT Press.

Laffont, J. and **Tirole, J.** (1986) Using cost observation to regulate firms, *Journal of Political Economy,* vol. 94, pp. 614–41.

Le Grand, J. and **Robinson, R.** (eds) (1984) *Privatisation and The Welfare State,* London: Allen and Unwin.

Littlechild, S. (1983), *Regulation of British Telecommunications Profitability,* HMSO.

Mandelker, G. (1974) Risk and return: the case of merging firms *Journal of Financial Economics*, December, vol. 1, pp. 303–35.

March, D. (1991) Privatisation under Mrs Thatcher, *Public Administration*, vol. 69, winter, pp. 459–80.

Marsh, D. (1992) *The New Politics of British Trade Unions*, Basingstoke: Macmillan.

Marshall, J. (1986) Economic privatisation: lessons from the Chilean experience, in W. Glade (ed.) *State Shrinking*, Austin: University of Texas.

McCarthy, Lord. (1988) Privatisation and the employee, in V. Ramanadham (ed.) *Privatisation in the UK,* London: Routledge.

McAllister, I. and **Studdlar, D.** (1989) Popular vs elite views of privatisation: The Case Of Britain, *Journal of Public Policy*, vol. 9, pp. 157–78.

Milne, R. (1987) Competitive tendering in the NHS: an economic analysis of the early implementation of HC(83)18, *Public Administration*, vol. 65, no. 2, pp. 145–60.

Mitchell, J. (1990) Britain: privatisation as myth? in J. Richardson (ed.), *Privatisation and Deregulation in Canada and Britain*, Aldershot: Dartmouth.

Musgrave, R. A. (1958) *The Theory of Public Finance*, McGraw-Hill.

NEDO (1976) *A Study of UK National Industries*, London: HMSO.

Newberry (1990) Reform in Hungary: sequencing and privatisation, mimeo, presented at Fifth Annual Conference, European Economics Association, Lisbon, September.

Niskanen, W. A. (1971) *Bureaucracy and Representative Government*, Chicago: Aldine.

Okun, A. (1975) *Equality and Efficiency: The Big Trade off*, Washington, DC.: Brookings Institution.

Osborne, D. and **Gaebler, T.** (1992) *Reinventing Government*, Addison Wesley.

Ott, A. F. and **Hartley, K.** (1991) *Privatization and Economic Efficiency*, Aldershot: Edward Elgar.

Parry, R. (ed.) (1989) *Privatisation*. London: Kingsley.

Pitt, D. (1990) An essentially contestable organisation! British Telecom and the privatisation debate, in J. Richardson (ed.) *Privatisation and Deregulation in Canada and Britain,* Aldershot: Dartmouth.

Posner, R. (1971) Taxation by regulation, *Bell Journal of Economics*, vol. 2, pp. 22–51.

Price, C. M. and **Weyman-Jones, T. G.** (1993) Malmquist Indices of productivity change in the UK gas industry before and after privatisation, Economic Research Paper 93/12, Loughborough University of Technology.

Ramanadham, V. (ed.) (1988) *Privatisation in the UK,* London: Routledge.

Rowthorn, B. and **Chang, H-J.** (1991) Public ownership and the theory of the state, mimeo, presented at St Andrew's University Conference on Privatisation, Strategies and Practices.

Savas, E. (1987) *Privatisation: The Key to Better Government,* Chatham, New Jersey: Chatham House.

Schumpeter, J. A. (1961) *The Theory of Economic Development,* New York: Oxford University Press.

Sen, A. (1982) Carrots, sticks, and economics, *Indian Economic Review.*

Sherman, R. (1989), The Regulation of Monopoly, Cambridge: Cambridge University Press.

Singh, A. (1971) *Takeovers: Their Reference to the Stock Market and the Theory of the Firm,* Cambridge: Cambridge University Press.

Singh, A. (1975) Takeovers, economic natural selection and the theory of the firm: evidence from the post war UK experience, *Economic Journal,* vol. 85, September.

Spring, P. (1992) An Investigation of RPI-X: price cap regulation using British Gas as a case study, Public Finance Foundation: Centre for the Study of Regulated Industries, Discussion Paper No 1.

Stewart, J. (1986) *The New Management of Local Government,* London: Allen and Unwin.

Stigler, G. (1971) The theory of economic regulation, *Bell Journal of Economics,* vol. 2, pp. 3–21.

Stiglitz, J. (1985) Credit markets and the control of capital *Journal of Money Credit and Banking,* vol. 17, no. 2.

Thomas, D. Kay J. *et al.* (1986) *Privatisation and Regulation: The UK Experience,* Oxford: Clarendon.

Thompson, G. (1990) *The Political Economy of The New Right,* London: Pinter.

Train, K. (1991), *Optimal regulation,* MIT Press.

Veljanovski, C. (1987) *Selling the State: Privatisation in Britain,* London: Weidenfeld and Nicolson.

Veljanovski, C. (1990) Privatisation: progress, issues and problems, in D. Gayle and J. Goodrich (eds) Privatisation in Global Perspective, London: Pinter

Veljanovski, C. (1991), *Regulators and the Market,* London: Institute of Economic Affairs.

Veljanovski, C. (ed.) (1989) *Privatisation and Competition: A Market Prospectus,* London: Institute of Economic Affairs.

Vernon-Wortzel, H. and **Wortzel, L.** (1989) Privatization: not the only answer, *World Development,* no. 17, pp. 633–42.

Vickers, J. and **Yarrow, G.** (1988) *Privatisation: An Economic Analysis,* London: MIT Press.

Vogelsang, I. and **Finsinger, J.** (1979) A regulatory adjustment process for optimal pricing by multiproduct monopoly firms, *Bell Journal of Economics,* vol. 10, pp. 157–71.

Williamson, O. E. (1985) *The Economic Institutions of Capitalism,* New York: Free Press; London: Macmillan.

Wilshire, K. (1987) *Privatisation, the British Experience: An Australian Perspective,* Melbourne, Australia: CEDA.

Yarrow, G. (1989) Does ownership matter? in C. Veljanovski (ed.) *Privatisation and Competition,* London: Institute of Economic Affairs.

Yotopoulos, P. (1989) The (RIP) tide of privatisation, lessons from Chile, World Development, vol. 17, no. 5, pp. 683–702.

Young, S. (1986) The nature of privatisation in Britain 1979–85 *West European Politics,* 9, pp. 235-52.

CHAPTER 2

Divestiture of public sector assets

Mike Wright and Steve Thompson

Introduction

Although the UK has experienced privatisation for over a decade, the wave of similar activity sweeping the world is generally a more recent phenomenon (Vuylsteke, 1988). The extension of privatisation to the post-Communist countries of Europe and beyond emphasises the importance of this aspect of industrial policy and the need to analyse objectively the economic issues involved rather than merely accept the slogan that private ownership of assets is *per se* better than ownership by the state.

Most attention has focused on privatisation through stock market flotation since it is this form of ownership transfer which has tended to involve the largest enterprises. Some but by no means all of these enterprises have been so-called natural monopolies (such as BT, British Gas and Water), although even here it is debatable how many truly fit this description. Flotation is not the only means of transferring publicly owned assets to the private sector. Sale to management or other groups of whole or parts of publicly owned firms are also possible options and may be more appropriate in certain circumstances.

There is no centralised record in the UK of just how many transfers of public assets to the private sector have occurred. Neither individual ministries nor it seems the state-owned firms themselves maintain sufficiently detailed records to enable such an assessment to be made (Wright, Chiplin and Robbie, 1989). Surveys of privatisation activity, however, have undoubtedly understated its extent (Pirie, 1988; Vuylsteke, 1988; Bishop and Kay, 1989).

Counting each multiple flotation as a separate case, there have been 48 such privatisations, with a total market capitalisation in current prices of £44.2 billion. In contrast, there have been 158 management and employee buy-outs from the public sector, although their total value is probably less than £2 billion. In addition, although comprehensive data are difficult to obtain there have probably been in excess of a hundred sales to third parties.[1] Hence it is appropriate in this chapter to set out a framework of the forms of organisation that privatisation might take and the methods of effecting them. The following chapter analyses in detail the privatisation and subsequent regulation of natural monopolies.

These points raise a number of important issues about the conduct of privatisation policy which concern whether the policy has been carried out in a way which meets the objectives of government discussed in Chapter 1. That is, has the method and organisation structure chosen been such as to be consistent with the achievement of objectives of increasing competition and economic efficiency both at the level of firms and for the wider public interest? Have objectives for wider share ownership been achieved? Has the privatisation been priced optimally and have sufficient safeguards been introduced to ensure that unacceptable levels of underpricing have not occurred? Is the cost of the privatisation acceptable? Has the whole process of privatisation been carried out in an acceptable manner? Moreover, it also needs to be borne in mind that conflicts between objectives may make it difficult to achieve one without at the same time compromising another. For example, attempts to maximise the sale proceeds on the privatisation of a monopolist through the establishment of a relatively weak regulatory regime or failure to enforce divestiture to produce a more competitive structure may mean that the objective of enhancing allocative efficiency fails to be achieved. Similarly, attempts to achieve the objective of wider share ownership by offering individuals and employees various incentives to hold shares may also conflict with the maximisation of sales proceeds. The discussion in this chapter draws attention to these issues.

The conduct and effects of the UK privatisation policy may have lessons and implications for more recent programmes elsewhere, but there may also be a need to use alternative approaches. This chapter addresses the above issues as follows. Section 2.1 analyses the rationale, form and method of privatisation, both in principle and in relation to UK experience. Section 2.2 examines the key issues which arise on privatisation in the context of the objectives being pursued by government, that is competition, wider share ownership, pricing of sales and devices to ensure that assets are not sold too cheaply, expenses incurred in the privatisation process and investigations by the National Audit Office concerning how effectively the process has been carried out, and the impact on firm efficiency. The issue of competition is developed further in the following chapter, particularly in respect of natural monopoly firms. Section 2.3 extends the discussion to the particular case of privatisation and restructuring in the post-Communist countries of Europe.

2.1 The rationale, form and method of privatisation

In a public sector firm, neither incentives nor sanctions are closely related to performance. Most managers are likely to be hired on contracts offering job security with additional monetary gain limited to advancement within a promotional hierarchy. The absence of an external equity market means the public enterprise escapes both the scrutiny of market analysts and the sanction of potential takeover. While the state-owned firm may rely on the capital market for debt finance, the removal of the bankruptcy threat weakens the bonding of managers to meet debt-servicing obligations.

Public ownership entails some monitoring via the political process. However, this appears to be more successful in exposing gross misconduct than in monitoring commercial performance (Chiplin and Wright, 1982; Jackson, 1982). Furthermore the objectives of state-owned enterprises are likely to include certain social obligations which may be poorly defined and which are almost certainly hard to quantify. The resulting looseness of the objective function of the state company makes its performance that much harder to monitor (Garner, 1982; Wright, 1984; Whynes, 1987). Where state-owned firms possess monopoly power in the product market, which may be a natural monopoly or one reinforced by legal barriers to entry, the detriments to efficiency resulting from the above may be reinforced by a lack of product market competition.

However, given the variety of circumstances in which state-owned firms occur, simple transfer to the private sector by the obvious process of stock market flotation may not be the most appropriate means of achieving government objectives in all circumstances (Kay and Thompson, 1986). There is a need to examine both the most appropriate organisational structure and the most suitable ownership form (Table 2.1). Organisational structure refers to whether the entity or entities to be privatised involve a complete state-owned firm, the vertical or horizontal separation of an existing state-owned firm, or one or more subsidiaries of a state-owned firm while the 'core' part either remains in public ownership or is subsequently privatised. In the last case, the subsidiaries may have some form of trading relationship with their parent or may simply be peripheral activities.

The three principal ownership forms which privatisation may take are stock market flotation, sale to incumbent management and employees (management or employee buy-outs) and sale to a third party (an already existing company, sometimes referred to as a trade sale).

The UK privatisations which have involved stock market flotation are shown in Table 2.2. A straightforward share flotation ought to raise the value of a firm, that is reduce agency costs, through the clear specification of profit objectives, the introduction of a bankruptcy threat, the transfer of monitoring from the political process to the stock market, and the potential for improved managerial incentives. However, these changes may not necessarily occur. Flotation of a state-owned business does nothing of itself to alter the reward structure of management; although in practice they are usually offered shares on preferential terms.

Furthermore, if the newly privatised company retains market power and if the share disposal leaves equity ownership widely dispersed, there may be few pressures for internal improvement. A survey of the evidence by Vickers and Yarrow (1988) confirms there is little indication of private firm superiority where product market competition is degenerate. The size of some privatised undertakings probably prohibits their being taken over, even with a highly leveraged takeover bid. The 'unbundling' which is often a key part of a leveraged acquisition may be difficult in former state enterprises with a narrow spread of product areas, although break-up via

Table 2.2   Stock flotations and gross equity proceeds of sale

Company	Equity Proceeds* (£m)	Date
BP	7,200	Oct. 87
British Gas	5,600	Dec. 86
10 Water Cos.	5,400	Nov. 89
12 Elec. Cos.	5,180	Nov. 90
British Telecom	3,920	Dec. 84
Scottish Power/Hydro-electric	2,900	Mar. 91
British Steel	2,500	Dec. 88
National Power/Powergen (60%)	2,100	Jun. 91
TSB	1,360	Oct. 86
Rolls-Royce	1,360	May 87
BAA	1,280	Jul. 87
British Airways	900	Feb. 87
Cable and Wireless	600	Dec. 85
BP	565	Sep. 83
British Aerospace	550	May 85
Britoil	548	Nov. 82
Britoil	450	Aug. 85
Enterprise Oil	393	Jul. 84
Jaguar	294	Aug. 84
BP	290	Nov. 79
Cable and Wireless	275	Dec. 83
Cable and Wireless	224	Nov. 81
British Aerospace	149	Feb. 81
Amersham International	63	Feb. 82
Assoc. British Ports	52	Apr. 84
Assoc. British Ports	22	Feb. 83

Sources: Financial Times; Privatisation International; National Audit Office; Mayer and Meadowcroft (1985).
Note: *excludes proceeds from debt repayment.

regionalisation may be an option. Government equity retention and 'golden share' provisions may in some cases reduce or eliminate the possibility of takeover, although recent UK experience in this respect suggests too much weight ought not to be placed on this point.

Table 2.3   UK privatisation buy-outs

Source	Number
Whole state firm:	
National Freight	1
British Technology Group (core)	1
Break-up of state firm:	
National Bus	39
Scottish Bus	5
Divestment of parts:	
British Aerospace	1
BL/Austin Rover	13
British Rail	7
British Shipbuilders	12
British Steel	10
BTG/NEB	12
Local authority and other governmental sectors:	
Bus services	9
Non-bus services	28
Ancillary health and other agencies	16
Buy-ins	4

Source: CMBOR

In a buy-out debt and quasi-debt instruments are used to produce a considerable concentration of equity in the hands of the management team and their financial supporters. Efficiency benefits ought to accrue from the introduction of equity-based incentives for managers, the bonding effect of managers being required to meet tight financing targets, and the close monitoring by outside financiers. Additionally, a wider spread of employee ownership, which as will be seen below is common in privatisation buy-outs, may provide a greater degree of horizontal monitoring to supplement management's increased incentive to engage in vertical monitoring, and be particularly relevant where tasks are non-routine and employee-specific skills are important making traditional monitoring difficult. Employee ownership may influence worker involvement to the benefit of performance, although the evidence is ambiguous in the absence of participation (Estrin *et al.*, 1987). There are further potential benefits from management and employee buy-outs when trading relationships exist and are expected to continue. Severing the ownership link may convey a credible message that the former parent is no longer responsible as lender of last resort. For former employees, the possibility that poor performance will not be bailed out is made more transparent. Moreover, where the former subsidiary is more dependent on its former parent for trading activities than vice versa (asymmetric interdependence), and there are alternative suppliers or customers, the power of the former parent to enforce good quality performance is enhanced (Wright, 1986). This threat may be muted where a close working relationship is involved, because of the costs to the former parent of searching out and working with a new relatively unknown partner. In the longer term, each may reduce their dependence on the other so that the former parent's bargaining power may be reduced. For a buy-out to be feasible as an independent entity there is a necessity for sufficient managerial skills, a viable market and the ability to meet external finance servicing costs. In the absence of such conditions, but where employee specific skills are important, a sale to joint arrangement of a buy-out and an industrial partner may be warranted. The extent and sources of privatisation buy-outs in the UK are shown in Table 2.3.

Sale to a third party may be appropriate where an activity would not initially be viable if privatised independently through either a buy-out or a flotation or where there are clear economies of scale and scope to be gained which are not outweighed by other factors. The principal sales to third parties are shown in Table 2.4.

Table 2.4 Main privatisations by sale to another company

Nationalised industry/Local authority	*Approximate nos (notes)*
British Shipbuilders	7
BTG/NEB	
British Rail	3
British Airways	2
British Gas	1
Rover Group	11 (1986–89; including itself)
British Steel	18 (1980–81 to 1984–85)
National Bus	27 (11 of which were acquired by companies subject to earlier buy-outs)
Royal Ordnance	2

Source: Various annual reports; author's research. (Based on published information, up to 1991)

The problems of the structure of a privatised natural monopoly-type industry have been examined by Vickers and Yarrow (1985) in respect of British Telecom, by Hammond, *et al.* (1985) and Wright (1987) in respect of British Gas, by Pryke (1987) in respect of electricity, by Vickers and Yarrow (1988) in respect of water, and by Lapsley and Wright (1990) in respect of British Rail. Natural monopolies may be privatised intact through stock market flotation with a regulatory system also being imposed. Alternatively, a regulatory framework may be constructed and vertical and/or horizontal separation may occur on privatisation. In both cases, the intention may be to increase competition, but in the latter the effect may be more immediate than waiting for new entrants to emerge (O'Brien, 1986; Thompson and Wright, 1988).

Franchising involves bidding for the exclusive right to supply a good or service for a specified period. Hence competition occurs at the bidding stage whereas it may not be possible in the production of the good or service. Serious problems with franchising concern efficient organisation of the bidding system and ensuring a means of transferring assets at the end of the franchise period which is consistent with incentives to invest optimally during it.

Vertical separation could substantially reduce the extent of monopoly power exerted by any one part of the system. Horizontal separation may have the attraction of increasing the realistic threat of takeover and regulatory agencies may obtain more comparative information on performance. However, there may be offsetting problems in vertical and horizontal separation. Landon (1983), writing in the context of the US electricity utility industry, argues that the costs of contracting, which disintegration would introduce, versus ownership would be increased. This increase arises from the existence of technological interdependence and idiosyncratic capital, the requirements for long-term contracting, the informational and transactional requirements involved and the difficulties of appropriate pricing between vertical levels. In respect of horizontal disintegration, the need to maintain a network may also introduce co-ordination problems.

The following chapter addresses these issues in more detail. At this point it may simply be noted that, although there were clear possibilities for vertical and horizontal separation, early experience with natural monopolies (BT and British Gas) saw them privatised intact with only modest efforts to stimulate new competition. Later experience with the water and electricity industries saw a mixture of horizontal and vertical disintegration being adopted, although to some extent this was a continuation of the *status quo ante*. Various separation options have been suggested in respect of the privatisation of British Rail (Lapsley and Wright, 1990).

In competitive markets, the process may be somewhat different. State firms which as a whole are in competitive (national and international) markets, which are profitable and where employee-specific skills are not critical may be sold by stock market flotation as in such cases as Amersham International, and British Aerospace. Such firms may not be as large as the natural monopoly firms but may be difficult to sell to third parties. From the viewpoint of maximising sales proceeds, stock market flotation may offer the best option.

The only case to date in the UK of a buy-out of a complete state-owned firm is National Freight Consortium (NFC), the road freight transport firm (McLachlan, 1983). The core of BTG was eventually sold in this manner after many subsidiaries of the former NEB had been disposed of to the highest bidder, of which twelve were buy-outs (Pirie, 1988). NFC had been close to bankruptcy in the late 1970s, as is clear from a perusal of the company's annual reports and accounts in this period. As a result, flotation on a stock market was a difficult option to pursue. NFC faced direct competition from other private sector freight operators in many of its market segments. It may have been possible to sell the company, as a whole or in parts to one or more of the other groups in the industry. However, senior management was able to argue successfully against such moves, including the need to ensure employees' cooperation in a sector dependent upon individual efforts, to dissuade both the government and other bidders from alternative sell-off routes. Here, widespread employee share participation was important in reducing the agency costs of control in the large number of geographically dispersed depots (Wright and Petrin, 1990).

The most important break-ups on privatisation involved the state-owned National Bus Company (NBC) and Scottish Bus Group (SBG), which ran bus and coach services. The privatisation of the latter drew heavily on experience with the former. Local authorities also ran bus services which were not generally in competition with either company prior to deregulation which occurred with the Transport Act, 1985. Besides providing for deregulation the Transport Act, 1985 also laid down that NBC was to be split up or privatised and that local authority bus transport companies were to be formed into separate passenger companies, operating at arm's length from the local authorities. Given the local nature of bus services and the low level of economies of scale in the industry (Glaister and Mulley, 1983), break-up with a preference for management/employee bids appeared to offer the best possibility of meeting government privatisation objectives of increasing efficiency (Mulley and Wright, 1986). The substitution of market or quasi-market transactions for internal organisational relationships after break-up was both feasible and cost-effective. The alternatives were sale as a whole to management and employees, which may have had adverse market power consequences, or flotation on a stock market where the positive effects from employee ownership and from the control effects of debt noted earlier may have been weakened. As it was, the individual subsidiaries of NBC were generally dominant providers of bus services in their local areas. The privatisation of NBC involved 73 separate sales, of which 39 were buy-outs. In a further eleven cases, subsidiaries were acquired by companies which had been bought-out earlier in the 20-month long privatisation process. Five of the buy-outs involved a wide spread of employee involvement, with a further seven making provisions for employee share ownership. Among trade purchasers, both Stagecoach and Drawlane/Endless bought four subsidiaries each while Carlton/ATL bought two. These companies played an important role in the subsequent acquisitions which occurred as the industry became the subject of further restructuring (see below).

A relatively small number of privatisations of local authority bus operators have been completed, partly because of the need for the political will on the part of the local authority to ensure that these take place and some concern that local authority bus operators would be vulnerable to acquisition by the companies formerly part of National Bus. The general use of employee-led buy-outs in these cases, rather than management buy-outs (Wright, *et al.,* 1989) has been influenced by political factors, the pioneering People's Provincial buy-out from NBC and a desire to avoid a management team selling the company in a relatively short period of time against employees' wishes.

Subsidiaries may be divested as state enterprises seek to restructure their activities to reduce losses or in preparation for their own privatisation. Some of the activities sold have been those which were peripheral to the state firms' main forms, having often been nationalised 'by accident' and carrying no strategic, monopoly or job-saving element. The relative size of inside and outside bids has been important in determining the successful purchaser in contested cases. Sometimes management have succeeded where their bid has not been the highest but where the vendor considered that this option held the best prospects for the business and the welfare of employees (Wright, Chiplin and Robbie, 1989), with at times various forms of vendor financial support being made available. Occasionally, doubts over the ability of management to survive independently have been influential in the decision to sell to third parties or in managers being unable to find financial support. There is also marked evidence of sale of activities as buy-outs where some continuing trading relationship exists with the state-owned parent. Significant examples in the UK include Istel from BL/Austin Rover and RFS Industries from British Rail. The first of these continued to be a major supplier of computer services to its former parent. The second was a major repairer and supplier of railway wagons to British Rail and indeed was heavily dependent upon its former parent. In such cases, the vendor may retain an equity stake in order to exert some control (as in the case of Istel) or exercise control through competition for contracts and in detailed cooperation in product development (as in the case of RFS Industries).

Structural and ownership form issues are also raised in respect of the privatisation of British Coal. The privatisation of the UK coal industry has been a difficult and highly contentious process, not least because of major questions concerning the longer term viability of the industry and its close vertical relationship with electricity generation. In principle, stock market flotation could only be considered in respect of British Coal as a whole. However, although British Coal recorded a profit of £170 million in the 1991–92 financial year the relatively low level of profits and market uncertainties cast doubt on its attractiveness to the stock market. While total closure is politically impossible, the closure option is likely to continue to be used at the pit-by-pit level, as events in the autumn of 1992 brought into sharp focus. If the industry were to be fragmented, which may be feasible in principle given its non-natural monopoly nature, such a route would be likely to introduce increased scope for sale to various buyers, including buy-outs, international mining companies seeking entry to the European market, UK companies (especially those involved in construction and mining) interested in the purchase of local pits, electricity generators or distributors with aspirations to develop their own generating capacity and buy-ins by managers with mining experience. The establishment of long-term contracts with the electricity generators could in principle form the basis for stable cash flow and is a key influence in establishing a meaningful valuation for the industry, both of which would be important in the assessment of a buy-out. Cost savings and further efficiency improvements might be expected to arise from the incentives incorporated in the buy-out. However, the level of investment funding required by the industry raises questions as to the extent to which a typical buy-out structure would allow for sufficient such funds after external funding costs are met. Uncertainties about future performance and investment needs suggest that some form of price-ratchet/earn-out mechanism or retained equity stake may be required in the case of buy-outs associated with a commitment by the electricity generators to take certain levels of coal for a given period. Pit-by-pit sales as buy-outs may be suitable in relatively isolated cases. But as a general policy they would appear to be too vulnerable to survive long as independent entities, not least because the profitability of individual pits can vary from year to year because of geological and other factors outside management's control.[2] Sale of regions or as an entity may go a considerable way to dealing with these problems, especially if sold together with the generally more profitable opencast mines.

A high level of employee and trade union identification with the industry is particularly acute in coal, adding to the well-known monitoring problems in an industry where employee specific skills are high and tasks are less routine.[3] As such, there are strong indications of a need to include some form of employee equity holding in any form of privatisation, either through a joint bid or the ability to participate in an acquirer's share ownership scheme. However, to obtain funding any buy-out with strong union involvement would have to be operated on strict commercial principles and the unions would need to clarify their role in the newly created employee-owned enterprise, as has been seen in the bus buy-outs discussed earlier. In general the position of employees and unions may be such as to be able to exert some influence on the nature of the privatisation. First, in earlier privatisations it has not been unusual to make requirements for prospective purchasers to give undertakings concerning employment and investment, which may strengthen the position of a buy-out bid *vis-à-vis* an outside purchaser. Second, the extent to which incumbent management would be considered acceptable to lead the newly created entity and the acceptability of certain outside purchasers who might be viewed as being little interested in the long-term future of the industry are likely to influence whether sale is to an outside buyer or to some acceptable form of buy-out. Anti-privatisation stances by unions may make outsiders unwilling to bid, leaving the way clear for a buy-out, although earlier experience suggests that different attitudes to privatisation by different unions are unlikely to prevent privatisation. Given the major review of the coal industry following from the government's closure announcements in the autumn of 1992, detailed consideration of the form and timing of privatisation has been delayed. What seems to be emerging is that if it is accepted that the future is likely to see considerably fewer viable pits and that there is a perceived need to maintain a viable skills base, then the sale of British Coal's coal-getting activities as a single entity to a trade buyer or some form of buy-out seems the most viable option. This route still leaves open the possibility for the sale of some individual pits and ancillary activities as buy-outs.

Similar arguments to those examined in relation to state industries have been used in the context of state and local government activities. Activities may at one extreme be considered to be no longer appropriate for local or state government involvement as they are totally unrelated to core government interests (such as quasi-governmental agencies like the Water Research Council and Washington Development Corporation). At the other extreme, government may continue to be heavily dependent upon the provision of a service by an existing agency with little prospect of a viable competitor emerging. In between, management may face the possibility of competition for service provision. As in the sales of subsidiaries of state firms considered above, divestiture may make it possible to take advantage of growth opportunities which was not possible under public ownership.

A major area of interest, examined further in the chapter in this volume by Peter Jackson, is local authority services such as cleaning, laundry, refuse collection, etc. In many cases, when contracts to provide such services have been put to tender, outside firms have won the contracts at the expense of authorities' own in-house providers. Studies of the effects of this process have shown that real efficiency improvements of the order of 20 per cent have been achieved and that where in-house providers have won the contract the service has been provided more efficiently than beforehand (Cubbin, *et al.,* 1987). It would also appear that the actual process of competitive tendering, irrespective of whether the tender is won by in-house or outside contractors, gives rise to real productivity gains which are not attributable to reductions in wage rates but to increases in productivity (Szymanski and Wilkins, 1992). The Local Government Act, 1988 introduced compulsory competitive tendering for certain defined services. By contracting-out, a local authority may become an enabler rather than a provider of a service, which may have attractions where the need for a service is declining or erratic. Lower costs of service provision may be obtained from new methods of working which could not be obtained under previous arrangements.

In a number of such services, the human capital contributed by management and employees may be quite significant. Suitably incentivised management and employees may help produce a better quality of service at a lower cost. Buy-outs may also offer advantages from it being more acceptable to transfer management control to a known group of individuals rather than rely on unknown outside contractors. In particular, it might be expected that quality control and compliance monitoring problems will be lower where a contract is operated by former employees with compatible perceptions of what constitutes an acceptable standard of service.

However, question marks are raised concerning the capability of managements to operate independently in a new commercial environment. In addition, the viability of the newly independent enterprise carrying out a contract is also important in ensuring continuity of service provision. The scope of the buy-outs for independent pricing and marketing (particularly in leisure service buy-outs) may be crucial to ensuring viability. The length and number of contracts awarded is also important, but authorities may need to be aware that long contracts may make them vulnerable to poor performance. Of course, there is a trade-off to be made between performance levels and administrative costs.

2.2 Privatisation issues

In Section 2.1 we outlined the principal objectives of privatisation. In this section we analyse the extent to which such objectives have been achieved.

Greater product market competition

The main issues in respect of competition concern the extent to which privatisation, liberalisation and possible separation have led to increased competition both in natural and non-natural monopoly firms. In this section attention is focused upon the effects in respect of non-natural monopoly sectors. The issues concerned with increasing competition in the natural monopoly industries are analysed in the next chapter. In both cases, the structure of the industry at divestiture has implications for the role of regulation afterwards. The principal competition issue in the non-natural monopoly sector has involved the privatisation of the bus industry.

The effects of privatisation in the bus industry have been compounded by the parallel introduction of deregulation in the industry. The industry is undoubtedly undergoing a degree of 'deregulation turmoil', characterised by a fundamental shake-up, business practices changing, and firms entering and leaving the industry. Structure and performance has changed across the industry, though as the market stabilises it is not at all clear that liberalisation has achieved its objective of making the markets truly competitive. In fact, the industry may even be regressing to its previous state. Sale of NBC in one unit, as originally envisaged, was considered to pose the threat of entry forestalling action against possible new competition (Mulley and Wright, 1986). Hence the decision to break up the company and allow market forces to decide the structure of the industry in the medium term, through a mixture of new entry and mergers. Six years on, however, the incumbent firms are still dominant having seen off most new entrants and the deregulated markets remain highly concentrated. For instance, Gwilliam (1989) and Evans (1990) report significant new entry only in Manchester, Preston, Stockton-on-Tees, Lancaster, and Oxford.

There has also been extensive merger activity, which was not unexpected. An understanding of the nature of competition in the industry is crucial to policy towards shaping its future structure and conduct. High concentration and lack of new entry is not, of course, in itself a sign of market failure, it could even be a sign of virtue. Firstly, the incumbent firms may simply be very efficient in providing good quality services at low prices which other firms could not compete with. Furthermore, it is conceivable that competitive outcomes can arise with only two firms in the market – consider the Bertrand duopoly model. Secondly, from the theory of contestable markets competitive outcomes even in monopoly markets may arise from the threat of new entry. Thus while incumbent firms remain in the market they are subject to competitive pressures from potential competition, so that if they earn significant rents (profits) other firms will enter the market reducing profitability and possibly displacing the incumbent. For this competitive process to work entry barriers would need to be minimal. Certainly, economies of scale and firm size do not seem to be a particularly important source of advantage, except that there may be some economies of scope arising from operating a large network and using a travel card scheme (though alliances with other operators are allowed for this purpose). However, the incumbents do seem to have a number of (naturally occurring) first mover advantages, which entail newcomers having to incur sunk (i.e. irredeemable) costs. In this market 'innocent' barriers to entry (Salop, 1979) would appear to arise from the brand name established during the regulatory era (which may be important in uncertain market conditions), information advantages through customers having incumbents' timetables, the incumbents' experience and having an established operational fleet of buses along with the necessary trained staff. Entrants then face the additional costs of having to inform customers of their services through advertising and distributing timetables. Furthermore, unless they are already established bus operators from neighbouring markets or from the special contract service sector, new entrants would have to recruit new staff and build up a fleet of buses suggesting that only small-scale entry is possible. Such innocent barriers may then be harnessed into strategic action to deter entry, the financial strength of incumbents enabling them to survive prolonged price wars (the so-called 'long purse' story) especially if cross-subsidisation from profitable routes is possible (which may well be the case if new entry is small-scale and selective). The reputation earned from fighting off a new entrant would then serve to deter further entry.

This threat is made all the more credible by the difficulty government competition agencies have in proving predatory behaviour. In the five-year period following deregulation the Office of Fair Trading received 105 complaints concerning predatory behaviour. Only four investigations of such behaviour were initiated (Elliot, 1991), with two cases dismissed and OFT finding evidence of predatory behaviour in the other two. Apart from the requirement that there are no sunk costs, for a market to be perfectly contestable entrants should be able to enter the market and slightly undercut the incumbents' prices and 'steal' the market before the incumbents have time to react. The key requirement is that incumbents cannot change their prices immediately in response to entry. Moreover, in the absence of sunk costs the entrants can freely exit the market when it ceases to be profitable. Given the ease with which firms can change their prices in this market, the 'hit and run entry' story relies on the element of surprise. However, in the bus market there is little chance of 'surprise' entry with entrants having to give 42 days notice to the local authority when applying for a route licence, thus allowing the incumbents time to take defensive action. Furthermore, simply offering a lower price than incumbents will not automatically mean that the entrants capture a sizeable part of the market, consumer loyalty to incumbents will take time to overcome and the market is such that different prices can be temporarily sustained (given that consumers waiting at a bus stop will often simply take the first bus that comes along as long as price differences are not too excessive).

At best then, the bus industry would seem to be only an imperfectly contestable market and greater reliance should probably be placed on actual competition. The problem is that there is currently very little active competition on routes. The evidence, by no means comprehensive, suggests that shortly after deregulation only 3 per cent of bus-kilometres were involved in direct 'on the road' competition; this increased rapidly to 10 per cent in 1987–88 but has since declined (Evans, 1990). Moreover, in Evans's (1990) study of four towns and cities where major entry has occurred he concluded that operators tacitly collude in matching fares, making simultaneous price movements, and that there was little difference between fares on actively competitive routes and non-competitive routes, and also on high-demand and low-demand routes. Attention by the Monopolies and Mergers Commission to the significant number of mergers taking place between bus buy-outs and other operators in the sector has resulted in no less than six reports being published in less than two years. In all but one of these the merger has been found to be against the public interest. The first acquisition of one ex-NBC buy-out by another in adjacent areas was referred to the Monopolies Commission in October 1988, with the report being published in March 1989 (MMC, 1989). The Commission was in agreement that the merger could bring benefits from better management of a larger bus fleet and the reintroduction of interavailability of tickets between routes and operators. However, members of the Commission were split as to the possibility for collusion and exclusion of other competitors in tendering for local authority services. The minority considered there was sufficient evidence of significant increases in competition in the period after deregulation. The majority argued that the parties should give undertakings not to collude and that if this was not done divestment should be ordered.

This report highlights the issue as to whether the bus industry can essentially be regarded as contestable, that is whether the threat of entry will provide a sufficient spur to efficiency when the bus sector is comprised of a few large groups and whether any economies of scale, both technical and managerial, in large groups outweigh the effects of competition. It was noted earlier that economies of scale in the bus industry are limited, though there may be a newly privatised and deregulated environment. Since 1986 there has been a period of transition in the market, in which entry has occurred. However, in many cases incumbents have been able to marginalise new entrants and head-to-head competition between large ex-NBC buy-outs has been seen to be costly and futile. Hence, incumbents may have forestalled future entry. In respect of Stagecoach/PCB, PCB was divested following MMC recommendations. However, in apparent scepticism that divestment by itself will increase competition the Commission has recommended other measures to try and meet this objective, such as undertakings on price and service levels and measures to prevent retaliation against new entrants.

The whole issue of investigating mergers in the bus industry was brought into question through a High Court ruling, following an appeal by South Yorkshire Transport against the Commission's recommendations that it divest itself of certain acquisitions. The Commission was held to have exceeded the powers contained in Section 64(3) of the Fair Trading Act, 1973 in concluding that the area covered by the South Yorkshire Transport referral constituted a substantial part of the UK. As a result, in June 1991 the OFT suspended investigations of all mergers where the question of what constitutes a 'substantial' part of the UK was at issue. In late November 1991, the Appeal Court upheld the High Court ruling by a majority of two to one. The Appeal court argued that the word 'substantial' in the 1973 Act was used in a comparative sense, the comparator being the whole of the UK. The areas covered by the South Yorkshire acquisitions could not in this sense be regarded as substantial. This point is of particular concern given the comment by the CPA (1991) that the Department of Transport, while having taken measures to promote competition at the time of sale, did not subsequently regard themselves as responsible for judging the adequacy of competition but rather left it to competition policy. Utton (1991) has also questioned the OFT/MMC's approach to the bus industry, arguing that there are low barriers to entry in the industry and that profitability is below the risk-free rate of return. However, Utton considers that it is right to be sceptical about the spate of mergers in the industry following deregulation and privatisation as the optimal market structure is unclear and that if mergers go unchecked it might take the industry further from the optimum without the market being able to adjust at a later date.

Difficult though it may be to maintain competitive market conditions in such circumstances, it may be less problematical than trying to stimulate competition when a monopoly, which might feasibly have been broken up, has been privatised intact. The experience of the gas industry, examined in the next chapter, demonstrates the difficulties faced by the regulator and the MMC in attempting to increase gas to gas competition following divestiture. The possibility of post-privatisation break-up was also being actively considered in the MMC investigation of gas under way in 1993.

Wider share ownership

The objective of extending share ownership involves both shareholdings by the general public in privatised entities and employee share ownership.

It is clear that privatisation has led to widespread individual ownership of shares, almost by definition. However, it is debatable whether such ownership is long term or generates sustainable increases in performance. As shown in Table 2.5, there have been marked reductions in the number of shareholders in privatised companies. Employees in buy-outs arising on privatisation will own a greater share of the equity than is the case for those former state firms floated on a stock market (Bishop and Kay, 1988; Buckland, 1987). In the latter, nominal amounts of free shares have been distributed to employees and discounts have been used to encourage further share holdings by employees (Vickers and Yarrow, 1988). However, there is also extensive evidence of share sales by employees very shortly after privatisation, so reducing further the extent of employee share ownership (Buckland, 1987; Vickers and Yarrow, 1988). In the case of Scottish Power and Hydro-electric, some two-thirds of individual shareholders had retained their shares six months after the flotation. This was higher than in the flotations of the 12 electricity companies and National Power and Powergen, where approximately half of shareholders had retained their shares six months after the sale and was largely attributable to the lower premiums in the Scottish Power and Hydro-electric cases (NAO, 1992a).

Table 2.5 Percentage of retained shareholdings one year after privatisation (principal cases)

Company	% of original number
Amersham International	13.2
British Telecom	73.6
BAA	48.7
British Gas	70.6
British Airways	38.2
Jaguar	43.3
Assoc. Brit. Ports	34.4
Enterprise Oil	103.3
Rolls-Royce	46.2
12 Electricity Companies*	40
Scottish Power/Hydro-elec.†	67

Source: Bishop and Kay (1988), Does privatisation work – lessons from the UK, LBS, and NAO reports (various).

Note: *Of those with incentives attached, some 70 per cent remained after one year.
†After six months.

The extent of employee ownership in the National Freight case is well documented (McLachlan, 1983; Bradley and Nejad, 1989). The smaller earlier buy-outs which occurred on the divestment of the more peripheral parts of state enterprises tended to be management buy-outs with ownership concentrated in the senior team. In the larger buy-outs there has tended to be more widespread employee involvement especially where this has been perceived as important to persuade unions to support a buy-out attempt, where employee motivation and commitment has been important in effecting turnround and where the individual skills of employees are important to the success of the buy-out. It has become more usual for employees to be offered the chance to participate in share ownership as a condition of privatisation.

The privatisation of National Bus shows a variety of employee involvement (Wright, *et al.,* 1990). Only five buy-outs can be classified as having the characteristics of employee buy-outs. The majority of buy-outs involved only a small team of the most senior managers or a wider group of senior managers, although in the others there were intentions to extend share ownership. The buy-out at People's Provincial was effected using an ESOP with an equal equity stake for all concerned from the managing director downwards. Those National Bus subsidiaries sold to third parties fared less well with few obtaining any initial share participation.

More recent and larger buy-outs from BL/Austin Rover, such as Unipart (Boley, 1989) and Istel have involved wider employee ownership. In the buy-outs from British Shipbuilders, VSEL offered shares to employees (and local residents) at the outset while Vosper Thornycroft employees were only able to obtain an equity stake after the buy-out.

The particularly high frequency of employee share participation buy-outs is also linked to countering trade union hostility. In the UK the trade unions have formally opposed the Conservative government's privatisation programme – although the extent of opposition has varied across unions and even between local and national levels of the same union. This was seen in the NFC case where opposition from the TGWU was particularly strong.

As to the effects of wider employee share ownership, studies of privatised utilities have shown little or no evidence of a change in attitude, nor a reduction in 'us versus them' feelings, and that there is no significant difference in these regards between employee shareholders and non-shareholders (Nichols and Davidson, 1992; Colling, 1991). However, in these cases employee ownership stakes in the company were generally very low. Evidence from UK public sector buy-outs provides some contrasting evidence. A study of the National Freight employee buy-out by Bradley and Nejad (1989), which compared the attitudes of shareholders and non-shareholders, found that the act of buying shares was more important than the amount of shares owned, that employee share ownership was perceived to have a greater effect on 'cooperation' than on performance, that there was no statistically significant difference between managerial and non-managerial employee share-owners in respect of 'cooperation' but that there was some support for the proposition that employee share ownership improved employees' cost consciousness. However, the Bradley and Nejad study involved only one division of National Freight and the authors express some caution as to the generalisability of their results. A second study which examined employee attitudes in four privatised local authority bus companies, where virtually all employees became shareholders, found that attitudes and performance are not simply distinguished by whether employees actually own shares. Whether employees felt they owned part of the company, their likelihood to quit, and whether they were managerial employees were all significantly related to a positive attitude towards employee ownership and to increases in various performance, satisfaction, motivation and participation variables resulting from the introduction of employee share ownership (Wilson, *et al.*, 1993).

The development of employee buy-outs where management lead the transaction and establish an ESOP to permit wider ownership may not occur without some trade union resistance. A change in attitudes to privatisation by unions has been signalled by the appearance of trade union led employee bids. In these approaches, management will have the freedom to take operating decisions, but will be subject to control by employee shareholders. These attempts have been clearly influenced by the People's Provincial buy-out from NBC and a desire to avoid a management team selling the company in a relatively short period of time. Such employee buy-outs need not be a permanent arrangement, as some would like to think. There is no reason, of course, why employee shareholders should not vote to sell to a trade buyer at an attractive gain on their original investment.

Valuation and pricing of privatisations

The principal valuation methods relevant to the privatisation of state assets are well known: net asset value; price/earnings ratios or multiples; and discounted present values of future income streams. These methods aim to provide an approximate objective measure of what is essentially a subjective exercise. Each method relies heavily upon accounting data and may therefore be influenced by the techniques that firms may use in preparation of their accounts. These techniques may involve major changes to accounting policies, such as changes to depreciation lives and the nature of assets which are capitalised as well as changes between historic cost and current cost accounting. Even in stable advanced market environments these techniques can produce wide variations in values. The different parties involved in a transaction may have differing valuation perspectives: the vendor is likely to wish to maximise the sale price, the buyer to purchase at the lowest price possible, and advisers to set a price range within which the activity can be sold satisfactorily. Notwithstanding the valuations which may emerge from the various techniques applied by managers, for a sale transaction actually to be completed requires that for a given price, the buyer values the firm more highly than the seller. Moreover, the whole valuation process may be affected by an interrelated set of factors which may be grouped under the headings of 'presentational' institutional economic and accounting. The pricing of a privatisation share issue is likely to be influenced by government's desire to have the issue perceived as a success in that all shares offered will be subscribed for.

The introduction of enterprises to the Stock Exchange is always risky. The enterprise to be sold is, from the point of view of the stock market, more or less unknown to the investor. This lack of information and the risk involved must be reduced by an introductory discount. The discount (the difference between the offer price and the price at the first dealings in the shares) has to be large enough to win over potential buyers, but at the same time the minimisation of the discount is in the interest of the seller. The magnitude of the discount appears to depend on various factors. Theoretically, there exists an optimum discount but each party to a transaction is interested in increasing it above the optimum. The interested parties are, to a certain extent, the owner because he wants to play safe, the underwriters, because they are reluctant to take over unsold shares, the stockbrokers, as the success or failure influences their further business opportunities and finally, the buyers, because they would like to make as much profit as possible. If the privatisation process is too rapid and the level of institutional funds available to be invested is limited, then there may need to be a significant reduction in the offer price if capital markets are to absorb a planned level of privatisation.

Estrin and Selby (1991) also argue that the existence of a derivative securities market will mean that post-privatisation premiums above offer prices will be greater than they otherwise might have been and that the UK government has failed to take this problem into account in pricing new privatisation issues. Lower prices may also be introduced to encourage the sale of problem cases so that the burden of monitoring remaining activities can be reduced. The introduction of an auditing body such as the National Audit Office (NAO) in the UK, whose findings are made public, which examines each privatisation, provides some pressure, albeit *post hoc,* to make the process reasonably transparent. Economic influences on valuation are wide-ranging. A desire to reduce government deficits may induce an objective of maximising sale proceeds, possibly through the use of competitive bidding. But, bidders may be unwilling to pay more if future profits are expected to fall because of increased competition, the introduction of regulatory regimes which limit price increases, and the effects of vertical or horizontal separation of a firm on privatisation to increase competition. Pre-privatisation restructuring and redevelopment potential may increase the valuation price which may be placed on an entity to be privatised. However, where the information concerning these benefits is subjective or not in a form which can be made public, managers who possess an informational advantage as to the likely extent of the undeclared benefit may be able to use that information to their own advantage.

In respect of accounting policies, there is extensive evidence that changes in UK state enterprises' acccounting policies have had a marked effect on their reported profits (Wright, 1979, 1980, 1985). These changes include, for example, shortening depreciation lives and introducing inflation accounting to reduce reported profits in high profit making state firms such as British Gas and the opposite action in weaker industries so as to reduce reported losses. There is also at least circumstantial evidence that the basis of accounting can change immediately if the enterprise in question approaches privatisation (Likierman, 1983). British Telecom and British Airways changed immediately from their usual current cost accounting method to historical cost accounting to display higher profits and thus increase their potential market value as their privatisation came on the agenda. British Gas also reversed its depreciation lives policy prior to its own privatisation, producing an upward effect on profits (Wright, 1987). The valuation of assets such as land and buildings poses particular difficulties. The Royal Institution of Chartered Surveyors in the UK has developed guidelines concerning the methods of valuing land and buildings, but only from 1991 was it mandatory for valuers to state whether or not they had followed the guidelines, or if not, the reasons why (Cherry, 1991). In the case of subsidiaries, detailed published accounts may not in any case be available. Moreover, where the activity has been run at a cost centre rather than a profit centre under state ownership, it may be extremely difficult to construct reliable profit and cash flow information.

Under full information and a large number of bidders, the interests of the public as shareholders in state firms are most obviously achieved in an open auction. In the case of larger state firms, there may be few obvious buyers, particularly ones which would meet the requirements of the Monopolies and Mergers Commission. A policy which explicitly or implicitly favours managers when state enterprises are sold will tend to reduce the set of bidders and the eventual price. The potential problems of management anticipating disposal and taking action to depress the deal price may be worse than in the case of private sector sales. First, there may be greater informational asymmetry problems between the vendor and the management of the subsidiary. Second, where a proposed privatisation sell-off is on the agenda for a prolonged period, the potential for management to engage in action which is not clearly in the vendor's interest is more acute.

We now examine valuation and pricing issues which have arisen in UK privatisation firstly in respect of stock market flotations and secondly regarding asset sales.

Stock market flotations

Sales of state assets by public share flotation has been observed to involve significant discounting of price, that is the difference between the price at which the state sells the shares and the prices at which they are initially quoted on the stock market. There are various ways in which the discount may be measured. The simplest method is to compare the initial opening price with the sale price, which in some cases may be a first instalment on a larger full price. In the cases of TSB, British Airways, Rolls-Royce and BAA this method produced discounts of 71, 68, 73 and 46 per cent, respectively. In respect of the major natural monopoly privatisations Table 2.6 shows a wide variety of initial premia, ranging from about 20 per cent in the cases of the power generators to 86 per cent for BT.

The estimated average differences between the privatisation share prices of flotation and the trading prices after one week range from 15.9 per cent to 26.5 per cent (Buckland, 1987; Mayer and Meadowcroft, 1985).

Table 2.6 Opening share premia and dividend yields: major sales

Company	First instalment (p)	Opening price (p)	Gain (%)	Dividend yields (%)
British Gas	50	62.5	25	n.a.
BT	50	93	86	n.a.
Water				
Anglian	100	140	40	8.51
Northumbrian	100	168	68	8.91
North West	100	142	42	8.73
Severn Trent	100	135	35	8.25
Southern	100	141	41	8.35
South West	100	143	43	9.68
Thames	100	140	40	8.10
Welsh	100	138	38	9.31
Wessex	100	148	48	8.45
Yorkshire	100	143	43	8.57
Electricity				
Eastern	100	147	47	8.03
East Midlands	100	164	64	8.36
London	100	151	51	8.28
Midland	100	157	57	8.36
Northern	100	155	55	9.03
Norweb	100	153	53	8.68
Manweb	100	176	76	8.89
Southern	100	153	53	8.03
South Wales	100	163	63	8.87
South West	100	158	58	8.44
Yorkshire	100	170	70	8.58
National Power/ Powergen	100	119/126	19/26	
Scottish Power/ Hydro-electric	100	120	20	

Source: Financial Times

However, private sector flotations also demonstrate significant discounts on the issue price (Buckland, *et al.*, 1981) and the important question is whether public sector sales produce different results. A recent direct comparison, using a market adjusted excess returns model, between discounts on privatisation and private sector initial flotations shows, after controlling for size of issue, that the former provide average excess returns above those of the latter of 31 per cent over a 32-week period (Menyah, *et al.*, 1990).

The privatisations of Water and Electricity distribution raised particular issues because they involved multiple flotations of the different regional firms. In both privatisations, common share prices were set for each regional firm. However, with marked differences between the actual and potential performances of each region, a common share price though offering the benefits of simplicity ran the risk that some firms would attract little interest and that others would rise to very high premia on the first day of sale. In order to even up the attraction to investors the government set different dividend yields for each firm, with the weaker firms being compensated by higher yields. The yields were based on notional full year dividends for the relevant year. In respect of water, the dividend yields ranged from 8.1 per cent for Thames to 9.68 per cent for South West. In the case of electricity, the weighted average yield was 8.4 per cent, with a range from 8.03 per cent in the cases of Eastern and Southern to 9.03 per cent for Northern. The yields set had also to take into account the need for the eventual yield once flotation had occurred to be in line with those for other utilities. The difficulties resulting from the absence of full information on which to base these dividend yields were shown in the opening premia (Table 2.6). The premia were all substantially above analysts' expectations, with a large range being observed between the lowest and the highest and with their rankings being different from those of the notional dividend yields. It might be expected that further differences will occur as institutions become more able to distinguish between individual companies and managements. In the cases of the privatisations of electricity generators, the opening premiums were noticeably lower.

The process by which shares are offered to the public in privatisation through stock market flotation illustrates one aspect of the conflict between government objectives. In principle, fixed price offers may be better for spreading share ownership to small investors although they are more likely to lead to higher initial premia than tender offers which may be a better means of maximising sales proceeds.

Asset sales

Valuation issues arise whether assets are disposed of to incumbent management or to a third party. The difficulty is to value not only assets but future income streams, the latter being especially important in the divestiture of service activities which may not previously have been viewed as commercial ventures. The problem may, however, be more general since assets pre- and post-privatisation are being assessed under two different regimes, one where the objective is not to maximise the discounted flow of future income streams and one where it is. While, as will be seen below, there are grounds for trying to ensure that sales take place at a price which represents a fair return to the state, it is not clear that the state should reasonably expect to receive a price equivalent to the present value of future income streams when this was not the state's objective nor in all probability could the state have earned such returns. This latter aspect may especially need to be taken into account in respect of buy-outs where managers obtain significant incentives to perform, which were previously absent.

In the case of buy-outs the extent of discounts may be estimated by comparing the deal price with the accounting value of the company's assets at the time of the buy-out. An analysis of the mean price/net assets ratios of the trade sales and buy-outs from National Bus found that for the latter category at 0.9 to be significantly below that for the former at 1.57 (Thompson, Wright and Robbie, 1990). However, it is not clear how much of this premium is attributable to the favourable treatment of buy-outs. First, buy-outs were particularly common among the earlier disposals when there was still considerable uncertainty over the consequences of deregulation and hence fewer rivals in the bidding. Second, in the later disposals the emerging buy-out companies themselves became buyers, so strengthening the market. Third, the average mean price/net assets ratio for trade disposals is inflated by a small number of highly priced deals.

All buy-out teams along with their financial backers, clearly, wish to pay a price for a company which will both enable financing to be obtained and serviced, and enable them to obtain a return commensurate with their efforts. The vendor management, however, have a duty to act in the best interests of the current shareholders, whether the transaction is taking place within the public or private sectors. Such a requirement essentially means obtaining the best price for the assets being sold. A buy-out bid may not always offer the highest price. There may be offsetting factors which need to be taken into account, which may encourage vendors to favour a buy-out. In the case of privatisations, employee ownership consideration, as seen in the previous section, may be influential. The importance of continuing trading relationships has also been key to a buy-out of a subsidiary of a state-owned firm succeeding. While some state-owned firms have introduced policies to encourage and support buy-out attempts, not all bids have succeeded even when price discounts have been on offer. Subsidiaries have been sold to other private sector firms (Wright, Chiplin and Robbie, 1989). Besides the question of price, buy-outs may not succeed because of weaknesses in management teams or an absence of independent viability of some subsidiaries. Critics of the public sector have argued that its traditional work practices and salary levels discourage those with entrepreneurial preferences and encourage those seeking security. If management teams fail to convince potential financial backers, then the buy-out cannot go ahead. It may, however, be possible to supplement or replace weak management by recruiting outside entrepreneurs.

In some cases the importance of management has been recognised by the trade acquirer in the form of allowing them to obtain a significant share of the equity. In addition, management in some cases have mounted a joint bid with another group in order to succeed against an unwelcome outside bid (e.g. BREL from BR). In the case of Harland and Wolff a joint bid was necessary because a bought-out firm would not have been viable on its own (Wright, Chiplin and Robbie, 1989).

It is possible to allay some concern about the under-pricing of buy-outs, and indeed sales to third parties, by the use of delayed payments contingent upon performance and/or by the vendor retention of an equity stake. For example the initial sale price of VSEL from British Shipbuilders was £60 million, but this could rise to £100 million depending upon subsequent profitability. Similarly the sale of Unipart from Austin Rover included a price escalation clause which depended on profits and market capitalisation on flotation. Several Austin Rover and British Steel buy-outs have left the vendors with a retained equity stake as a check on initial under-pricing. In the sale of the National Bus subsidiaries, clauses were introduced in several cases to allow the government to claw back gains on the future development of town centre bus depots.

Nevertheless there is evidence that some privatisation buy-outs are resold – via a flotation or a trade sale – within very short periods at premiums considerably in excess of the buy-out price. Almost a third of privatisation buy-outs had exited in these ways by 1992, compared with 19 per cent of all buy-outs and buy-ins (Wright, *et al.*, 1993). The period between buy-out and exit is also shorter than the four years average for all types of buy-out which have exited. These exits may be deemed necessary from the point of view of the strategic development of the business, but the extent of the gains has been a cause of concern. However, in any analysis of the extent of the gains, due account needs to be taken of the changing price of assets generally since the privatisation occurred and the contribution of management to the increased value of the company before the extent of any under-pricing can be assessed.

Trade sales may frequently occur against direct competition from a buy-out attempt. Hence, if they are successful it must be assumed that a fair price has been paid. Similar safeguards to those adopted in some buy-outs, as noted earlier may also be introduced. Trade sales may also be a feasible means of privatisation when a company would not be viable as an independent entity. However, safeguards may need to be introduced where a continued trading relationship with the state-owned parent is envisaged. The incentives that government may have to give to encourage another group to make the acquisition may attract attention. The most notable case was the disposal of Austin Rover to British Aerospace (National Audit Office, 1989b). As will be seen below, the NAO considered that the disposal had occurred at a price which was highly advantageous to British Aerospace.

Concern about pricing has been particularly expressed in relation to the privatisation of local authority and government agency activities. The privatisation of local authority services is discussed in more detail in the chapter by Peter Jackson in this volume. In essence, the valuation issues identified earlier may be heightened in the context of this type of disposal because of the conflicts of interest when management may be acting both on behalf of the local authority and their own buy-out attempt, of uncertainties in valuing future income streams in previously non-commercial activities, and because of the difficulties in persuading outsiders to bid if they perceive that insiders have an unfair advantage. Both the Audit Commission (1990), in respect of local authorities, and the National Audit Office (NAO with CMBOR, 1991), in respect of government agencies, have sought to establish ground rules to ensure that such activities are disposed of at a fair price. In order to resolve conflicts of interest, the Audit Commission suggested several solutions, including entering arm's length negotiations between authorities and management teams, ensuring competitive bidding takes place, the establishment of an independent contract monitoring inspectorate, and close control of the length and nature of contracts. The status of the buy-out team during the negotiating period is a difficult issue since it raises questions as to the management of the operation in the meantime, and the position of a buy-out bid *vis-à-vis* a bid by a Direct Service Organisation. The Commission has suggested independent valuation of assets, determination of the market value of assets through competitive bidding, clawback arrangements, or retention of assets by authorities.

A more general approach adopted by the NAO (NAO with CMBOR, 1991), directly addresses the appropriate form of disposal as the first step in the divestiture process. If a buy-out is the most appropriate form of sale, then it needs to be assessed whether a buy-out would be viable (particularly important if a continued trading relationship exists), that appropriate control and information mechanisms are introduced, that variable pricing mechanisms are introduced if appropriate, etc. These concerns reflect those raised in respect of private sector buy-outs of companies quoted on a stock market, but as Amihud (1989) has observed great care is required in such approaches. If the anticipated returns to management are reduced by the introduction of stringent rules, they may be unwilling to bid in the first place so that all the gains to vendors may be lost.

Privatisation expenses

The cost of privatising state-owned assets has attracted a great deal of attention. Very large privatisations, especially British Telecom, British Gas, the Water Authorities and the electricity industry have required massive marketing campaigns to ensure that the government's objectives of a successful transition to the private sector and a wide spread of share ownership are met. As a result, the total privatisation expenses in these cases are far in excess of those of the more modest sales (Table 2.7). As a proportion of the proceeds from the sale, the expenses involved in these privatisations are exceeded only by the case of Associated British Ports. However, it is notable that in the last four major privatisations, total expenses have been between 2.4 and 2.8 per cent of equity proceeds, considerably below the levels seen in BT and British Gas.

These reductions reflect the effects of efforts to reduce costs of flotation in response to earlier criticisms. The problem, especially in the larger privatisations, has been to balance the objective of containing the costs of sale with that of ensuring that the sale is seen to be a success, that is achieves sufficient levels of subscriptions. It has now become typical to pay much closer attention to project management in flotations, including the use of staff with prior experience of the process. In the sale of the regional electricity companies a tendering process was introduced for primary underwriting, with the result that the overall rate of 0.17 per cent of the share price was one of the lowest for a major privatisation. The costs of incentives given to potential shareholders to encourage them to subscribe and to hold shares have been closely monitored both by sponsoring departments and, as will be seen below, by the NAO. In the sale of National Power and Powergen, clear indications were obtained before the offer had to be priced of the likely demand from institutions at different prices. This procedure demonstrated to the sub-underwriters the likely strength of demand at the offer price and enabled the sponsoring department to dispense with primary underwriters, so reducing costs. In addition, close monitoring of the marketing campaign produced savings of £1 million in relation to the original budget. Similarly in the case of Scottish Power and Hydro-electric, some £1.2 million was saved in comparison with the original budget as advertising was reduced so as not to create too much demand during the offer campaign.

Table 2.7   Privatisation expenses as a percentage of equity proceeds

Company	Date	Expenses/equity proceeds (%)	Expenses (£m)
Cable & Wireless	1981	3.1	7
British Aerospace	1981	3.8	6
Amersham International	1982	4.6	3
Britoil	1982	3.2	17
Assoc. Br. Ports	1983	11.2	2
Enterprise Oil	1984	2.8	11
British Telecom	1984	6.8	263
British Gas	1986	6.4	360
British Airways	1987	4.7	42
Rolls-Royce	1987	–	29
BAA	1987	3.4*	43
British Steel	1988	1.8	46
10 Water Authorities	1989	2.5	131
12 Electricity Companies	1990	2.4	191
National Power/ Powergen (60%)	1991	2.7	79
Scottish Power/ Hydro-electric	1991	2.8	98

Source: National Audit Office, various reports.
Notes: *Excluding £53.9m cost of bonus shares.

In comparison to the above, the cost of the sale of National Bus was at 2 per cent of gross sale proceeds well below that for most privatisations involving stock market flotations.

The privatisation process: National Audit Office (NAO) investigations

The NAO has become involved in the regular appraisal of the privatisation process, assessing how well and to what extent government departments have met their objectives for individual privatisations. The themes addressed centre around whether value for money has been obtained and to identify lessons for future privatisations. In particular, the NAO has examined whether the sale has been achieved in a timely fashion, whether sales proceeds have been maximised, whether the costs of sales have been reasonable, whether objectives of widening and deepening share ownership have been met, whether there is overall recognition that the sale has been a success, and in the case of stock market flotations whether a modest premium has been achieved. The privatisations covered in the NAO's reports include major flotations, divestments of individual assets, sales of companies to private sector groups and the break-up and privatisation of state-owned activities. It is worth noting, however, that the NAO cannot question matters of policy, only how well policy was implemented and that it does not have statutory access to the papers of state enterprises, only those of the sponsoring departments (Beauchamp, 1990). The experience of the NAO in these investigations and an approach which is perceived as neutral and constructive suggest that these points are not likely to have a materially adverse effect on the investigations (Garner, 1982; Wright, 1984).

Several major themes emerge from an analysis of the reports' findings. Almost invariably, the NAO has found that the relevant departments have successfully achieved the objectives of a transfer to the private sector within a given time scale. Objectives of achieving wider share ownership also receive favourable comments from the NAO, although it has at times questioned the necessity of using share incentives, particularly in the cases of BA (NAO, 1987b) and BAA (NAO, 1988). The NAO has noted with approval the attempts to reduce the costs of privatisations, examined in the previous section, but has continued to emphasise the need to evaluate in the circumstances of each sale what type and level of incentives might be required to attract the required level of subscription from investors. In the case of the regional electricity companies, the NAO considered that further market research could have been undertaken to identify more carefully the nature of incentives which ought to have been offered in order to market the sale successfully (NAO, 1992c).

As might be expected, the scope for greatest criticism has focused upon whether sale proceeds have been maximised. One area of concern relates to whether the entity has been properly valued in the first place and whether effort to strengthen a company financially prior to sale is likely to increase market value sufficiently to offset the cost of doing so

(Beauchamp, 1990). In respect of privatisation by flotation, the NAO also has been sceptical as to whether the extent of marketing costs (British Gas, NAO (1987a)) or bonus shares (BA and BAA) helped to maximise sale proceeds. In the case of the disposal of the regional water authorities, the NAO concludes that it was a notable achievement to privatise successfully ten companies with limited trading track records in a short time (NAO, 1991). The NAO also notes that the level of achievable proceeds was determined largely by the K factor in the regulatory formula, which determined revenue and in turn dividends. Hence, any significant increase in proceeds for the taxpayer would have been at the expense of the consumer.

Considerable debate has arisen about the form in which shares have been offered to the public. As a result of problems in correctly judging prices with both fixed price and tender offers in uncertain market conditions, and especially in early privatisations as seen above, there have been suggestions by the Public Accounts Committee to sell shares in tranches. The Treasury has opposed this approach on the grounds that where blocks of shares remain unsold this would overhang the market, affect proceeds and damage future sales. In the case of the 12 regional electricity companies, which involved a 100 per cent sale, the NAO notes that the novelty of the industry and a number of other uncertainties at the time of the sale made it particularly difficult to price the issue and suggests that a partial sale might have been preferable. In the sale of National Power and Powergen, some 40 per cent of the shares were retained, which the NAO considers to have yielded worthwhile gains to the taxpayer.

An alternative approach is the use of the back-end tender, whereby a proportion of shares is earmarked for offer to the highest bidders from institutional and overseas investors after the close of the offer period. This mechanism was used for the first time in the privatisation of the electricity generating companies (where it resulted in an extra £41.5 million proceeds) and subsequently in the sale of Scottish Power and Hydro-electric (where it resulted in £42.25 million extra proceeds). The NAO considers that such an approach could usefully have been employed in the sale of the regional electricity companies without adversely affecting the sale (NAO, 1992a,c).

In those privatisations examined which did not involve a stock-market flotation, the NAO has expressed concern about the lack of supervision by sponsoring departments of direct sales of subsidiaries by state enterprises themselves (Beauchamp, 1990). It has also frequently drawn attention to the need to consider greater use of clawback provisions to enable the taxpayer to benefit from subsequent gains arising on property development or sale of the company, as in the cases of the disposal of New Town Assets (NAO, 1986), Royal Ordnance (NAO, 1989a), Rover Group (NAO, 1989b), and Herstmonceux Castle (NAO, 1990b) and in the privatisation of work in English New Town bodies (NAO, 1990c). Later sales seem to have gone some way to meeting these concerns. In the case of National Bus (NAO, 1990c), it was considered that considerable care had been taken to safeguard the taxpayer by either selling property separately or through the use of clawback provisions. The operation of the clawback mechanisms embodied in some sales had produced an extra £6 million of revenue between the date of privatisation and the time of the NAO report. The possibility of undervaluation has subsequently been raised in other public sector bus buy-outs and there does appear to have been an extension of the lessons learnt in the National Bus case. For example, in respect of the West Midlands Travel company, where preference was for a buy-out on privatisation, mechanisms were introduced to increase the eventual price to be paid to well above that being considered initially.

In respect of the buy-out of the Skills Training Agency, the NAO noted that proper measures were taken to ensure that purchase by incumbent management did not give them an unfair advantage and although the method of disposal chosen represented only the fourth highest return it was the one which best met all the sales objectives. Clawback provisions on property appeared to be adequate, but proceeds were adversely affected by downturns in the property market at this time.

Clawback provisions on property disposals have also been introduced in recent stock market flotations, such as Scottish Power and Hydro-electric and National Power and Powergen. Although also used in the sale of regional electricity companies, the NAO considered that higher net proceeds might have been achieved in this case if some provision had been made to claw back a proportion of profits in excess of the cautious forecast which had been made. However, the positive effects on proceeds of such a measure would have to be offset against any corresponding negative effects on dividends and hence share prices.

Across all types of privatisation that it has examined, the NAO has frequently noted the need to offset against apparently less than maximum proceeds the adverse effects of uncertain or volatile markets and the influence of timetables for privatisation imposed by government.

Efficiency benefits and performance.

Subsequent chapters deal with increases in efficiency in the natural monopoly sectors. Attention is focused here on management and employee buy-outs, since information in respect of state assets sold to third parties is not available from the accounts of their new parent companies.

A number of consistent themes emerge from analyses of privatisation buy-outs: privatisation *per se* frequently enabled diversification and rationalisation of unprofitable product lines to take place; privatisation enabled more appropriate financial control systems,[4] employment contracts and negotiating machinery to be introduced; and frequently released former subsidiaries from the constraints on investment resulting from cash constraints on loss-making parents (see e.g. the case of Victaulic in Wright and Coyne, 1985; Coated Electrodes in Wright, *et al.*, 1991; NFC in Bradley and Nejad, 1989; RFS Industries in Wright, Thompson and Robbie, 1992b; and Unipart, in Wright, Thompson and Robbie, 1993). Key contributory factors to post- buy-out development also emerged as extensive restructuring prior to privatisation, including debt write-offs, the disposal of large amounts of under-used property the latent profitability of which incumbents had been able to identify prior to privatisation, and the general economic buoyancy of the late 1980s. Case study interviews of 20 of the NBC buy-outs, undertaken by the present authors in the first year after buy-out, found clear evidence that break-up had given a great deal of freedom to introduce more appropriate organisation structures, purchase appropriate fleet vehicles, to reduce costs bases and to obtain fuel at lower costs than available through central purchasing. Privatisation also provided scope for greater organic growth through diversification into related travel and leisure areas. The negative side was some loss of central co-ordination of new management training. Also in respect of NBC, break-up was reported to allow more localised and flexible remuneration structures which were seen as important in meeting increases in competition which came from the deregulation which accompanied the privatisation process. Costs would seem to have fallen in the bus industry as a result of both deregulation and privatisation. Glaister, *et al.,* (1990) report that competitive tendering for subsidised bus services has resulted in subsidy costs falling by some 20 per cent, though Heseltine and Silcock (1990) have observed a fall of 50 per cent in a number of areas.

Besides these positive factors, a number of danger signals are apparent: diversification which has been too rapid and outside areas of core skills and has consequently been unsuccessful; erosion of market as a result of new entry; loss of core contracts in some local authority buy-outs; and problems with commercially inexperienced managers and strong competition from established firms making it difficult to maintain a viable critical mass (see e.g. Paddon, 1991 and Wright, 1991 in respect of local authorities; and the case of Coated Electrodes in Wright, *et al.,* 1991).[5] These problem areas raise the need for financial control systems to be both strategically and operationally based.

It should also be noted that the initial privatisation form may need to change if the company is to continue to develop. In respect of NFC, for example, the company was floated on the official market in London in 1989, at a market capitalisation of £890 million. There were important needs to provide access to further capital to finance future expansion and to augment the internal share market. With a workforce which was relatively stable in size and with little staff turnover, there was a danger that the internal market would soon run out of sufficient liquidity to operate effectively. The Stock Exchange authorities gave exceptional permission for a special share to be created which would give employee shareholders double votes in the event of a hostile takeover bid, so helping to preserve employee control.

2.3 *Privatisation in Central and Eastern Europe*

In the newly emerged democracies of Eastern Europe, considerable interest has developed in the use of privatisation as a means of restructuring centrally planned economies (CPEs). In a CPE, the state is the maker of all formal entrepreneurial decisions. The central authorities attempt to co-ordinate *ex ante* supply and demand for all resources. The classic problem with central administration is that if state employees begin to behave in an opportunistic self-interested fashion, this can lead to control loss on a large scale. Such a problem is likely to arise where decision-making by employees is non-routine and where the exercising of judgement in the face of unanticipated events is likely to go unacknowledged and unrewarded by those higher up the vertical hierarchy. An economic system that depends exclusively on vertical monitoring of decision-making processes for the application of rewards and penalties when a high proportion of non-routine decisions must be made will produce high economic performance consistent with a lack of decentralised entrepreneurship, that is high production costs, low product quality and a lack of enthusiasm for innovation. These characteristics are those associated with the notion of soft budgets (Kornai, 1986). An enterprise faces a relatively soft budget constraint when it anticipates that monitoring, penalties and rewards will be permissive. The result is that the enterprise will tend to overconsume inputs, underproduce output and pay little regard to the mix of output that consumers would prefer. It could be argued that privatisation may not be necessary to resolve these problems since different techniques are available to those at the top of a vertical hierarchy to improve control and harden budget constraints. In a CPE with markets being absent the partial hardening of constraints may be ineffectual (Buck *et al.*, 1991). Further, the absence of effective private property rights causes serious governance problems in socialist systems.

Privatisation is thus seen as key to enabling a rapid shift to a market economy to take place. Despite a perceived need for privatisation, the obstacles to it are formidable. The issues involved have some parallels with privatisation experience in the West, but also raise a number of other fundamental questions. Aside from the need to introduce a legal and regulatory framework to establish the institutions of a market economy and provide the basis for a privatisation and restructuring programme (Hare, 1991), key questions concern whether assets should be sold or given away and to whom assets should be privatised. These questions are themselves influenced by the need to weigh issues concerning the speed of the privatisation process, the acceptability of various forms of privatisation, the governance of firms after privatisation and valuation problems.

The method of sale raises key issues concerning corporate governance (Table 2.8). In the CPE, where product market competition is often weak, there is hostility towards absentee shareholders, the market for corporate control is undeveloped and state enterprises can only be transformed into commercial entities at significant cost, indirect control by outsiders may have potentially adverse implications for performance. Hence, stock market flotation which is in any case restricted because of the as yet undeveloped nature of such markets, may have serious shortcomings. An alternative is to distribute shares in firms for free (Lipton and Sachs, 1990). Several variations on the distribution of free vouchers to allow all adults to bid for a certain percentage of major companies are being actively considered in the Czech Republic and Poland, but are regarded with some scepticism elsewhere. Major implementation problems and loss of revenue implications notwithstanding, it may provide a rapid and acceptable means of privatisation which avoids valuation problems (see below). However, where it involves the privatisation of a majority of a company's equity there is the risk of replacing existing problems with the classic problem of the divorce between ownership and control which arises from diffuse shareholdings (Corbett and Mayer, 1991; Kornai, 1992). This problem may be partly solved if blocks of shares are held by mutual funds. However, there remains the problem of finding enough well qualified managers and in any case such funds may essentially be the industrial ministries of state socialism (Ellerman, *et al.*, 1991).

Table 2.8 Alternative privatisation approaches and governance

Type of privatisation	Direct shareholder control by individuals	Direct shareholder control by institutions	Indirect shareholder control (through share sales)
Absentee shareholders:			
Trade sale	medium	medium	quite high
Flotation	low to medium	low to medium	high
Mass voucher schemes (without mutual funds/institutional shareholders)	insignificant	insignificant	high if shares immediately tradeable
Holding company/Mutual fund voucher schemes	low	high, if capable institutional managers available	low in long term
Incumbent shareholders:			
MBO	high	high	low
EBO	quite high	quite high	low

As an alternative, direct control by insider shareholders such as managers and other employees may be preferred, even on efficiency grounds. While shares for insiders invariably involve restrictions on the tradeability of shares, and thus inhibit indirect control by outsiders on an external, competitive capital market, they also offer the potential benefits of closer monitoring and horizontal monitoring by employees with insider knowledge who wish to raise the value of their shares. It can be argued that in the case of Japan and Germany, banks and other financiers effectively become 'insiders', enjoying long-term relationships with firms rather than short-term shareholdings. Buy-outs represent a means of introducing insider control with ownership and control closely held between incumbent management and funding institutions (Thompson, Wright and Robbie, 1992). The problems relate to questions about skill levels, concern about people associated with the previous regimes benefiting from privatisation, a reluctance to carry out necessary restructuring as insiders will be reluctant to vote themselves out of a job, concern that gains will be unevenly distributed depending on whether employees find themselves in a viable enterprise or not, and the difficulty in ensuring adequate institutional monitoring. This last point is of particular relevance in the light of the governance problems experienced in the Yugoslav workers' self-management regime and which may be exacerbated in the conditions of transition (Estrin, 1991).

Where voucher schemes are not used, the valuation issue has to be addressed. Although many enterprises are effectively worthless, others have considerable value. Techniques used in the West, such as price/earnings ratios, asset values and discounted cash flows, are difficult to apply in the absence of a market for corporate assets, with accounting information which is also an inappropriate base on which to value a company, uncertainty as to future performance and the problem of unenforceable inter-enterprise debt (Valentiny, Buck and Wright, 1992). A discounted future cash flow method may also be unacceptable as it rests on the implausible assumption that the state owns and is selling the full profit potential of the privatised company. However, the problem is that the state cannot generate the profits of the privatised companies. Selling at a price which discounts these gains is likely to remove the very incentive which is required (Ellerman, *et al.,* 1991). These kinds of difficulties have also arisen in respect of privatisations in the West, as seen earlier. Attempts to deal with the problem of undervaluation in the privatisation of former GDR assets include purchase price adjustment clauses and clawback clauses which require capital gains to be repaid to the *Treuhandanstalt* (THA), the privatisation agency, on a sliding scale if the enterprise is sold within a relatively short period (Carlin and Mayer, 1992). The THA is also able to sell firms without the accompanying property, which may be leased on a long-term basis but with the granting of an option to buy the property. In addition, penalties can be incurred if investment and employment guarantees made by the purchaser are not met.

The problem of who actually owns public assets has also had to be clarified since, despite a general perception that assets were publicly owned, its precise meaning was often not clear. The closest parallel in the UK to this issue involved the problem of establishing ownership of the Trustee Savings Bank prior to its stock market flotation. The absence of clear ownership in Hungary and other countries left scope for 'spontaneous privatisations' with managers taking action unilaterally, sometimes in the form of the nomenklatura buy-outs, and the potential for public assets to be disposed of at excessively low prices. It has thus proved necessary to enact legislation to establish ownership and create a joint stock company before privatisation can be satisfactorily progressed. However, an additional ownership issue which has subsequently emerged and which remains to be resolved concerns claims made by pre-communist regime owners to be reinstated (re-privatisation) or to be compensated.

The introduction of privatisation agencies, such as the SPA in Hungary and similar structures elsewhere, may help to regulate the problem of nomenklatura buy-outs but may only help to speed the process of privatisation if a decentralised approach is pursued whereby the company makes all the preparatory steps and the agency approves the sale. There does, of course, remain the well-known problems of regulatory capture and access to information, which may be exacerbated by a widely acknowledged shortage of skilled human resources to conduct the approval procedure. In September 1991 self-privatisation was introduced in Hungary principally for smaller firms. Buy-out teams are required to select a consultant from a government-approved list to provide an independent valuation of the company. Consultants are required to give priority in purchasing the firm to management and employees. While reputation and the threat of removal from the approved list gives consultants an incentive to make a fair valuation, this may be difficult in an uncertain environment where incumbent managers may be in a strong position to influence the apparent true value of a business.

The political attractiveness of voucher-based mass privatisation schemes for some segments of the population has frequently meant that they have been seen as in direct conflict with buy-outs. However, both schemes can co-exist for different sizes of companies and recent developments indicate that it may be possible to include both elements in the privatisation of a particular firm. Hence a minority of shares in a company may be acquired through vouchers, including the possibility for employees to exchange vouchers for shares in their company, with the majority of the shares being sold in auction to incumbent management and employees. This is particularly true of the privatisations in Russia which began in late 1992.

Trade sale, probably to foreign owners is likely to bring superior management skills, technical know-how, hard currency and much needed investment funds. It might also provide an acceptable level of corporate governance. However, it also carries the risk of bringing unacceptable levels of rationalisation. Moreover, given the difficulties in accessing information, there are some indications that foreign buyers may prefer to wait until a company has been privatised, say through a buy-out, and at least partially restructured before wishing to acquire it.

Conclusions

This chapter has examined divestiture of public sector assets in the light of government objectives. It was seen that in a number of cases, the appropriate organisational and ownership form was not consistent with objectives of increasing competition and hence allocative efficiency, especially in early privatisations. Moroever, early and large privatisations in particular appear not to have been associated with maximising sales proceeds either. The overriding issues were seen as ensuring that privatisation was perceived to be a success in the sense that a state enterprise was transferred to the private sector in a timely fashion without an embarrassing undersubscription of shares and in achieving at least short-term wider share ownership. These latter two objectives conflict to some extent with the two former ones. NAO investigations have noted substantial improvements in the costs of privatisation, but key issues continue in respect of ensuring that an appropriate competitive structure is achieved on privatisation and that a robust framework is in place so that sale occurs at a fair price. In respect of valuation issues there remains a need to ensure a balance between protecting the public interest and encouraging investors to invest and in the case of buy-outs to give managers the incentive to undertake such transactions in order to realise the wider benefits of productivity improvements. There has been increasing attention to both these issues. Problems remain in dealing with those industries already privatised and indicate a need to address structural issues at the time of privatisation and its implications for post-privatisation regulation. These issues are addressed more fully in the next chapter.

Notes

1 Buy-outs are considerably smaller on average than flotations. Even flotations vary considerably in size from the 47 employees in Enterprise Oil to the 238,384 in British Telecom. Using data from the flotated state firms' annual reports, the average number of employees on privatisation was 44,100. The average for those buy-outs with known employment levels is 1,466.
2 The Monktonhall Colliery in Scotland had at the time of writing been the subject of a quasi-buy-out in the form of a leasing arrangement by a group of employees and a similar arrangement in respect of Thurcroft Colliery in South Yorkshire was under discussion.
3 Management have to some extent been successful in turning an institution into a business and in changing corporate culture (Monopolies and Mergers Commission, British Coal Corporation, Cmnd, HMSO, 1989).
4 Of both an operational and strategic nature. This is particularly important to identify and monitor closely appropriate diversification activity.
5 Coated Electrodes grew rapidly post buy-out and achieved a stock market flotation. However, problems with diversification attempts and the entry into the market by a competitor with a product which superseded Coated Electrodes core product led to the firm being the subject of a rescue takeover.

References

Amihud, Y. (1989) *Leveraged Management Buy-outs: Causes and Consequences,* Dow Jones Irwin, New York.

Audit Commission (1990) Management buy-outs: public interest or private gain? *Management Paper No. 6,* Audit Commission, London.

Beauchamp, C. (1990) National Audit Office: its role in privatisation, *Public Money and Management,* Summer, pp. 55–8.

Bishop, M. R. and **Kay, J. A.** (1988) Does privatization work? Lessons from the UK, mimeo, London Business School.

Bishop, M. R., and **Kay, J. A.** (1989) Privatisation in the United Kingdom: lessons from experience, *World Development,* vol. 17. no. 5.

Boley, (1989) The Unipart buy-out: helping employees to a share of the action, *The Director,* Feb. pp. 89–90.

Bouin O. and **Michalet, Ch-A.** (1991) *Rebalancing the public and private sectors: developing countries' experience,* OECD, Paris.

Bradley, K. and **Nejad, A.** (1989) *Managing Owners – The NFC Buy-out,* Cambridge University Press.

Bruce, A. (1986) The Case of Sealink, in J. Coyne and M. Wright (eds), *Divestment and Strategic Change,* Philip Allan, Deddington.

Buck, T. and **Wright, M.** (1990) Control in Vertical Hierarchies, Soft Budgets and Employee Buy-outs, *Economic Analysis and Workers Management,* vol. XXIV (4), 377–94.

Buck, T., Thompson, S. and **Wright M.** (1991) Post-communist privatisation and the British experience, *Public Enterprise,* 11 (2–3), pp. 185–200.

Buckland, R. (1987) The costs and returns of the privatisation of the nationalised industries, *Public Administration,* vol. 65, pp. 241–58.

Buckland, R., Herbert, P. J. and **Yeomans, K. A.** (1981) Price discounts on new equity issues in the UK, *Journal of Business Finance and Accountancy,* vol. 8, pp. 79–95.

Calvo, G. A. and **Frenkel, J. A.** (1991) Credit markets, credibility and economic transformation, *Journal of Economic Perspectives,* vol. 5 no. 4, pp. 139–48.

Carlin, W. and **Mayer, C.** (1992) Restructuring enterprises in Eastern Europe, *Economic Policy,* 15, Oct., pp. 312–52.

Cherry, A. (1991) The statements of asset valuation practice and guidance notes (The Red Book). *Journal of Property Valuation & Investment,* vol. 9, no. 3.

Chiplin, B. and **Wright, M.** (1982) Competition policy and state enterprises in the UK, *Anti-trust Bulletin,* Winter, XXVII (4), pp. 921–56.

Chiplin, B., Wright, M. and **Robbie, K.** (1992) *Management buy-outs in 1991 and the first quarter of 1992,* CMBOR.

Colling, T. (1991) Privatisation and the management of IR in electricity distribution, *Industrial Relations Journal,* vol. 22 (2), pp. 117–29.

Committee of Public Accounts (CPA) (1991) Sale of National Bus Company, Ninth Report 1990/91, HC 119, HMSO.

Corbett, J. and **Mayer, C.** (1991) Financial reform in Eastern Europe: progress with the wrong model, *Oxford Review of Economic Policy,* 7 (4), pp. 57–75.

Cubbin, J., *et al.* (1987) Competitive tendering and refuse collection: identifying the sources of efficiency gains, *Fiscal Studies,* vol. 8, pp. 49–58.

Dehesa, G. de la (1991) Privatization in Eastern and Central Europe. Group of Thirty's occasional papers No. 34, Washington, DC.

Ellerman, D., Korze, U. and **Simoneti, M.** (1991) Decentralised privatisation: the Slovene ESOP program, *Public Enterprise,* 11 (2–3), pp. 175–84.

Elliot, D. (1991) The role of the OFT following bus deregulation, mimeo, OFT.

Estrin, S., *et al.* (1987) Profit-sharing and employee share ownership, *Economic Policy,* vol. 2, pp. 13–62.

Estrin, S. (1991) Privatisation in Central and Eastern Europe: what lessons can be learnt from Western experience, *Annals of Public and Cooperative Economy,* vol. 62, no. 2, pp. 159–82.

Estrin, S. and **Selby, M.** (1991) Privatisation: underpricing and the role of the derivative securities market, *Public Money and Management,* Autumn, pp. 43–5.

Evans, A. (1990) Competition and the structure of local bus markets, *Journal of Transport Economics and Policy,* vol. 24 (3), pp. 255–82.

Fama, E. and **Jensen, M.** (1983) The separation of ownership and control, *Journal of Law and Economics,* XXVI, pp. 302–24.

Filatotchev, I. (1991) Privatisation in the USSR: economic and social problems. *Communist Economies and Economic Transition,* vol. 3, no. 4.

Filatotchev, I., Buck, T. and **Wright, M.** (1992a) Privatisation and buy-outs in the USSR, *Soviet Studies,* vol. 44, no. 2, pp. 265–82.

Filatotchev, I., Buck, T. and **Wright, M.** (1992b) Privatisation and entrepreneurship in the break-up of the USSR, *World Economy,* 14 (4), 505–24.

Garner, M. (1982) Auditing the efficiency of the nationalised industries: enter the MMC, *Public Administration,* vol. 60, no. 4.

Glaister, S. and **Mulley, C.** (1983) *The Public Control of the British Bus Industry,* Gower Press, Aldershot.

Glaister, S., Starkie D., and **Thompson, D.** (1990) The assessment: economic policy for transport, *Oxford Review of Economic Policy,* vol. 6, no. 2, pp. 1–21.

Gwilliam, K. (1989) Setting the market free, *Journal of Transport Economics and Policy,* vol. 23, pp. 29–43.

Hammond, B., *et al.,* (1985) British Gas: options for privatisation, *Fiscal Studies,* vol. 6, pp. 1–20.

Hare, P. (1991) Hungary: in transition to a market economy, *Journal of Economic Perspectives,* vol. 5, no. 4, pp. 195–202.

Heseltine, P. and **Silcock, D.** (1990) The effects of bus deregulation on costs, *Journal of Transport Economics and Policy*, 24 (3), 239–54.

Hurdle, G., *et al.* (1990) Concentration, potential entry, and performance in the airline industry, *Journal of Industrial Economics*, vol. XXXVIII, no. 2, pp. 119–39.

Jackson, P. (1982) *The Political Economy of Bureaucracy*, Philip Allan, Deddington.

Jensen, M. (1989) The eclipse of the public corporation, *Harvard Business Review*, Sept/Oct.

Kay, J. and **Thompson, D.** (1986) Privatisation: a policy in search of a rationale, *Economic Journal*, 96, pp. 18–32.

Kornai, J. (1986) The soft budget constraint, *Kyklos*, 39 (1), pp. 3–30.

Kornai, J. (1992) The principles of privatization in Eastern Europe, *De Economist*, 140, no. 2, pp. 153–76.

Landon, J. (1983) Theories of vertical integration and their application to the electric-utility industry, *Anti-trust Bulletin*, vol. 28, pp. 101–30.

Lapsley, I. and **Wright, H.** (1990) On the privatisation of British Rail, *Public Money and Management*, vol. 10 (3), pp. 49–54.

Likierman, A. (1983) Evidence on accusations of manipulating profitability: adjustments for inflation accounting by the nationalised industries 1976–1981, *Accounting and Business Research*, vol. 14, no. 53, pp. 29–34.

Lipton, D. and **Sachs, J.** (1990) Privatization in Eastern Europe: the case of Poland, *Brookings Papers on Economic Activity*, 2, pp. 293–333.

McLachlan, S. (1983) *The NFC Buy-out – The Inside Story*, Macmillan, London.

Mayer, C. P. and **Meadowcroft, S. A.** (1986) Selling public assets: Techniques and financial implications, *Fiscal Studies*, vol. 6, no. 4, pp. 42–56.

Menyah, K., Paudyal, K. and **Inyangete, C.** (1990) The pricing of initial offerings of privatised companies on the London Stock Exchange, *Accounting and Business Research*, vol. 21, no. 81, pp. 50–6.

Monopolies and Mergers Commission (1989) *Badgerline and MRW Holdings*, HMSO, London.

Mulley, C. and **Wright, M.** (1986) Management buy-outs and the privatisation of National Bus, *Fiscal Studies*, August, pp. 1–23.

National Audit Office with CMBOR (1991) *Auditing Management Buy-outs in the Public Sector*, NAO, London.

National Audit Office (1986) *Disposal of New Town Assets,* NAO-HMSO, London.

——, (1987a) *British Gas,* HC 22, 1987/8, HMSO, London.

——, (1987b) *British Airways,* HC 37, 1987/8, HMSO, London.

——, (1987c) *Royal Ordnance,* HC 162, 1987/8, HMSO, London.

——, (1988) *BAA,* HC 312, 1987/8, HMSO, London.

——, (1989a) *Further Examination of Royal Ordnance,* HC 448, 1988/9, HMSO, London.

——, (1989b) *Sale of Rover Group to British Aerospace,* HC 9, 1988/9, HMSO, London.

——, (1990a) *British Steel,* HC 210, 1989/90, HMSO, London.

——, (1990b) *Herstmonceux Castle,* HC 341, 1989/90, HMSO, London.

——, (1990c) *Privatisation of Work in New Town Bodies in England,* HC 447, 1989/90, HMSO, London.

——, (1990d) *National Bus,* HC 43, 1990/1, HMSO, London.

——, (1991) *Skills Training Agency,* HC 484, 1990/1, HMSO, London.

——, (1992a) *Sale of Scottish Power and Hydro-electric,* HC 113, (1992/3), HMSO.

——, (1992b) *Sale of National Power and Powergen,* HC 46, (1992/3), HMSO.

——, (1992c) *Sale of Twelve Regional Electricity Companies,* HC 10 (1992/3), HMSO.

Nichols, T. and **O'Connell Davidson, J.** (1992) Employee shareholdings in two privatised utilities, *Industrial Relations Journal,* 23 (2), 107–19.

O'Brien, D. (1986) Divestiture: the case of AT&T, in J. Coyne and M. Wright (eds), *Divestment and Strategic Change,* Philip Allan, Deddington.

Paddon, M. (1991) Management buy-outs and compulsory competition in local government, *Local Government Studies,* 17 (3), pp. 27–52.

Pirie, M. (1988) *Privatisation: Theory, practice and choice,* Wildwood House, London.

Pryke, R. (1987) Privatising electricity supply, *Fiscal Studies,* vol. 8, pp. 75–88.

Salop, S. (1979) Strategic entry deterrence, *American Economic Review,* vol. 69, pp. 335–8.

Szymanski, S. and **Wilkins, S.** (1992) Competitive tendering: evidence from the public sector, *Business Strategy Review,* Vol. 3 (3), pp. 101–13.

Thompson, S. and Wright, M. (eds) (1988) *Internal Organisation, Efficiency and Profit*, Philip Allan, Deddington.

Thompson, S., Wright M. and Robbie, K. (1990) Management buy-outs from the public sector: ownership form and incentive issues, *Fiscal Studies*, vol. 11, no. 3, pp. 71–88.

Thompson, S., Wright, M. and Robbie, K. (1992) Buy-outs, divestment and leverage: restructuring transactions and corporate governance, *Oxford Review of Economic Policy*, vol. 8, no. 3.

Utton, M. (1991) *Competition Policy in the Deregulated Bus Market*, NERA, London.

Valentiny, P., Buck, T. and Wright, M. (1992) Privatisation and the valuation of public sector assets: experience from the UK and Hungary, *Annals of Public and Cooperative Economy*, 63 (4), 601–20.

Vickers, J. and Yarrow, G. (1985) *Privatization and Natural Monopolies*, London: Public Policy Centre.

Vickers, J. and Yarrow, G. (1988) *Privatisation: An Economic Analysis*. MIT Press, Cambridge, Massachusetts.

Vuylsteke, C. (1988) *Techniques of Privatisation of State-owned Enterprises*, vol. I, *World Bank Technical Papers No. 88*, World Bank, Washington, DC.

Whynes, D. (1987) On assessing efficiency in the provision of local authority services, *Local Government Studies*, Jan./Feb., pp. 53–68.

Wilson, N., Wright, M., Robinson, A. and Robbie, K. (1993) Privatisation of local-authority owned bus companies: evidence on employee attitudes, mimeo.

Wright, M. (1979) Inflation accounting in the nationalised industries: a survey and appraisal, *Accounting and Business Research*, Winter,

Wright, M. (1980) Real rates of return on capital: some estimates for British Gas, *Journal of Business Finance and Accounting*, Spring, vol. 7 (1), pp. 89–104.

Wright, M. (1984) Auditing the efficiency of the nationalised industries: exit the CAG?, *Public Administration*, vol. 62 no. 1, pp. 95–101.

Wright, M. (1985) Auditors' qualifications and nationalised industry accounts, *Accounting and Business Research*, Spring.

Wright, M. (1986) 'The make-buy decision and managing markets: the case of management buy-outs', *Journal of Management Studies*, vol. 23, no. 4, pp. 434–53.

Wright, M. (1987) Government divestments and natural monopolies: the case of British Gas, *Energy Policy*, June

Wright, M. (1991) Buy-outs of local authority services, in M. Wright (ed.), *Economist Guide to Buy-outs*, 6th edn., Economist Publications, London.

Wright, M. and **Buck, T.** (1992) Employee buy-outs and privatisation: issues and implications for LDCs and post-communist countries of UK experience, *Public Administration and Development,* vol. 12, pp. 279–96.

Wright, M., Chiplin, B. and **Robbie, K.** (1989) Management buy-outs, *Public Money and Management,* vol. 9, no. 3, pp. 59–65.

Wright, M. and **Coyne, J.** (1985) *Management Buy-outs,* Croom-Helm, London.

Wright, M., Dobson, P., Thompson, S., and **Robbie, K.** (1992) Does privatisation achieve government objectives? The case of bus buy-outs, *International Journal of Transport Economics,* October.

Wright, M. and **Petrin, T.** (1990) Transformation of public enterprises into employee stock ownership companies, in J. Prokopenko and I. Pavlin (eds), *Entrepreneurship Development in Public Enterprises,* ILO Management Development Series, No. 29.

Wright, M. and **Robbie, K.** (1992) Employee Buy-outs, in N. Wilson (ed.), *ESOPs,* Macmillan, London.

Wright, M., Thompson, S., Chiplin, B. and **Robbie, K.** (1991) *Buy-ins and Buy-outs: New Strategies in Corporate Management,* London: Graham and Trotman.

Wright, M., Thompson, S. and **Robbie, K.** (1989) Privatisation via management and employee buy-outs: analysis and UK evidence, *Annals of Public and Cooperative Economy,* vol. 60, no. 4, pp. 399–430.

Wright, M., Thompson, S. and **Robbie, K.** (1993) Finance and control in privatisation through buy-out, *Financial Accountability and Management,* vol. 9, no. 2, pp. 75–100.

Wright, M., Thompson, S., Chiplin, B. and **Robbie, K.** (1990) Management Buy-outs, trade unions and employee ownership, *Industrial Relations Journal,* 21 (2), 137–146.

Wright, M., Thompson, S., Robbie, K., Romanet, Y., Bruining, J., Joachimmsson, R. and **Herst, A.** (1993) Realisations, longevity and the life-cycle of buy-outs: a four country study, in B. Bygrave and M. Hay (eds), *Harvesting Venture Capital Investments,* FT-Pitman.

CHAPTER 3

Economic regulation of privatised monopolies

Catherine Price

Introduction

Five monopolies in the UK privatised between 1984 and 1991 are regulated to curb their dominant market power. This chapter explains why such regulation is necessary and outlines its implementation in Britain. Section 3.1 discusses the nature of the industries concerned and the objectives of such control; section 3.2 presents alternative models for achieving such outcomes, concentrating on rate of return regulation, price cap and public ownership; section 3.3 outlines the development and application of regulation in the UK; and the chapter concludes with a survey of relevant regulatory components and an assessment of future trends.

3.1 Objectives of regulation

Economic regulation attempts to improve on the outcome of unfettered market interactions and is motivated by some form of market failure. Usually this is market dominance by one producer but environmental considerations are increasingly significant, especially for water and the fuel sector where industries may cause pollution without themselves bearing the costs of the consequent injurious effects. Economic regulation can counteract such negative externalities and abuse of market power. But the industries in question (chiefly the utilities: water, gas, electricity and telephones) are also prone to other government objectives. Once a regulatory structure is imposed governments are tempted to use it for other objectives, including macro-economic policy. This section will concentrate on the more overt micro-economic objectives which motivate establishment of economic regulation in such industries. Discussion in section 3.3 reveals that the implementation of regulation is often affected by other factors.

Much of the rhetoric surrounding privatisation suggests that private markets should be superior to public ownership without the need for regulatory intervention. However the presence of monopoly power prevents such a happy outcome, since a profit maximising monopolist raises price above its most efficient level and restricts output. One obvious solution is to abolish monopoly power wherever feasible. But some monopoly power is inevitable in industries which deliver services through fixed networks (wires or pipes) to consumers. Indeed monopoly may be desirable in such industries in so far as it produces output more cheaply than duplicating the network. The traditional definition of natural monopoly of this kind has concentrated on economies of scale over the whole area of market demand; recent developments have defined natural monopoly more generally as including economies of scope, where the cost of producing a variety of products is lower than that of making each separately. Natural monopoly of this kind is inherent in all the utilities, though other parts of the industries could sustain competition. Much depends on how the firm is structured. Because regulation is required primarily to counteract monopoly power its extent and nature are determined by the industry's structure and the existence of actual or potential competition.

The natural monopoly element of utilities is in provision of services through a fixed network, and for such activities competition is neither feasible nor desirable. For telecoms this element is the local network of wires; for gas and electricity the national transmission and local distribution systems; for water the pipes which deliver water and remove waste. But competitive supply does coexist with such monopoly: telecommunications equipment and long-distance services; gas production and electricity generation; industrial waste disposal services. The distinction between potentially competitive activities and inevitably monopolised services has been much more closely reflected in the structure of industries privatised in the later phase of the programme; electricity was vertically and horizontally separated at privatisation in contrast to the integrated monopolies of telecommunications and gas. The separation of electricity supply into a service distinct from distribution was an innovative concept, demanding much more selective and specific application of regulation to 'those parts which competition cannot reach', while allowing development of competition wherever possible.

Regulation is also influenced by how those activities which must remain monopolistic are structured. For example the horizontal disaggregation of electricity distribution into Regional Electricity Companies (RECs) with local monopolies enables application of 'yardstick' regulation (where the rewards for an individual supplier depend on its performance relative to the average); such a solution is not applicable to the integrated gas or telecommunications industries as originally privatised.

The coexistence of inherently monopolistic activities requiring regulation and potentially competitive areas within each industry gives the regulator a dual role in monitoring both these sectors and in overseeing the vital access for competitors to the network; this is complicated where the incumbent monopolist owns the network and may want to restrict competition. The regulator's options in providing a framework for such an industry can be explored by defining the objectives of regulation. Kenneth

Train suggests the following criterion. 'Effective regulation establishes a situation in which the outcome that is socially optimal also generates most profit for the firm, such that the firm chooses it voluntarily.' (Train, 1991). Such a definition underlines the difference between regulating private firms so that they choose socially optimal outcomes, and owning nationalised companies which can (in principle at least) be directed to such decisions.

A distinction should be drawn between objectives identified when the regulatory structure is initially constructed and those of the regulator in operating later within these constraints. *Ex ante* objectives of regulation were first made explicit for the UK by Stephen Littlechild (Littlechild, 1983); then the criteria were developed in relation to British Telecom, but Littlechild has since been able to apply these principles as the first regulator of the electricity industry.

Littlechild suggested five objectives for regulation: first, protection against monopoly; second, encouragement of efficiency and innovation; third, low cost of implementation; fourth, promotion of competition; and fifth, maximisation of proceeds from sales and enhancement of the private company's commercial prospects.

This list contains some repetitions and contradictions; for example, promotion of competition may be a means to achieve protection from monopoly. Indeed competition itself may be undesirable if it raises costs of supply (i.e. contradicts the second objective). Moreover share sales proceeds are directly related to market power and so a further contradiction arises between the first objective and the fifth. However such conflicts are not new in government policy, particularly with respect to these sensitive industries which are so significant in both domestic and industrial sectors.

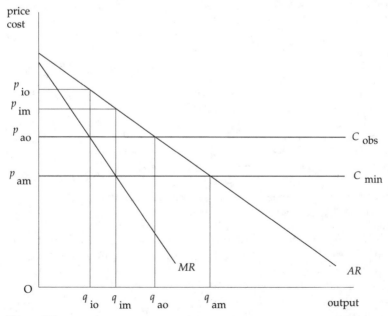

Figure 3.1

In economic terms the objectives suggested by Littlechild describe a regulator maximising the industry's welfare (the weighted sum of consumer surplus and profit). The relative weights of these two components in the regulator's objective function affect the preferred outcome: the greater the weight of consumer surplus the lower the price. For simplicity we shall assume that the weights are equal, so that allocative efficiency is achieved by marginal cost pricing. If this yields insufficient revenue for the firm to cover total costs, prices should be raised above marginal costs most for products whose demand is least responsive to such price increases. Demand is then disturbed as little as possible from the ideal (first best) pattern. The consequent prices may however raise questions of equity if they result in disproportionate gains or burdens for particular consumer or income groups or industries. Though Littlechild does not explicitly mention this, it is likely to be an important political issue for governments.

Allocative efficiency concerns the relation of price to appropriate costs, while productive efficiency is concerned with minimising the level of these costs (Littlechild's second ojective). These objectives may conflict in choosing regulatory regimes.

The regulatory options can be illustrated in Figure 3.1. Figure 3.1 shows constant returns to scale for simplicity, though this chapter is concerned with natural monopolies. This entails no loss of generality. C_{obs} represents the observed costs; C_{min} the minimum achievable costs; p_{ao} is the allocatively efficient price with the higher level of C and p_{am} an outcome which is both allocatively and productively efficient. p_{io} and p_{im} are the monopoly prices with observed and minimum cost levels and the corresponding output levels are indicated by q_{ao}, q_{am}, q_{io}, and q_{im}. The regulator's task is to achieve p_{am}, q_{am}. This can be characterised as the following paraphrase of the Littlechild objectives:

(1) enabling the industry to capture economies of scale through monopoly production;

(2) preventing abuse (high price and restricted output) of the consequent monopoly power;

(3) encouraging productive efficiency (low operating costs); and

(4) minimising the regulatory costs.

The need to address the second and third issues arise directly from lack of competitive pressures in the monopoly, which is itself needed to take advantage of economies of scale and would probably arise anyway from a free market process through bankruptcy and/or merger.

These objectives are addressed through a series of regulatory bargains. The first is the privatisation bargain itself in which the government sells a share in profits. This is struck at a price determined by expected profits which depend *inter alia* on the severity of regulation. Other pertinent factors are the structure of the industry and expected limits on sectors not subject to explicit regulation. The conditions which the government imposes in each of these categories determines the expected profitability and share price. The nature of the 'flotation bargain' renders the initial period different from its successors with implications for the level of regulation imposed which will be apparent later.

In each regulatory period (including the first) another bargain is made: between the profit-maximising industry and a regulator aiming for objectives discussed above. The regulatory regimes imposed represent an agreement between these parties for the relevant time period. The enforceability of both the privatisation and regulatory bargains has become increasingly controversial. Proposals by the gas regulator to restructure the industry raise questions about security of the initial privatisation bargain. Splitting up British Gas would be no different in principle from the divestiture of the American AT&T telephone company in the 1970s, but those who bought shares in British Gas as recently as 1986 might feel cheated by a government which changed the rules after play had commenced but when it had safely pocketed the privatisation proceeds.

Similarly regulators are often under considerable pressure to intervene during the regulatory period if firms declare high profits or particular consumer groups are adversely affected by charges which satisfy the constraints imposed on the industry. If the profit level is not an explicit target of regulation then tightening restraint in response to higher profits involves reneging on the relevant bargain. Governments may also try to intervene for other reasons, macro-eonomic or distributional, or to protect a supplying industry. Before the history of such 'bargains' in the UK is reviewed the next section considers what structures are available to achieve the regulatory objectives outlined above.

3.2   Models of regulation

The previous section has highlighted the nature of regulation as a bargain between government, regulator and industry which changes market outcomes from those of an unfettered market. There are a variety of structures which may facilitate such objectives, four of which were considered by Littlechild. To these can be added public ownership, the traditional British method of regulation until the 1980s. (Though regulation was very non-specific, as we shall see, nationalisation represents one implicit form of industry control. Hence the confusion in terminology in the United States and Britain, where a similar move to more reliance on market forces is named deregulation in the US, and regulation in the UK. Reregulation is perhaps a better description of the latter experience, see Chapter 4.)

Littlechild's paper focused on the relative merits of rate of return regulation and a cap on some of the prices charged by the company. Rate of return regulation, which restricts the company's profits to a defined proportion of its capital, had encountered problems in the US where it had been used for some years. Tying profit to capital encouraged over-use of capital, the so-called Averch–Johnson effect (Averch and Johnson, 1962). Moreover the regulator was intimately involved in defining the costs of the industry to determine profit; later the concept of allowable and non-allowable capital expenditure drew the regulator still further into a mire of detail. All this was exacerbated by the litigious nature of the American system, and might have posed less acute problems in the more secretive British framework. By the time explicit regulation was required in the UK the failings of the US system were abundantly clear.

In meeting the four objectives defined at the end of the previous section, rate of return regulation can prevent monopoly abuse and achieve allocative efficiency if the allowed rate is set very close to the cost of borrowing (Train, 1991). However rate of return does not achieve productive efficiency because of the incentive to over capitalise, and the regulation is very expensive for both firm and regulator to implement.

Direct control of prices avoids both these problems. The regulated firm can increase profits only by reducing costs, and will therefore seek the least cost input combination. Indeed regulators have been concerned that this message will be too strong, resulting in a fall in quality which consumers are unable to avoid because of the lack of alternative suppliers. In operation a price cap is easy and cheap to monitor, so costs are low for both parties. However though input choice is not distorted some forms of price cap may induce an inappropriate output mix, as we shall show later.

Given these benefits the UK government's enthusiasm for price cap is not surprising. As a short-term measure, which regulation was originally perceived to be, it had obvious advantages. Littlechild expected that price cap would be an interim arrangement until rapidly developing competition in telecommunications rendered it redundant. Once the initial price cap was determined as part of the privatisation bargain its administration was relatively straightforward.

Such benefits remain however only so long as the determination of the level of price cap is exogenous to the industry and the firm cannot affect its level. If the industry believes that the regulator will choose the cap according to the firm's performance then it will adapt its behaviour accordingly. Since regulators have few criteria other than rate of return to determine the appropriateness of price levels, the necessity to review the price cap induces the firm to reduce rate of return, and introduces the familiar incentives to overcapitalise. 'Repeated' price cap bargains inevitably become rate of return regulation when price cap is determined; during the course of a regulatory bargain the industry can reap the short-term benefits of efficiency gains, but expects that these will be transferred to consumers through a tighter price cap at the next review. The constraint becomes a hybrid with some elements of the costs and advantages of both price cap and rate of return regulation.

The net outcome is likely to be a similar mixture. An industry subject to average revenue constraint, which aggregates prices according to current quantities sold, is likely to raise prices in high cost markets and lower them in low cost markets, relative to the optimum level; this would probably slant seasonal tariffs so that peak prices (where both costs and demand are high) are above the optimum, and off-peak prices lower than optimum (Bradley and Price, 1988). However a rate of return/cost of service regulation might have the converse effect, since the industry would wish to expand its capital base, and therefore peak capacity, and would lower price at peak to raise demand at this time. Thus to the extent that an industry subject to short-term average revenue regulation acts strategically to raise the capital base for the time at which regulation was reviewed, the two effects might fortuitously counteract each other. Conversely the worst effects of both might be apparent.

The two regulatory regimes differ fundamentally in that price cap applies only to monopolistic sectors while rate of return covers the entire industry. Indeed costs and infrastructure shared by different markets make it virtually impossible to separate rates of return for different sectors in any integrated industry, though this may be easier where the industry is disaggregated. Where price cap is periodically reviewed according to achieved rates of return the profitability of the 'uncapped' sector will inevitably play a significant role.

The extent of price cap is crucial. It should be restricted to areas where both competition and its prospect are absent; otherwise the firm can combine predatory pricing in the competitive sector with exploitation in the monopolistic sector within an average price cap applied to both markets. Such behaviour might result either from short-term attempts to exclude competition or, if the potential profitability of higher prices in the monopolistic market exceeded lost profits, from subsidising the potentially competitive one. Where consumers need temporary protection until competition develops the market should be subject to a separate price cap, though care should be taken that potential entrants are not discouraged by the prospect of restrictions. Another argument for separate caps might arise for distributive reasons within markets to protect specific consumer groups. The allocatively efficient pattern of prices which exceed marginal costs most for services which are least price responsive may place a disproportionate burden on the poor. Limiting price increases for specific groups or products provides protection, but at the expense of preventing the company from rebalancing prices in the most allocatively efficient way.

If the uncapped sector is genuinely competitive, or potentially so, the firm will choose those prices efficiently (indeed the market will determine the price charged). But regulation may have a profound effect on cost allocations. If profits in this sector are included in rate of return calculations the firm has an incentive to inflate the capital base and use an inefficient input combination throughout the company. Alternatively, if an attempt is made to calculate rate of return separately for the regulated sector the firm will allocate to it as many costs and as much capital expenditure as possible to deflate profits and raise capital base and so argue for a laxer price cap. This may focus the undesirable incentives of rate of return regulation within the capped sector.

Where a choice must be made between price cap and rate of return Beesley and Littlechild (1989) have suggested that it be determined by the characteristics of the industry concerned. An industry moving towards a competitive structure may be regulated by a price cap, partly because the problem of incentive is reduced by the industry itself having both opportunity (through changing technology) and reason (potential competition) to reduce costs. Where the chance of competition is small and there is a single firm within the industry the prospects of cost reduction, and so the importance of incentives, are less, suggesting that rate of return or cost of service regulation may be more appropriate. In general, recent development in the literature suggests that initial enthusiasm for price cap regulation may have overstated its advantages, particularly where there is uncertainty (see for example Schmalansee, 1989).

Most such industries were nationalised, or rationalised if already in public ownership, by the Labour governments which held office between 1945 and 1951. Little specific attention was paid to their operation (though there was a vigorous political debate about the effect of nationalisation on the operation of the coal industry), and no specific guidelines were given about their management. Such guidance was regarded as unnecessary, since these industries were expected to operate in the public interest, and the appropriate management decisions were assumed to be largely self-evident. The nature of this 'public interest' was identified in three areas: to act fairly as employers (particularly important in the context of troubled labour relations in the pre-war period); to cover costs 'taking one year with another'; and not to practise undue discrimination between consumers (see for example the 1948 Gas Act).

Interpretation of these clauses was left to the industries and various governments in the period up to 1979. The requirement to cover costs originally implied the inclusion only of historical cost depreciation, an understanding later amended to include some allowance for replacement costs by introducing target rates of return over and above 'break even' (HM Government, 1961). In contrast to rate of return regulation this was a minimum rather than a maximum constraint. Similarly the requirement not to discriminate between consumers was probably intended to indicate uniform pricing, while more recent work (Phlips, 1983) defines discrimination as failure to reflect relative costs of supply in prices.

Covering costs meant that price levels had to reflect average costs. However in 1967 a White Paper recommended marginal cost pricing, a policy adopted as official policy even though it was not fully accepted by the industries themselves. The losses which such a policy would cause in industries which had falling average costs were never adequately addressed, even in the later (1978) White Paper which did try to resolve some of the misunderstandings about definition of marginal cost. Allowing natural monopolies to make losses would contravene the nationalisation Acts whose sparse guidelines did include the requirement to break even.

Another confusion arose for nationalised industries in their responsibility for broader government policies. The prices and incomes policies of the 1960s and 70s emphasised this through the special expectations imposed on government-owned industries, both as exemplars and because their own products were a significant component of the Retail Price Index. As a result the wages, prices and morale of nationalised industries were severely depressed, an inevitable result of 'leading the way' in a voluntary policy where few others followed. Moreover it was not clear how their obligations as leaders in macro-economic policy related to managerial obligations in terms of pricing policies, financial targets and investment policies. Since there was no formal mechanism to ensure consistency even between these micro-economic objectives, the confusion over their role in the macro-economic arena further muddied an already murky scene. Ironically at the beginning of the 1980s the emphasis on restricting the Public Sector Borrowing Requirement required these industries to raise prices in order to be less of a burden on the exchequer in pursuit of the same low inflation goal. None of this helped provide clear guidelines for management, but it did raise their profitability usefully prior to privatisation.

Other government objectives also impinged on nationalised industries even at the end of the period when the damage from ministerial intervention was widely recognised. For example the fuel industries were subject to government pressures: first in holding down gas prices in 1979 against the recommendations of the Price Commission, and later raising real gas prices by 30 per cent over the next three years, then by introducing a standing charge rebate scheme for users of small amounts of gas and electricity (the political nature of this policy was betrayed by its announcement at a Conservative Party conference in the year prior to a general election). Such confusions and contradictions were used as a powerful argument in favour of privatisation, though the difficulties resulted from interference by the very government which criticised such intervention; similar difficulties continue to affect regulatory agencies.

The implication of their ill-defined role for nationalised industries was that the lack of clear direction and the receipt of conflicting messages caused significant difficulty for management. This left considerable scope for development of independent objectives, and managers and workers were able to pursue goals of expansion, high employment and wages with little effective control (see for example Rees, 1984). This came to be seen as 'public' failure parallel to the market failure which nationalisation had been designed to cure.

Most industries practised some form of average cost pricing, conscious that either profits or losses would attract opprobrium: the former because of suspected consumer exploitation and the latter on grounds of inefficiency. The fact that breaking even guarantees neither efficiency nor lack of exploitation, particularly where industries are statutory as well as natural monopolies, would not detract from the attractiveness of such a policy for managers pursuing their own ends and hoping to avoid the close scrutiny of either media or politicians. The outcome was somewhat haphazard, and was criticised by the National Economic Development Office (1976) which recommended far-reaching changes. However, events were somewhat overtaken by the privatisation programme. The patterns of this privatisation programme have been outlined in the first two chapters of this volume; the next section of this chapter concentrates on how regulatory structures for these industries developed.

3.3 *Regulatory development in the UK*

Regulation in the UK reflected a very different approach both in structure and style from that in the United States (see for example Stelzer, 1991). The US had a much longer history of regulation which was embedded in a culture emphasising due process and open hearings, and resulted in a tardy and expensive process. In contrast, closed negotiations and confidential hearings are traditional in the UK. This makes regulation quicker and cheaper, but somewhat more haphazard since the regulators themselves must take account of a variety of interests where these are not guaranteed a separate hearing. Much confidential negotiation between regulator and industry is held 'in the shadow' of the law, which is often perceived as a threat if negotiations are unsuccessful. Regulators themselves are only weakly accountable; they are conscious of judicial review which may be implemented if they act *ultra vires,* but there is little other formal control. This is in stark contrast to the US where regulators' actions are open to constant public scrutiny.

The privatisation Acts created for each industry a partner regulator specifically concerned with its decisions, and acting in concert with other regulatory bodies. Three of these can affect the industries' operations. The minister of the sponsoring government department shares some responsibilities with the regulator under the privatisation Act and holds separate powers, for example to control entry to the industry or define a legally protected monopoly market. The Office of Fair Trading (OFT) has a special responsibility for general competition policy; and the Monopolies and Mergers Commission (MMC) has power to alter the licences of the companies and investigate the existence or exploitation of monopoly power. Each of these 'regulators' has a more general remit, and different objectives, for example political considerations in the case of government ministers. The regulatory bodies themselves are constituted as non-ministerial government departments, so they are clearly an arm of the government but with an apolitical emphasis. The inter-relation between the regulators, not always obvious at privatisation, became increasingly complex and significant as regulation developed.

While the OFT and MMC pursue general competitive objectives, the industry specific regulators are also responsible for encouraging competition. As well as overseeing regulation of the monopolistic sector of the industry, each regulator had a duty, variously expressed, to encourage or enable competition in the unregulated part. This usually involves access to the natural monopoly elements which are owned by the incumbent monopolist; terms of access for potential competitors are vital for their entry into the market and the regulator is responsible for ensuring reasonable terms. The relation between the sectors has become increasingly delicate, particularly when regulation is reviewed.

The first explicit economic regulation was introduced in 1984 for British Telecom. Privatisation was accompanied by considerable changes in the competitiveness of some parts of the industry (notably equipment supply) and by the establishment under licence of a protected 'line' competitor, Mercury. Just over half BT's revenue was regulated.

This regulation was of a price cap tariff basket kind. The prices which BT was allowed to charge were limited by a constraint on the revenue which would have been raised if the previous year's quantities had been sold at the current year's prices. The constraint was of the so-called 'RPI – X' type, since it required the average price so defined to decline by X per cent annually in real terms. X is a measure of the managerial efficiency improvement expected in each year. This constraint is consistent with one which induces the firm to balance prices in the most allocatively efficient way (Vogelsang and Finsinger, 1979).

RPI rather than some industry cost-related index was used to avoid the problems of an index which could be influenced by the dominant regulated firm, and so enable excessive costs to be passed on in higher prices. The RPI not only has the merit of being independent of industry influence but is significant for consumers whom the government were trying to reassure about the adverse effects of privatisation. Initial choice of X was in all cases a political decision, emerging from private debate between the industry and the government. The identity of the regulator was often not disclosed at this stage. Here the link between the structure of the privatised industry and the extent and severity of the regulation is most obvious. An industry privatised to maximise competitive potential would require regulation to control a smaller proportion of its activities than one which was maintained as a monopolistic entity. But the government's desire to maximise sales proceeds (an important objective recognised in Littlechild's 1983 paper) suggested maximum monopoly power with minimum regulation. The initial level of regulation reflected this requirement for a 'successful' (i.e. fully subscribed) flotation, and X would be correspondingly depressed. This was particularly evident in the gas industry where potential competition and vigorous regulation were sacrificed to the political and financial expedient of the industry's quick (and profitable) sale.

British Gas (BG) was privatised in 1986 and the British Airports Authority (BAA) in 1987. BG's senior management demanded light regulation in return for their co-operation in the swift transfer to the private sector which the government wanted. Regulation applied only to the tariff market, then defined as sales of gas to consumers using less than 25,000 therms each year, and to whom a published tariff applied, unlike consumers of larger amounts of gas who negotiated individual and confidential contracts with BG. The majority of tariff market consumers are domestic, though many small industrial and commercial users also buy under the tariff. BG had a legal monopoly on sales to tariff consumers, though its monopoly in the contract market was merely *de facto*.

Average revenue in the tariff market was constrained by a price cap. This was a current weighted average price, an obvious choice in an industry which had a uniform charge per unit of gas sold regardless of place, season or time of day. Any other weighting system would have been irrelevant so long as uniform pricing remains and would have seemed to be a contrived introduction of categories not used in the tariff.

However such an average revenue constraint may be undesirable if such differentiation between regions, seasons or times becomes likely. In the gas industry there are clear cost differences both between regions (since British Gas is primarily a gas purchasing and distribution company whose costs depend on distance over which gas is delivered from beach-heads) and seasons (because of the variation between summer and winter demand). The failure of BG to differentiate these prices in the past probably results from mixed motives: a sense of public service, a desire to maximise the long-term (domestic) market, and some rather strange concepts of the functions of prices (evidence to Energy Committee, 1985). BG's belief that consumers do not want differentiated tariffs persists, as its managers remind us (Simon Kirk, 1993). It is not at all clear that the present uniform gas tariff is appropriate, and BG's introduction of seasonal weights in its bulk price schedules and transport charges suggests there is at least a *prima facie* case for the introduction of similar differentiation in the tariff. Indeed an optional seasonal element has been introduced for large tariff consumers. Arguments for distinguishing according to average distance over which gas is delivered are even stronger, given the ease of implementation and the imposition of distance-related charges to competitors hiring space in the transmission system. Competition will encourage BG to introduce regional differentiation in the contract market where continued average pricing would make the cheap markets most attractive to competitors; BG must either reduce its prices there to compete or lose the business and subsidy which currently supports the more expensive markets.

In the event of such differentiation the present average revenue constraint would encourage distortions in the balance of the tariff compared with the most efficient pattern of prices. Arguments outlined in section 3.2 suggest that this might be partially counteracted by the effect of the rate of return element inherent in price cap review. However this seems a somewhat haphazard way in which to regulate an industry, and is unlikely to be the reason for the government's original decision, which merely reflected the existing uniform tariff.

More surprising, perhaps, was the lack of any regulation in the industrial and commercial contract market, where BG supplied over one-third of the non-transport fuel demand and 100 per cent of the gas. The absence of regulation in this sector has been consistently criticised, and constraints have increased significantly since privatisation, culminating in the decision to divest the industry of half this market and to separate gas transport activities by 1994. Such an outcome has resulted from the regulator honouring his duty to 'enable persons to compete effectively', a task he has pursued vigorously. Interventions from other competitive bodies (notably the MMC and OFT) have spawned the publication of a rapidly changing set of price schedules both for sale of gas to the contract market and for transport services. While the MMC and OFT have significantly altered competitive conditions in the contract market, the regulator has tightened the price cap by raising X and restricting the ability of BG to pass on gas purchase costs to consumers. Almost simultaneously the remaining regulator, the government minister, reduced the boundary of the guaranteed (and regulated) monopoly market from 25,000 to 2,500 therms sold per annum. This apparently independent regulation of different aspects of BG's operations resulted in a self-referral of the whole industry to the MMC in July 1992, a move which carries the risk of dismemberment for BG.

BAA is not a natural monopoly but, endowed with ownership and control of London's three airports, it required economic regulation. The industry continued under the control of the Civil Aviation Authority, which combines both economic and other regulatory responsibilities for the company. As with British Gas and British Telecom regulation was partial, and did not include the duty-free shops which generated a significant part of the profits and revenue. Excluding these activities from regulation (even though they can hardly have been said to be competitive) introduced incentives to expand them at the expense of regulated services. The regulated portion of the Authority had shrunk from 45 per cent to 40 per cent of its revenue during the first five-year regulatory period (MMC, 1991).

Despite the somewhat obscure process of privatising BAA there was considerable consultation about the form of price cap to be applied, partly because revision of price cap requires referral to the MMC. Two candidates were already in force, the tariff basket formula applied to British Telecom, and the average revenue constraint imposed on British Gas. We have seen that the former is superior because it gives the firm incentives to price efficiently, though average revenue may be a more obvious choice where a single product like gas is sold at a uniform price. The CAA commissioned an independent report (NERA, 1986) which recommended a tariff basket constraint, mainly on operational grounds. However the government chose average revenue regulation. The debate was repeated for Manchester Airport and a tariff basket was again suggested, this time by the MMC, and again the Department of Transport chose average revenue regulation. One explanation for this choice is that average revenue constraint seems to yield a higher level of profit for the airports than does tariff basket regulation with the same X. A higher X appears to provide more protection for consumers, while average revenue grants the firm greater profits, so the combination offers an attractive compromise between these interests.

The next industries to be regulated, water in 1989 and electricity from 1990, complete the public utilities in this category but differ from the first three in constituting horizontally disaggregated firms rather than a single monopoly. (British Rail, which the government is proposing to transfer to private operation through franchises, has many similar economic characteristics, but is not technically a utility.) Both industries are divided into regional companies with *de facto* if not permanent legal local monopolies over much of the market, and the electricity industry is further divided vertically into generation, transmission and distribution (supply) companies with generation also split horizontally. The existence of several companies operating at similar levels in different locations offers potential yardstick regulation, the subject of much discussion before privatisation. In the event comparisons have initially been left largely to regulators on an informal basis rather than being included explicitly in the regulation structure.

Regulation of water prices is complicated by a charging system based on rateable value and levied per household, rather than depending directly on quantities consumed. In effect water bills constitute a (variable) standing charge and zero commodity charge. Regulation is based on a tariff basket, appropriately amended for these circumstances. This acts as an incentive for water authorities to introduce water saving methods, and for the move towards metering which the regulator is encouraging. This would almost certainly increase economic efficiency (the only doubt concerns the cost of introducing metering) but might require considerable protection for low income users. Each water company has its revenue limited by RPI + K where K varies according to investment expenditures required by each firm particularly in responding to EC directives.

Electricity regulation is confined to the public suppliers (successors to the regional boards) and transmission charges on the basis that there is sufficient competition in generation to make regulation unnecessary. The regulation formula is complex and allows for a number of costs to be 'passed through' without being subject to the constraint, including generating and transmission costs and the surcharge to support the nuclear generating industry. Most commentators consider that the generation market is insufficiently competitive (with two dominant producers) to justify its unregulated state (Newbery and Green, 1991).

Substantial competition has developed among independent suppliers in response to the duopoly power of the private generators, with subsequent problems for coal supply. These difficulties demonstrate both the desire for responsiveness of supply to potential profit and the RECs' desire for political and economic independence from the generators. The argument over alternative fuel supplies has also focused attention on the role of the regulator, who steadfastly refuses to interfere on the basis of broader government concerns. Despite being the last of the utilities to be privatised the electricity industry has shown the quickest and most dramatic changes, largely because of its disaggregated structure.

While at privatisation the imposition of regulation can be seen as a means for reaching those markets where competition cannot be introduced, after privatisation the close control of incumbent firms may discourage new entrants. This raises the question of how much of the industry's activities should be regulated and how such activities should be defined for regulatory purposes. The exact coverage of regulation depends on the government's view of both actual and potential competition, and regulation will generally be applied to those activities where monopoly power is strongest and most intractable.

In each privatised industry the unregulated sector generally represents an area where potential competition is considered feasible, i.e. a contestable market. But these industries are natural monopolies by virtue of their transmission networks. Competition in a network industry depends crucially on terms of access to the distribution system, owned by the incumbent monopolist. In potentially competitive areas the monopolist can choose between continuing to supply the 'unregulated' market itself, and making its distribution system available to competitors for rent. The form of regulation will influence this decision through its effect on the profitability of various alternatives (Laffont and Tirole, 1990).

In both gas and electricity competition had been very slow to develop before privatisation, despite the removal of legal protection for the nationalised industries in the early 1980s. The effect of industry structure on potential entry is dramatically demonstrated by the different experiences of these industries since flotation. No significant competition developed in the vertically and horizontally integrated gas industry, despite the industry adopting the recommendations of the 1988 MMC report to encourage entry. By 1992 the industry had agreed to divest itself of half its industrial market and split transportation and storage from supply, and the regulator was recommending separate ownership of the two halves. In contrast, supply competition in the disaggregated electricity industry had developed so fast that within two years of privatisation the choice to build new gas-fired generation plant caused major problems for the traditional supplier, coal, and for the government in consequent political implications. Indeed, even the limited stimulus which had occurred for private use of gas pipelines was mainly for electricity generation. In telecommunications entry was thought feasible only if the entrant was protected, so a single new entrant was admitted with a guaranteed position until 1991, though the market was later opened to other competitors.

3.4   Characteristics of regulation and their development

Preceding sections of this chapter have explained the philosophy, background and development of regulation in the UK. This section considers in more detail and summarises the development of different characteristics of the price cap. Five characteristics are considered: the type of cap; the extent of regulation and to which market it is applied; the element of costs passed direct to consumers outside the cap; the period between reviews; and the level of the cap and changes at revision. These characteristics are then summarised in tabular form to identify a pattern of development.

Tariff basket or average revenue price cap

Section 3.2 explained the difference between a base-weighted tariff basket and a current weighted average revenue (sometimes called revenue yield) price cap. Tariff basket constraint is more likely to induce the firm to choose allocatively efficient prices subject to the limit imposed by the cap. There has been little public debate about the type of cap, as indeed about most initial imposition of regulation, though the issue was raised with respect to the British Airports Authority, and there was some discussion at the first reviews of regulation for BT and BG.

Tariff basket has been applied to British Telecom and to water charges (even though these are not strictly prices since they are largely unrelated to consumption). Average revenue constraints apply to British Gas, BAA and the various regulated electricity charges.

Extent of regulation

The regulation of integrated monopolies such as BT and BG poses different questions from that applied to the disaggregated electricity industry. Later privatisations have been of separated industries, partly because the government was prepared to strike a different privatisation bargain, which in turn was significant for the regulatory bargains. Where the privatised company was integrated, regulation and competition issues appeared only in final markets; some naturally monopolistic activities are intermediate inputs to both capped and uncapped markets, and this has raised questions of access terms which are generally subject to separate supervision by the regulator. For electricity, however, 'regulation by parts' enables the price cap to be applied more directly and selectively to the monopolistic sectors of the industry, but makes it more difficult to identify what proportion of final output is subject to regulation. For BT and BG this is an easier calculation: just over half their revenue was capped, and for water about 75 per cent. In electricity, generation is not regulated, but transmission and distribution are; supply is subject to price cap for the so-called 'franchise market', defined to dwindle to zero by 1998. Cost pass through is an important element in such successive vertical regulation, and is addressed below.

Cost pass through

All the industries privatised after British Telecom have formulae which allow certain categories of costs to bypass the formula (i.e. are not subject to its constraints) either in full or in part. The justification is that some costs are beyond the industry's control and cannot reasonably be reduced or absorbed. For gas these are costs of buying fuel from the oil companies which extract gas from the North Sea and sell it to BG at the beach-head. Such purchases are made under long-term contracts with prices indexed by some combination of wholesale or retail prices, exchange rates and world oil price. Clearly BG cannot influence any of these, and the index is subject to large fluctuations. Gas purchase costs are a major and growing part of the company's costs (about half total operating costs). Since the company could not absorb the risks of such fluctuations itself without demanding a much higher price level in compensation, the risks are passed directly to consumers by exempting these elements from the price cap.

The outcome, however, distorts incentives. Both suppliers and BG know that these costs can be passed on, and there is therefore no incentive to negotiate as tough as possible a contract. BG's counter argument is that allowing the price to rise may be unprofitable even in the regulated market if demand is sufficiently responsive to result in significant loss of sales. In the supposedly more competitive unregulated market (which also receives gas supplied under such contracts) the incentive to reduce costs would be even higher.

There will also be odd incentives for the industry between activities which are substitutes, where one falls into the category of 'allowed' costs and the other does not. The gas industry's allowed pass through of gas purchase costs can serve as an example. The seasonal nature of gas demand means that more gas is burned in winter than in summer. This variation can be met either by an uneven delivery at the beach-head, which is more expensive for the extractors and therefore for BG, or by taking a constant rate of delivery and placing some of the gas in storage during the summer for use during the winter. Storage is an expensive option, equal to about one-sixth of after tax profits. If BG chooses to buy gas more unevenly it will increase the costs it pays for gas purchase, and can pass these increased costs on to the regulated tariff market; if the variability is met by building storage this cannot be 'passed through' and is therefore subject to the reduction in real value required by the tariff constraint. Regulation encouraged BG to shift towards more uneven delivery and higher purchase costs and away from providing storage, inducing BG to be cost inefficient. These problems were recognised in the 1991 review which placed a cap on the gas costs which could be passed through, determined by an index outside the industry's control. The industry then has every incentive to choose the least cost option since it can retain any cost reduction which it implements.

Cost pass through in other industries has been at lower levels. British Airports Authority may pass on 85 per cent of costs incurred by government imposed safety regulations; water's costs from higher water standards, particularly those issued by the EC, and metering are 'allowed' in determining the amount permitted for capital expenditure; and the regional electricity companies can pass through various elements of their generating and purchase costs. Such allowance requires the regulator to keep a separate check that the RECs are purchasing efficiently, and he is considering some form of yardstick to provide a more direct reward to companies who purchase more cheaply than the average. Explicit incentives of this kind which remove distortionary pressures and reduce the discretion in the system are likely to produce outcomes which are more efficient in both the allocative and productive sense.

Regulatory review period

Arrangements for reviewing the type and level of regulation vary almost as much as the regimes themselves. In Telecom there was a built-in review after five years, for which the director issued a consultative document. The period before next revision was shortened to four years, with various arrangements for interim assessment. British Gas or its regulator could apply for alterations after five years. Ofgas published a consultative document in 1990 and recommended a significant tightening of the formula from 1992. The MMC reported on BAA's review in 1991 and suggested a tighter price cap but one which varied to take account of planned capital investment at Heathrow. Water's review period is much longer, ten years, with the regulator promising an interim assessment after five and suggesting variations to individual targets much more frequently. Electricity transmission prices were reviewed and tightened by the regulator immediately after privatisation, and the price caps applied to supply companies have been reassessed after three years.

The period between revisions is crucial in determining the balance between the appropriate pricing level and structure and the requirement for the company to share cost savings with consumers (the trade-off between allocative efficiency, managerial efficiency and equity reflected in the debate between rate of return and price control models). If the firm behaves myopically to maximise profit subject to a suitable price cap this can have desirable allocative consequences, but strategic behaviour is likely as regulation review is approached, when rate of return and other profit measures will determine the level of regulation for the subsequent period. The shorter the time between reviews, the more likely is such strategic behaviour, and the more likely rate of return regulation is the constraint; however a long revision period is rigid, does not enable changes in cost and demand conditions to be incorporated in the control and may result in 'excessive' (and politically unacceptable) profits. The relatively short review period in Telecoms and the longer period in water may reflect appropriately the different rates of technology change in the two industries. An indeterminate period before revision as in gas may have advantages in not concentrating the industry's strategic behaviour as it anticipates review. Alternatively it may merely encourage the industry to act strategically at all times in order not to 'trigger' a review which would be disadvantageous to the industry.

A trend towards more frequent formal review of regulation and interim investigations is clear, somewhat counteracting the original design of an arm's length regulation. Regulation is developing as a more complex mechanism than originally anticipated. Government complicates the situation by continuing to interfere, much as it did with nationalised industries. The independence of the regulator, not only from the industry but also from government interests, will be crucial as regulation matures.

Review of regulation is further affected by the partial regulation which was discussed above. Regulation, and therefore the review, is presumably properly concerned only with the part of the industry's activities covered by the constraint, and yet assets are invariably shared with the unregulated sector. The industry has an incentive to apportion costs and assets to the regulated sector in a situation where allocations have a large arbitrary element (Bradley and Price, 1991). Indeed, the gas industry's practice of using quite different cost allocations for different purposes led the MMC to demand a consistent allocation method. A joint review of cost allocation was undertaken by British Gas and Ofgas to inform the regulatory review, though its results were not published (an example of British discretion which seems quite inexplicable to North American observers).

More important than attempts to allocate costs in particular ways may be incentives to change real rather than accounting behaviour. If the regulation is effective, then marginal profitability must be negative, while it is presumably zero in the unregulated market. This will encourage the firm to shift activities away from the regulated to the unregulated sector. To the extent that this may reduce prices in the unregulated sector where this still contains some monopoly power, such incentives may be desirable, particularly if prices are effectively constrained in the regulated sector. However it may also give rise to charges of predatory pricing by potential competitors in the unregulated sector.

Level of price cap

All price caps are expressed as a limit of (RPI − X%) on revenue where X represents a reduction in the real price level. It is determined by expectations of potential cost reductions, which in turn depend on changing technology and demand. At review the original political considerations for flotation no longer apply, and one would expect regulation to be tightened. This has been the case for all industries (two BT reviews, BG, BAA and transmission charges in electricity) for which reviews had been concluded by 1992.

These characteristics of price cap can be summarised in Table 3.1.

Table 3.1 Summary of UK price regulation, February 1993

Industry	BT	BG	BAA	Water	Electricity
Price index*	t.b.	a.r.	a.r.	t.b.	a.r.
Review (years)	5	ind.	5	10	3
(revised	4)				
Pass through	none	gas	85% sec.	many	gen. costs
Initial X%	3	2	1	varied	varied
1993 level	6.25	5	4		
To	7.5		1		

*t.b. = tariff basket, a.r.= average revenue

As regulation proceeds the separation of regulatory powers to industry-specific offices of supply raises the question of consistency. This is particularly significant in related industries, for example gas and electricity, where gas is a feed stock for electricity generation while they remain competitors in the industrial and domestic markets. When gas regulation was revised the regulator introduced a new pass through element designed to encourage energy conservation, allowing BG to pass on to consumers 100 per cent of approved costs which contributed to energy efficiency in the industry. This might include the cost of subsidising insulation of homes but the outcome of such a scheme could be quite counter productive. If consumption switched from gas to electricity (for example by discouraging particularly inefficient uses of gas) the environmental effects might be adverse; electricity generated from coal and oil produces more emissions injurious to the environment than does gas consumption so the net effect might be to worsen global warming or acid rain. Some co-ordination between regulators might help to avoid such anomalies.

How effective has regulation been in achieving the four objectives identified in the first section: economic (or allocative) efficiency, managerial efficiency, equity, and cost of regulation? What assessment can be made of UK regulation under each of these headings after eight years experience?

The initial emphasis of British regulation was on managerial efficiency, partly in reaction to the experience of rate of return regulation in the US and partly to solve perceived inefficiencies in nationalised industries which were seen as fuelling inflation. Pure price cap regulation allows firms to keep any savings beyond the price cap, encouraging them to reduce costs. Indeed there were concerns that this message might be too strong, prejudicing quality in industries with monopoly control and where consumers were not always well informed about quality. Early post privatisation experience suggests that managerial efficiency was improving, since profits rose while prices of at least some of the industry's profits were pegged. However, similar trends occurred among corporations still nationalised (Bishop and Thompson, 1992), and it is impossible to measure potential cost reductions, which may have been even larger. Moreover the price reductions in the regulated sector were accompanied by vigorous protests of monopoly exploitation from customers and *potential* competitors in the unregulated sector. Much of this may have been reaction to (efficient) removal of cross-subsidies, eliminated in response to the greater transparency of explicit regulation. There is some evidence of decline in quality (for example in availability of public phone boxes and standards of service in fuel). Regulators have responded by enforcing explicit service quality measures and targets.

The strong incentives for managerial efficiency provided by initial regulation have been weakened considerably by increasing emphasis on the profits made by the firms. This is partly a political issue, arising from criticism of excessive profits (an interesting echo of the expectation that these industries when nationalised should break even). But the effects have been magnified by the intervention of regulators who have expressed concern about high profits. Regulation reviews must clearly take these into account, since rate of return is the only feasible guide to appropriate price cap levels; as review periods shorten the regulation resembles increasingly closely the US rate of return model, with a regulatory lag between reviews. Many of the disadvantages of that system are becoming apparent in the UK.

Given the problems of price cap, does this movement towards rate of return regulation increase allocative efficiency? We have seen that some distortion is inevitable in a partially regulated system which allows cost pass through, and that this is exacerbated where average revenue rather than tariff basket price cap is used. Unfortunately strategic behaviour by the firm, for example to increase the asset base by under-pricing peak consumption, becomes more likely with emphasis on the rate of return, so no clear gain is obvious.

Regulators are increasingly concerned with their remit to encourage or enable competition, and the terms of access to the naturally monopolistic system. The distinction between distribution and supply in gas and electricity emphasises the importance of access to the distribution system, and the thorough 1992–93 MMC review of the gas industry is motivated by the same issue. This highlights the basic task of regulation, to maintain and control monopoly where desirable, while encouraging competition where feasible. The importance of industrial structure has been much more clearly recognised as regulation has developed, even if restructuring means reneging on the privatisation bargain.

One phenomenon which has caused concern in the US is regulatory capture, where a regulator identifies with the industry rather than its consumers. So far there is little evidence of such capture in the UK despite the very small size of the regulators, though there is a worrying tendency for the government to intervene. Since such actions are often covert it is difficult to assess their effect, though there is evidence of some regulatory resistance (for example Stephen Littlechild urging the government not to delay competition in the electricity supply market to protect coal supplies).

The regulatory system has been relatively inexpensive to operate though this may be more a reflection of the traditional British use of 'expert commissions' rather than the expensive US judicial process. Regulation has certainly not proved the 'arm's-length' instrument envisaged by its original proponents, but neither was government influence on these industries in their former nationalised incarnations. Both reflect the inability of governments to resist intervention in industries which are so central to both domestic and industrial voters. Under privatisation the increased involvement of the regulators in the industries, particularly the so-called unregulated sectors, also demonstrates that monopoly power was often much more entrenched than optimists suggested and governments admitted at privatisation. Such detailed examination of the industries' activities must run counter to many of the cost reduction incentives which price cap control is supposed to provide, as well as increasing expense for both industry and regulator.

The effect of regulation on the industries' behaviour is difficult to measure given the number of changes which they have experienced, and the vagaries of the economy in the late 1980s and early 90s. Empirical studies of the effect of regulation will be a vital input into any review of the regulatory process, and the development of regulation both in the UK and in other countries where it is introduced. On the success of regulation rests any assessment of the privatisation programme itself and it is clear that regulation will take a different course when no longer dominated by the initial privatisation bargain.

Glossary of regulators and abbreviations

Industry	Economic regulator
British Telecom (BT)	Office of Telecommunications (Oftel)
British Gas (BG)	Office of Gas Supply (Ofgas)
British Airports Authority (BAA)	Civil Aviation Authority (CAA)
Water	Office of Water Services (Ofwat)
Electricity	Office of Electricity Regulation (Offer)

References

Averch, H. and **Johnson, L.** (1962) Behaviour of the firm under regulatory constraint, *American Economic Review*, 52: 1053–69.

Beesley, M. and **Littlechild, S.** (1989) The regulation of private monopolies in the United Kingdom, *Rand Journal of Economics*, 20: 454–72.

Bishop, M. and **Thompson, D.** (1992) Regulatory reform and productivity growth in the UK's public utilities, *Applied Economics*, 24, 11: 1181–90.

Bradley, I. and **Price, C.** (1988) The economic regulation of private industries by price constraints, *Journal of Industrial Economics*, 37: 99–106.

Bradley, I. and **Price, C.** (1991) Partial and mixed regulation of newly privatised UK monopolies, in W. Weigel (ed.), *Economic Analysis of Law*, Österreichischer Wirtschaftsverlag, Vienna, 212–21.

Energy Committee (1985) *Gas Depletion*, HCP 76, HMSO.

HM Government (1948) *Gas Act*, HMSO.

HM Government (1961) *The Financial and Economic Obligations of the Nationalised Industries*, Cmnd 1337, HMSO.

HM Government (1967) *Nationalised Industries: A Review of Economic and Financial Objectives*, Cmnd 3437, HMSO.

HM Government (1978) *The Nationalised Industries*, Cmnd 7131, HMSO.

Kirk, S. (1993) Address to IIR conference, London, 20 January.

Laffont, J-J. and **Tirole, J.** (1990) The regulation of multiproduct firms II, *Journal of Public Economics*, 43, 37–66.

Littlechild, S. (1983) *Regulation of British Telecommunications' Profitability*, London, Department of Industry.

Monopolies and Mergers Commission (1991) BAA plc: *a Report on the Economic Regulation of the South-East Airports Companies*, CAA, London.

National Economic Development Office (1976) First report, HCP 65, HMSO.

National Economic Research Associates (1986) *Economic Regulation of the British Airports Authority*, Department of Transport.

Newbery, D. M. and **Green, R.** (1991) Competition in the British electricity spot market, *Department of Applied Economics Working Paper 9108*, Cambridge.

Phlips, L. (1983) *The Economics of Price Discrimination*, Cambridge: Cambridge University Press.

Rees, R. (1984) A Positive Theory of the Public Enterprise, in Manhand, M., Pestieciu, P. and Tulkens, H. (eds.), *The Performance of Public Enterprises*, Amsterdam: North Holland.

Schmalansee, R. (1989) Good regulatory regimes, *Rand Journal*, 20, 3, 417–36.

Stelzer, I. (1991) Chapter 3 in Veljanovski (ed.) *Regulators and the Market*, Institute of Economic Affairs, London.

Train, K. (1991) *The Optimal Regulation*, Cambridge, Mass: MIT Press.

Vogelsang, I. and **Finsinger, J.** (1979) A regulatory adjustment process for optimal pricing by multi-product monopoly firms, *Bell Journal of Economics*, 10: 157–71.

CHAPTER 4

Deregulation

Tom Weyman-Jones

Introduction

The idea of deregulating a market often has a particularly attractive sound to economists, since it conjures up images of removing the dead hand of bureaucracy that has been stifling the entrepreneurial spirit. Alternatively, however, the image may be one of consumers exposed to the full exploitation of monopolistic firms no longer constrained by the control of a democratically elected government. The term deregulation is used in a great variety of ways, and is often confused with both privatisation and liberalisation. However, a useful working description can be adapted from Joskow and Schmalensee (1983) who say, (p. 4) that the central issue in deregulation is 'whether the role of government . . . should be reduced, with market forces replacing government regulation as the guarantor of acceptable industry performance'.

Initially, we must dispose of a couple of distracting issues: perfect competition and the distribution of the economy's wealth. Firstly, in a perfectly competitive market with free entry and no externalities, no form of regulation can yield net benefits in terms of economic efficiency. For deregulation to be more than a trivial or empty recommendation, we have to focus on relevant markets, i.e. where a competitive outcome comprising many firms each with price equal to marginal social cost and only making normal profit is unlikely to occur. Perfect competition is not a relevant policy option here. However, rivalry, contest, potential entry and deterrence are all possible alternatives to regulation where this regulation takes the form of government intervention to limit the role of market forces including entry and exit. Secondly, we will not be concerned with the equity or otherwise of the distribution of the economy's wealth in general, or a given industry's social surplus in particular. Our only criterion of economic welfare will be the sum of consumer and producer surplus however distributed. While this assumption removes what many political observers might regard as a critical issue, it has the advantage of allowing us to concentrate solely on questions of economic efficiency.

One issue has been to the fore in recent years: what is the relevant economic model for analysing deregulation? This is important because a group of economists, in particular associated with the Bell Lab of the American Telephone and Telegraph Company, and with the US Civil Aeronautics Board, have argued that there is a particular hypothesis, Contestable Market Theory, especially suited to analysing deregulation proposals. This is because contestable market theory analyses those circumstances in which a monopoly or a small number of oligopolies will choose to remain dominant in an industry while only making normal profit so that regulation in the traditional sense is redundant. Competing models of deregulation include the idea that industries actively seek to be regulated, and that regulations persist long after they have served any useful purpose. In other words as well as disagreeing about the consequences of deregulation, economists disagree about the most useful way to discuss the concept itself.

4.1 Traditional views on regulation

Throughout the economics literature on regulation and deregulation writers seem to adopt one of two broad theoretical platforms from which to analyse the issues: the public interest theory and public choice theory. The public interest theory takes the view that regulation or deregulation can be analysed in terms of whether it increases net economic welfare in the sense that the gainers could compensate the losers. Whether a particular set of regulations should be maintained then depends on evaluating its net effect on economic efficiency. This is still the position taken by the majority of economists commenting on regulatory proposals. The public choice theory instead says that producers, regulators and consumers will devote resources to achieving that set of regulations which maximises the real income or economic rent of the group of which they are members. From this viewpoint, regulations on industry conduct and structure are simply the means by which different groups associated with the market seek to maximise their economic rent, so that the prevalence of regulations can be explained as the outcome of rent seeking behaviour. Section 4.2 of the chapter discusses deregulation from the public interest point of view while section 4.3 adopts the public choice model.

The traditional economic argument for having government intervening to set prices in a market is well known. Suppose the typical firm in an industry exhibits decreasing long-run average costs. This might arise because there are very heavy fixed costs to setting up production but low marginal costs of varying output once production facilities are set up (the long run here is not so long as to include the possibility that no firms have yet entered the industry or all have left) or simply because there are increasing returns to scale. In this event the industry is a natural monopoly, so that it is socially efficient in the sense of achieving lowest cost production to have only one firm in the industry, perhaps simply in order to avoid the duplicate incurring of the fixed costs. However such a monopolistic firm is in a position to maximise its profits when facing the industry's downward-sloping demand curve by setting price above marginal and average cost. The consequence is a transfer of resources from consumers to the producer as consumer surplus is reduced and producer profit increased compared with the outcome that would prevail under competitive conditions where price is set equal to marginal cost. In the process of monopolisation not all of the consumer surplus is transferred to the producer since the higher price reduces the quantity sold and the consumer surplus associated with the unsold quantity of the product is lost. The size of the resource transfer, T, is equal to the price change multiplied by the new lower quantity sold, while the deadweight welfare loss, H, is equal to half the product of the price change and the quantity change:

$$T = [\Delta p]q \quad H = [\Delta p \Delta q]/2 \tag{1}$$

The resource transfer is clearly larger than the loss but given our assumption that the distribution of wealth is immaterial, the size of the transfer has no bearing on the efficiency argument for regulating a monopoly. The efficiency argument in the public interest model rests on using regulation to minimise the size of the dead-weight loss. Nevertheless many of the arguments in the public domain about the desirability of regulating monopoly are based on the equity consequences of the size of the transfer, T. It is worth noting however that some part of the transfer may accrue to the employees of the monopoly firm who may therefore develop an interest in retaining any regulations or other circumstances which actually confer monopoly power.

However, this is a very naive explanation for both the type and prevalence of economic regulations and government intervention in product markets, and so we must set out more carefully the nature and type of regulation before examining the arguments for and against doing without it. Very broadly regulations fall into three categories:

1. limitations on entry to a market or exit from it;
2. specifications relating to the quality of the products supplied;
3. formulae for determining the price of the products supplied.

In principle each form of regulation is designed to cope with a particular form of market failure, so that we have also to ask what is the nature of the market failure involved.

Limitations on entry and exit usually take the form of a licensing arrangement whereby a producer requires a form of legal permission from a government department or official authority in order to be able to sell a product or provide a service. The licensing authority may take various forms some far removed from what we normally think of as a government department. For example a taxi service may be licensed by an elected local council, while the television commercials produced by an advertising company may be licensed by an appointed broadcasting authority or the supply of adult cinema films may be licensed by an officially appointed censor. Among the most important licensed suppliers in the economy are those firms which supply a network service: telecommunications, transport and trans-shipment, and electricity, gas and water distribution. The licence arrangement may take one of two forms: a prohibition on entry to a market by new suppliers, or the prohibition on incumbent suppliers of moving into new segments of an existing market. Usually the licence will carry a corresponding obligation not to exit from a market or fail to meet all reasonable demands for the product or the supply. For example bus companies may only be given a monopoly franchise on certain busy routes in return for an obligation to provide a service, possibly of lower quality, on infrequently used rural routes.

Other examples of entry-limiting regulation are the allocation of particular air-routes to certain airlines, the award of broadcasting franchises (wavelengths) to a few television, cable and satellite companies, and the disallowing of supply permission to independent gas and electricity companies in certain sectors of the market after privatisation. The fundamental argument for such entry and exit licensing is that without a monopoly franchise the incumbent will not be prepared to accept the risks of constructing and maintaining the necessary capacity to serve the whole market. The form of market failure most obviously addressed by entry and exit licensing is the inability of suppliers to pass on the risk of large investment programmes with heavy fixed costs before revenues are received. In ideal circumstances individual risk-averse suppliers should be able to trade their risks with the risk-neutral mass of consumers or diversifying insurance companies. Guaranteed monopoly franchises are one way of bringing about this efficient trading of risks between individual risk-averse producers and the risk-neutral population as a whole represented by the licensing authority. The licensing authority may then devise some additional provisions to ensure the financial viability of the producer.

At the risk of oversimplification quality of supply regulation can be seen as covering another form of the entry and exit decision. The licence to supply a service or produce a commodity usually will contain provisions about the minimum frequency with which a service is provided or about the technical specification of the product in question. Sometimes the standard itself is the only licence, e.g. in the case of electrical appliances when faulty products could result in a firm incurring cost penalties which increase the risk of entering an otherwise competitive market. When a regulated industry produces a commodity at a given price there will be feedback effects running from the quality of supply or service to the price charged for the product and vice versa so that it is important to regard the price of the product and the quality of product as two aspects of the same problem. The market failure under attack is based on the problem of information. Quality of supply regulation is often adopted when it is felt by government that consumers may not be well informed about the nature of the goods that they are buying. When there is this asymmetry of information economists call it an adverse selection problem. This term arises in the literature on risk and insurance and reflects the idea that when the typifying characteristics of a consumer cannot be observed by the insurance company, the company is likely to attract the worst risks if it offers a standard contract. The efficient solution to the problem of adverse selection is to design a menu of contracts that indicate by their different choices the consumers' individual characteristics. In the context of quality of supply regulation the economics of adverse selection suggests that when consumers are ignorant of quality differences, the quality of the goods actually supplied, all of which must sell at the same price, will sink to the lowest common denominator. Since all goods have the same, lowest, quality the resulting outcome is called a pooling equilibrium, and quality of supply regulation attempts to maintain the acceptability of the pooling equilibrium standard. However a more efficient solution may be to allow for a separating equilibrium in which different qualities are available at different prices just as different forms of insurance protection are available. Hence quality of supply regulation that ensures all firms are at the same quality standard is not necessarily efficient in the sense of allowing for all the gains from trading risks. Note that another example of such quality regulation is the setting of fixed emissions standards for polluting industries.

Price regulation usually takes the form of setting maximum or minimum prices for a product, setting price by a formula, or of setting a formula for the rate of return on capital that a regulated firm is allowed to earn. In accounting terms, the price and rate of return regulation are related of course. Let Q be the firm's sales volume, P its price per unit of sales, OC its operating costs, K its stock of capital, and R the rate of return on capital, then: $R = [PQ - OC]/K$. As Catherine Price discusses in Chapter 3, recent UK privatisations of the major utilities regulated have focused on price caps. Other well known regulated prices include the television receiver licence fee which is the sole income source for the British Broadcasting Corporation. However, rate of return regulation has also been used in the UK, most notably for firms supplying pharmaceutical products for the National Health Service, and in the supply of condoms when that market was monopolised in the 1970s. The market failure that is the subject of price cap or rate of return regulation is the result of monopolistic or oligopolistic power which may give rise to two different types of inefficiency: (a) price or allocative inefficiency arising from the failure to relate price to marginal cost as would happen in a competitive market (this is is the loss measured by H in equation (1)), and (b) X-inefficiency that arises from firms failing to minimise costs because of a lack of concern with market disciplines and competitive constraints (see Leibenstein 1966). Of course all three types of regulation: entry, quality and price often come together in a single package of regulations applied to a particular industry if only because the types of market failure discussed above often go together.

4.2 Models for analysing deregulation I: contestability

Deregulation became a widespread topic of political debate in the 1980s as impatience with the apparently inefficient performance of public enterprises and regulated industries grew in both Europe and the USA. This debate coincided with the emergence in economics of a novel way of describing the possible equilibrium outcome in some types of market. In what were called perfectly contestable markets, (PCMs), Baumol, Panzar and Willig (1982), argued that an industry with increasing returns to scale (or other characteristics of a natural monopoly), might settle at an equilibrium where entry was free but did not occur, and where the incumbent monopolist kept price at the level of average cost and failed to make abnormal profits. The impetus was simply the threat of potential entry. In these circumstances the optimal government policy was to encourage the threat of low risk hit and run entry by removing regulations that hindered the entry and exit of firms.

A crucial preliminary idea for the issue of contestability is the notion of a sustainable industry equilibrium. This concerns the situation in which a single product or multiproduct monopolist is vulnerable to entry by a rival firm. The entry may take one of two forms. In the single product case the entrant may seek to supply only a small part of the monopolist's market by offering selected consumers (a market segment) a lower price than the incumbent monopolist. In the multiproduct case the entrant may offer to supply only one of the products (or a proper subset of the monopolist's products) at a price below that which the monopolist needs to break even when supplying both (or all) products. The monopolist is of course trying to recover the fixed costs of multiproduct production from sales of both commodities. We begin with the single product case.

The PCM model can be most easily illustrated in Figure 4.1 which shows a perfectly contestable market. With the demand schedule D_1 the industry is a natural monopoly since market demand can be satisfied at a point (q_1, p^*), on a single firm's average cost curve before minimum average cost or minimum efficient scale (MES), is reached at output level q_{mes}. This is not the only or indeed a necessary condition for the existence of natural

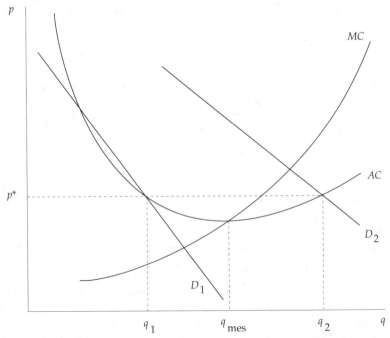

Figure 4.1 Natural monopoly in a perfectly contestable market where D_1 is unsustainable with D_2

monopoly, but it is sufficient. In fact one of the contributions of the PCM economists was to delineate the necessary condition for an industry producing one or more products to be a natural monopoly, this condition being cost subadditivity. This occurs when the total cost to one firm of producing all the industry's output is not greater than the total of the costs to all firms of their individual outputs: $C(\Sigma q_j) \leq \Sigma Cj(q_j)$, where q_i is the output of the ith firm.

In Figure 4.1, two possible average cost pricing equilibria are shown, i.e. both have the firm pricing at average cost despite its monopoly position. With demand schedule D_1 the firm will not be challenged by an entrant as long as p^* is maintained, but at a slightly higher price and smaller output it is vulnerable to entry because of the monopoly profits that would then emerge. As long as the incumbent firm keeps price at the level of average cost there are no profitable opportunities for entry, and the particular equilibrium (q_1, p^*) is then said to be *sustainable*. Price is already at the deterrent level so that the incumbent does not alter its price when a potential entrant emerges, and while entry is free it does not occur. Now suppose the demand schedule is shifted right to D_2. The equilibrium (q_2, p^*), while feasible, is not sustainable. This is because an entrant who is able to capture a share of the market between q_1 and q_2 can make abnormal profits by charging a price lower than p^* but still above average cost. A non-sustainable equilibrium if it exists and persists therefore need not carry any connotations of being unlikely or unstable, but it does imply that since abnormal profits persist there must be some form of entry barrier maintaining the non-sustainable equilibrium. As many economists have argued, a more lucid description of the sustainable equilibrium is to call it an average cost-pricing equilibrium with free entry. Now comes the crucial link between sustainability and contestability. Any market which only exhibits an equilibrium which is sustainable is said to be perfectly contestable. In other words any market for which the only feasible equilibrium when entry is possible is one at which price equals average cost is a perfectly contestable market. Note that this is more general than a perfectly competitive market. A perfectly competitive market has a sustainable equilibrium and is therefore perfectly contestable as well, but perfect competition with demand schedule D_1 is not a feasible outcome for Figure 4.1 since a price equal to marginal cost (the competitive market prediction) drives out the incumbent monopolist and scares away any entrant with a similar cost schedule.

What happens in the event that demand is such that natural monopoly is unsustainable? In Figure 4.2 two firms appear: an incumbent monopolist labelled I, and an entrant labelled E who has identical costs. In Figure 4.2 the entrant's cost schedules are drawn using the output level q_{mes} corresponding to the incumbent's minimum efficient scale as the origin for the entrant. At output level q^* the AC curves intersect and for higher output levels industry costs will be reduced by having both firms in the industry – a natural oligopoly.

In Figure 4.2 we can observe the following results.

(a) Output levels up to q^*: the industry is a natural monopoly, costs are subadditive and it is socially efficient to have only one firm in the industry.

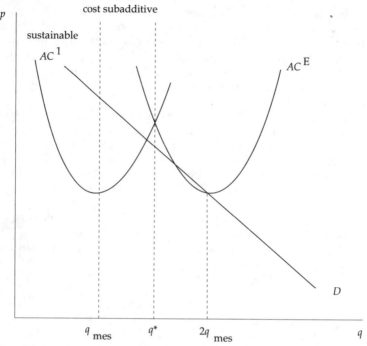

Figure 4.2 Natural monopoly and natural duopoly depend on cost and demand conditions

(b) Output levels up to q_{mes}: the natural monopoly is sustainable, since average cost pricing deters entry.

(c) Monopoly outputs between q_{mes} and q^* are not sustainable since average cost pricing offers profitable entry, even though such entry is socially inefficient by raising industry costs.

(d) Output levels between q^* and $2q_{mes}$: the industry is a sustainable natural duopoly, and so on.

These arguments make sustainable natural monopoly look like an unlikely phenomenon since the range of sustainable monopoly outputs is smaller than the range of cost subadditive outputs. However suppose that for each firm, the average cost curve flattens out at q_{mes} as many empirical cost studies have suggested. In that event, the average cost of q^* is no higher than the average cost of q_{mes}. The result is that with flat-bottomed cost schedules natural monopoly is sustainable, i.e. average cost pricing deters entry, over the whole range of output levels for which costs are subadditive, i.e. for which monopoly is socially efficient.

So far we have assumed that the monopolist produces only one product, but the analysis needs to be extended to the multiproduct case. This is because many natural monopolies and regulated industries supply a range of products. This is particularly the case where an industry produces a product which cannot be stored and must be consumed at the moment of production. The supply of the product at two different points in time is then best regarded as comprising two separate products. Many services fall into this category, as do products whose demand pattern over time consists naturally of peaks and troughs. Examples of such products are transportation services both for people, e.g. airlines, or other products, e.g. gas and electricity transmission services. There are then further reasons for expecting costs to fall with output, the most important of which is economies of scope, whereby the joint costs of producing two products together does not exceed the sum of the costs of producing each product separately at the same levels of output. In the multiproduct case, the equivalent to average cost pricing at a sustainable equilibrium is Ramsey pricing, in which the price of each of the firm's products is raised above marginal cost in inverse proportion to the elasticity of demand. The intuitive explanation for this latter result is as follows. We know that a profit-maximising monopolist selling in two different markets or making two different products will discriminate in the prices charged, raising price more in the market with the lower elasticity of demand. The same result carries over to the case where the monopolist is trying to find the lowest prices which will give him the minimum profit needed just to break even but without encouraging other firms to challenge his incumbency of each market. Once again he will discriminate on the basis of elasticity but instead of raising price proportionately above marginal cost by an amount exactly equal to one over the elasticity of demand, he will choose a price mark-up equal to a fraction of one over the elasticity of demand: for product j with elasticity e_j, he chooses:

$$[p_j - MC_j]/p_j = \theta[1/e_j] \qquad j = 1, \ldots, N \qquad (2)$$

The fraction θ is called the Ramsey number after the economist who first suggested the relevance of this type of pricing policy. It reflects the degree of freedom in choosing prices before running up against the break-even constraint. Note that if we take the result of equation (2) for two different products, then the ratio of the price mark-ups reflects the inverse of the ratio of the two elasticities.

However, it is easy to see that not all break-even price pairs for a multiproduct monopolist are sustainable. Imagine price pairs that satisfy equation (2). In this range there are values of p_1 that the producer of the single product q_1 can offer that will yield positive profit to him but undercut the monopolist who is supplying both products. The reason is that the entry-deterring price that the two-product monopolist is already charging on the second product reduces his ability to compete with the single-product entrant to the market for the first product. We get a generalisation of our earlier results that no sustainable price pairs might exist. On the other hand where sustainable price pairs do exist the possibility that the markets are contestable then arises, i.e. the only equilibrium may be one in which the monopolist chooses the Ramsey prices to deter entrants in each of the markets in which he operates. If this event does arise then it has very desirable efficiency properties because the Ramsey prices are precisely the second-best welfare maximising prices that are socially desirable for attaining overall Pareto efficiency subject to ensuring that firms are able to break even.

The PCM hypothesis therefore leads us to ask what the conditions are under which markets will be perfectly contestable, with second-best welfare maximising prices chosen voluntarily by the incumbent firm or firms in order to deter the threat of entry but with the socially 'right' numbers of incumbents in each market: one in natural monopolies, two in natural oligopolies, and so on up to indeterminately large numbers in competitive markets. Three conditions in particular have been identified:

1. Free entry to the industry in the sense that potential entrants and the incumbents do not face different entry costs.
2. Costless exit from the industry, in the sense that any firm can leave without additional costs to itself. This amounts in general to the assumption that any fixed costs associated with setting up production are neither sunk nor irreversible. In other words after a firm has entered an industry it can leave the industry at a cost that does not exceed the economic depreciation on its capital stock, perhaps by shifting the capital intact into some other market or disposing of it at the depreciated price in an efficient second-hand market.
3. The entrant is able to offer supply or sign a supply contract with the incumbent's customers before the incumbent can change its current price structure. It is the fear of the entrant's capability in this respect that makes the incumbent price at average cost permanently rather than only temporarily as in the limit pricing model.

The notion of free exit is important because to make the PCM hypothesis operational, we must assume the existence of hit-and-run firms for whom entry to an industry is a low-risk decision. Baumol, Panzar and Willig (1986) state the condition for a market to be perfectly contestable simply as the absence of sunk costs. It is critical not to confuse these with fixed costs. Fixed costs are those which must be incurred before production can be started up, and where fixed costs are large they lead to an average cost curve which falls over a large range of output levels. Such costs need not however be sunk if the assets which they represent are easily liquidated or easily transferable to another market. The more a firm's assets are specific to a particular market the more they give rise to sunk costs, and the less likely the market is to be contestable. Two classic examples are as follows. Electricity distribution to a particular region of the country requires the laying of cables down particular routes. The distribution company is unlikely to contemplate digging these up and moving to some other region if successfully challenged by an entrant, and any potential entrant is unlikely to lay cables in an attempt to undercut the price of an incumbent monopolist. On the other hand, an airline having invested in a fleet of aircraft prior to offering a service has the option of flying these to several different regions to undercut incumbent monopolists.

In simple terms where the conditions for contestability are satisfied, PCM theory asserts that regulation has nothing to offer even if the industry is a natural monopoly or naturally uncompetitive. Putting together the views expressed in Bailey and Baumol (1984) and Elizabeth Bailey's OECD report, (1985) we can summarise the policy conclusions of the PCM theorists as follows:

1. Contestable market theory should be used as a broad framework to analyse the consequences of deregulation.
2. According to this theory government should seek policies that promote contests for markets.
3. Impediments to entry and exit may be the primary source of interference with market efficiency (in the sense of promoting cost-minimising industry structures).
4. Regulatory policies tend to support cross-subsidisation, encourage a high-price and high-service product, draw artificial boundaries that interfere with the scope of a firm's operations, and fail to provide incentive for firms to act efficiently.
5. If the industries display the properties of contestability deregulation should lead to a dramatic lessening of cross-subsidies and the creation of a larger selection of products at different prices while providing enormous pressure to improve productivity.

The idea of a PCM therefore needs to be related to the earlier notion of barriers to entry. As Gilbert (1989) notes the usual entry barriers are defined as economies of scale, absolute cost advantages and product differentiation, and any of these would enable an incumbent monopolist to price in excess of average cost. In other words the earlier literature identified economies of scale with natural monopoly and concluded that a non-sustainable equilibrium with the incumbent making abnormal profits would be the usual outcome. In Figure 4.1, this would occur at an output like q_2 but with price at p^* or higher. Such monopolists could always see off potential entrants by limit pricing – when necessary dropping price to average cost to make entry temporarily or permanently unattractive. In such models economists assumed that entrants would believe that the monopolist would maintain output at its initial level and respond by price flexibility. The PCM hypothesis by contrast has the monopolist continuously pricing at average cost at a sustainable equilibrium in order to deter a permanent threat of entry. In addition PCM theory does not regard increasing returns to scale as an entry barrier in itself. The entry barriers PCM theory is concerned with are those set up by government as a form of regulatory control. Without regulations but with free entry PCM theorists would expect an industry with increasing returns to scale to be contestable, exhibiting Ramsey pricing and under permanent threat of entry unless the fixed costs of production are sunk as well.

4.3 Models for analysing deregulation II: public choice theory

Public choice theory offers a different, predictive model of why industries may become regulated and approaches the question of deregulation from an entirely different perspective from that of the public interest based PCM model. The basis is the idea of rent-seeking behaviour first suggested by Tullock (1967). The abnormal or monopoly profit associated with setting price above average and marginal cost is often referred to as rent. Utility-maximising individuals will always pursue rent-seeking behaviour as far as they are able, and one fruitful source of rent is the granting of political favours in the form of economic regulations. Hence there is a market for the granting of regulatory privileges with the supply being furnished by those in government designing and implementing regulations and the demand emanating from those firms likely to be favoured by the regulations, for example in limiting entry to an incumbent's industry. Now refer back to equation (1) above and in particular the resource transfer term, T. In an otherwise competitive industry, whichever firm can become the regulated monopoly will capture all the monopoly rents. It has an incentive to invest resources in pushing for regulations that will ensure its monopoly position. Once expended these resources are lost to the economy because the prospective monopoly rents including the present value of the future rents will have been dissipated in the attempt to capture them. The deadweight welfare loss to the economy is then the sum $H + T$ due both to price inefficiency and wasteful rent-seeking behaviour. (T and H are sometimes referred to as the Tullock and Harberger costs of monopoly after the economists associated with their analysis.) The immediate policy implication is that the monopoly conferred by entry-limiting regulation is a much more costly result than traditional economics recognises. The argument extends to all of the forms of regulation described earlier, including protectionist measures to improve the balance of trade in an economy since indigenous producers will waste resources in the attempt to establish favourable quotas and tariffs that enhance their own economic rents.

While the public choice theory provides a powerful argument against regulation, it also ironically contains the prediction that once regulations are established, they will not only be difficult to remove, but there will be a lack of interest in deregulation (see McCormick, Shughart and Tollison, 1984). The disinterest in deregulation arises because the Tullock costs, T, once expended are sunk. Deregulating a monopoly may recover the Harberger costs, H, but cannot recover the Tullock costs which represent resources lost to the economy for ever. Hence public choice theory argues: (a) the costs of imposing entry-restricting regulations may be much heavier than previously realised, but (b) the benefits of removing the regulations may be very small. Pressure groups opposed to rent-seeking producers may therefore concentrate on stopping new regulations, but will have little to gain from removing old regulations. As a consequence it may be expected that not only will industries seek regulation (because of the rents conferred) but old regulations are likely to persist long after they have yielded the rents that comprised the original objective. This conclusion is modified when the regulated firms have to spend current resources to maintain their regulatory privileges. The public choice theorists predict that deregulation is most likely in those industries where the incumbent finds it most expensive to maintain these privileges.

4.4 Applications of the deregulation models

In the UK the major impact of the deregulation programme occurred between 1979 and 1988, although it was not until 1990 that the largest privatisation, that of the the electricity supply industry took place. At the beginning of this period output from state-owned industries accounted for 11 per cent of gross domestic product but by 1991 the OECD concluded that the UK had one of the most open, liberal and competitive product markets among OECD countries (OECD, 1991). The model for deregulation throughout Europe in general and the UK in particular (as opposed to privatisation of nationalised industries), is the application of contestability to the airline industry in the USA, and it is worth noting the general lessons of that deregulation effort first. Forsyth (1983) and OECD (1985) describe these in detail. The US airline industry was a classic example of a heavily regulated industry. Airline service was composed of both trunk carriers and local services regulated by the Civil Aeronautics Board (CAB). New entry to the industry was limited by the regulations and the incursion of established airlines onto other routes was forbidden. In addition the fares structure was rigidly formularised with distance being the primary determinant of fares regardless of the marginal costs of different services or peak loads. By the beginning of the 1980s the US airline industry had been completely deregulated in all respects except safety, and prime movers in this like the economist Elizabeth Bailey concluded that the predictions of contestability theory in terms of the emergence of new products and more efficient and lower fares had largely been vindicated. Bailey and Baumol (1984) suggested four yardsticks for measuring the success of a deregulation policy change but first note that the actual market concentration after deregulation is *not* counted as a useful yardstick since one of the findings of contestability theory is that the number of incumbents in a market at any given time is a poor predictor of the efficiency of the market when entry and exit are unregulated. The yardsticks were:

(i) productivity improvements in labour and delivery systems
(ii) increases in the innovation and diversity of price–service options
(iii) adjustment of prices towards incremental costs and an end to cross-subsidy
(iv) transitions in market structure and profitability.

The first three of these yardsticks can be called respectively: productive, dynamic, and allocative efficiency.

The productivity improvements were most obviously noticeable in the emergence of hub and spoke route operations in which individual airlines were located at different major airport hubs into which fed many small-scale frequent services. There were large-scale services between hubs, and this combination replaced a multiplicity of infrequent services between different small airports. Linear routes were replaced by sunbursts of routes from different hubs. The flights between major hubs carried passengers from very different initial local airports and going to different local destinations rather in the manner of a motorway or turnpike road system. A variety of innovative pricing structures were adopted as different airlines competed across routes and across services looking for subsets of another producer's markets to enter. Prices tracked marginal costs more closely as peak and off-peak times were signalled. The evidence on profitability is mixed since during and after the deregulation process several external factors (strikes, oil price rises, and the economic cycle) induced a large degree of volatility in airline profits. Forsyth notes that one result of deregulation is that firms are free to suffer the bankruptcy consequences of bad management decisions as well as the profitable consequences of good decisions, and this effect does seem to have occurred.

The US airline deregulation has so far had only limited effect on the European airline industry which in addition to regulations similar to the US has had several other distortions such as cartel pricing to protect national carriers (Button and Swann, 1991). Forsyth argued that this 'nations' effect would delay the application of contestable deregulation to the European context. Button and Swann take the view that the beginnings of a proactive approach to competition are emerging in the aviation policies advocated by the Commission of the European Communities. However these authors point out that despite slow progress in European aviation other sectors of transport have been at the forefront of deregulation, and in the UK two in particular are notable: coach and bus deregulation.

Coach and bus deregulation began with express coaches and was followed by that of local services (see Davis, 1984 and Jaffer and Thompson, 1986). Bus and coach regulation prior to the 1980s showed all the characteristics of a heavily regulated structure: provision of a service required a licence which would only be granted if the regional Transport Commissioners felt the service was positively 'in the public interest'. Fares, frequency and routes were all strictly laid down and extensive bureaucracy with a presumption against change was pervasive even to the extent that competitors like British Rail and the National Bus Company entered the discussion (Davis, 1984). This preoccupation with a bureaucratic definition of the public interest as opposed to a presumption that competition in an industry is generally preferable unless evidence of large-scale economies is available has been a long-standing characteristic of UK competition policy in all its respects. Express coaches were deregulated as one of the first actions of the new Conservative government of Mrs Thatcher in 1980. Entry licensing was completely deregulated, and fare and route structures were set free. Over the next four to five years there were significant changes in market performance but not in market structure. Initially considerable new entry took place with between 20 and 30 per cent of the National Bus Company's market being captured. Fares fell by up to 40 per cent in nominal terms, and many new classes of service and routes were introduced. Subsequently, mergers and exit from the industry led to National Bus Company's dominant position being largely reinstated, and although the level and extent of the new services persisted, fares appeared to rise in real terms back towards the pre-deregulation level. Jaffer and

Thompson (1986) suggested two competing hypotheses to explain this history. The first hypothesis, effective competition, argued that the industry was subject to increasing returns to scale but contestable, and hence that the deregulation policy change was a once and for all improvement. The second hypothesis argued that effective barriers to entry remained after the deregulation, largely erected by the major incumbent, National Bus Company, and that this was evident in the rise in fares after a short period of entry deterring predatory pricing. To evaluate the competing hypotheses Jaffer and Thompson carried out an empirical study of coach fare-setting procedures. The effective competition or contestability model suggests that, given potential entry threats, prices will be determined by marginal costs and the price elasticities of demand along the lines of the Ramsey pricing formulae in equation (2) above. If, on the other hand, the barriers to entry hypothesis is valid then a measure of market structure should also be significant in explaining fares. The contestability hypothesis is therefore nested within the barriers to entry hypothesis. The market structure variable used was the Herfindahl index, H, based on the sum of the squared individual market shares, s_j, of each company supplying the product or service whose price constitutes the dependent variable to be explained: $H = \Sigma s_j^2$.

The market structure index, which takes a value of $1/N$ if all firms have equal shares and N is the number of firms, was found to be significant in explaining coach fares. Hence the authors had a qualified conclusion: deregulation had delivered efficiency improvements in all three of the Baumol–Bailey categories, but too many significant entry barriers remained to regard the industry as contestable. The subsequent privatisation of the incumbent after divestment into smaller companies would, they argued, improve the possibility of effective competition as would increased access to large-scale terminals for independent entrants. Nevertheless deregulation was felt to be worthwhile. Broadly similar conclusions appear to have applied to local bus services: deregulation has delivered efficiency improvements, but market structure has returned to concentrated levels after an initial period of rapid entry. While the entry and exit assumptions of PCM theory seem to be valid the ability of incumbents to respond rapidly with price changes has reduced the efficacy of the contestability model. It is essential that deregulation has an ongoing support in an active competition policy and this seems to have been largely absent from much of the UK government's policy initiatives.

4.5   Auctions and broadcasting deregulation

Among the many individual deregulations that have characterised UK government policy in recent years, that of the auction of television broadcasting licences has attracted considerable attention. The idea of auctioning the franchise for a regional public utility monopoly is associated with the classic question posed by Demsetz (1968): 'why regulate utilities?' It received its most eloquent counter-attack in Oliver

Williamson's (1976) analysis of cable television auctions in the USA. Train (1991) links auctions with the contestability theory by arguing that perfectly contestable markets are equivalent to a sequence of repeated franchise auctions.

Demsetz argued that competition in the field could be adequately replaced by competition for the field by allowing the contract to provide a public service to be awarded to the winner of an auction. The criterion for winning could either be the size of the bid or the price of supply commitment entered by the winning monopolist. In either case the government could ensure that all the monopoly rents from single firm supply accrued to the population as a whole. In the case of highest financial bid a competitive pool of bidders would bid up to the maximum discounted present value of the future monopoly rents (the Tullock costs), and the government could dispose of these by transfers in cash or kind. In the case of lowest price commitment, the price to supply would be bid down to the expected average cost and the rents would accrue directly to customers. Demsetz did not consider the auction mechanism in greater detail, but this does raise issues of economic substance. Williamson's counter-attack was directed at the principle involved, i.e. that franchise auctions could allow government to do without any regulatory mechanism at all. Williamson's argument contained three strands:

(i) both of the criteria left the quality of the service unspecified
(ii) the auction mechanism was unable to handle uncertainty
(iii) the auction mechanism did not evade the problem of market power.

The key to all three strands of Williamson's argument is that the subject of the auction is a contract to provide a service over some future period, but the government could not foresee all the factors including price and technology changes and exogenous shocks that would affect performance over the duration of the contract. Hence there would have to be a detailed specification of quality of supply which adds an extra dimension to the nature of the auction mechanism. How would the government decide between a low-price and low-quality bid as opposed to a high-price and high-quality bid? Secondly in the event of a long-term franchise it would not be possible to draw up a complete contingent contract, i.e. one that allowed for every possible eventuality. There would have to be a continuous monitoring of the franchisee's performance, and the franchisee would have an incentive to degrade the quality of supply or attempt to renegotiate the quality aspects after commencement. This would entail the need for continual regulatory oversight. If on the other hand the franchise is of short duration then the incumbent with a partially amortised but still effective capital stock would have a competitive advantage at the next auction. If the government tried to evade this by requiring the winner of the next auction round to purchase the incumbent's capital stock the winner might only offer a token price if the capacity is largely sunk and not transferable to another market. This would act as a disincentive for the first incumbent to invest in the specific assets needed to enhance supply quality. The situation at the second auction would more resemble bilateral monopoly with considerable market power than a competitive outcome.

Williamson concluded that franchise auctions offered only an illusory gain over detailed regulation.

The nature of the auction itself is important as Cave (1989) has argued. Since in the broadcasting case bidders are required to forecast a given total of advertising revenue the auction is a 'common value' model. This means that bidders do not have independent private valuations of the auction's object, the franchise. What other bidders think of the advertising revenue prospects *is* important. Common value auctions with the prize going to the highest bid in a sealed tender therefore carry the risk of the 'winner's curse': the winning bidder immediately realises that he/she has forecast a higher value for advertising revenue than all other bidders in the pool, and given the random distribution of the expected revenues about their mean, is likely therefore to make a loss. This can lead to extreme caution among careful bidders and bankruptcy among careless bidders.

In the case of the UK commercial television broadcasting franchises, prior to 1992 these had been awarded by a regulatory body, the Independent Broadcasting Authority (IBA) on the basis of detailed specifications of programming quality including both high-brow and low-brow tastes from different companies. The monopoly rents had been significant, and the system had deliberately fostered considerable cross-subsidy from large densely populated regional franchises to smaller rural franchises. This system was felt to be inequitable and inefficient. For the 1992 franchise auctions the IBA, after establishing a basic quality threshold, used a highest bid sealed tender auction to award the franchises. This imposed considerable risks on the bidders' shareholders, and one notable consequence was that one of the most profitable regions was won by a single unchallenged bid of a derisory amount by the incumbent. At the other extreme one former incumbent was eliminated despite making the highest bid for its franchise because the IBA felt that its advertising revenue forecast was so unrealistic as to render bankruptcy very likely. The outcome was met with a very mixed response. Many commentators felt that quality programming would be lost, while others felt that the resulting wide spread of winning bids meant that the IBA had induced unnecessary additional uncertainty into the broadcasting system. However, the franchise auction was not the only aspect of broadcasting deregulation, and the emergence of independent production companies from the previous producer-broadcasters has widened entry into the industry. This was reinforced by the requirement that the BBC take a quota of programmes from such independent producers. It is as yet too early to say what will be the consequences of the deregulation of an industry in which it was often argued that a paternalistic set of regulations had produced high-quality programming, assuming that that is the same as high-brow taste programming.

4.6 Future deregulation and the access issue

One way of avoiding the sunk cost problem of network natural monopoly is to keep the network in regulated or public ownership while opening up use of the network to deregulated competition. In this way the sunk costs are incurred by a single producer without an entry challenge. The prices charged by the network owner for access to the network are regulated either by a price cap or by rate of return regulation. In the case of a price cap of the RPI – X type the X factor will probably be reviewed on the basis of the utility's achieved rate of return so that it will in this case amount to rate of return regulation anyway. Competitive firms can then lease the use of part of the network for short periods to supply a service or deliver a product to final consumers. In this way the competitive firms do not incur large fixed costs which are sunk since they can relatively quickly exit from the market by not renewing an access contract or by reselling the lease in a secondary market. Two outstanding examples are the 1990 arrangements for electricity supply contracts and the proposals for rail deregulation.

Under the electricity industry privatisation of 1990 four distinct features of the product's delivery were distinguished: generation, bulk transmission at high voltage, distribution at low voltage, and supply. Generation was made a deregulated market without price regulation and freedom of entry. It could in principle develop into a competitive market since empirical studies from the USA in particular suggest that the minimum efficient scale at which average cost flattens out occurs at a capacity level that is about 10 per cent of the size of UK market demand (Weyman-Jones, 1989). At present the generation picture is less rosy than this suggests because the privatisation programme broke the incumbent nationalised monopoly supplier, the Central Electricity Generating Board, into only two rival firms and in the depressed aggregate demand conditions of the early 1990s the excess capacity of each allows significant room for predatory and entry-deterring price structures. Transmission and regional distribution are to remain as licensed network monopolies subject to price cap regulation, but supply contract services are expected to form a contestable market. Under supply contestability, an energy company can offer short-term supply contracts to final consumers after buying the power and leasing the use of the wires for common carriage. The supply revenues account for about 5 per cent of the industry's total turnover. In the 1990 privatisation free entry to this market was phased in with supply competition at first limited to customers taking more than 1,000 kw at the time of system maximum demand. This restriction on entry reduces to the market above 100 kw maximum demand in 1994 and is removed entirely in 1998. Customers in this open market for supply can sign short-term supply contracts with any licensed second tier electricity supplier, e.g. an independent generator or a distribution company in any part of the UK as long as that supplier can lease part of the transmission system to carry whatever electricity it has generated or purchased to fulfil the contract. The assumption in the electricity privatisation programme is that this market would become contestable sufficiently easily to make maintenance of the initial price regulation unnecessary. The key to the workability of this system is the availability and terms of access to the network. The transmission network is owned by a holding company in which all the distribution utilities have an interest and careful regulation of access conditions for third-party independent suppliers will be essential. Access terms became the first preoccupation of the industry's regulatory office, Offer, upon privatisation and if experience of access disputes amongst US gas and electric utilities is anything to go by this issue will remain critical to the developing deregulated industry (see Stalon, 1992).

An analogous idea is proposed for rail privatisation with the rail network remaining as a natural monopoly in public or regulated private ownership. Independent companies can then lease part of the network to run route-services in competition with the incumbent British Rail. As with the split between electricity distribution and supply it will be essential to treat the two parts of British Rail, network services and carriage services, as separate businesses or profit centres. Profitability forecasts are very uncertain for this deregulation proposal at present, but at least one potential entrant, Virgin (also a competitor for British Airways on international airline routes), has announced an interest.

4.7 Assessing the gains and losses from deregulation

All observers of deregulation experiences in both Europe and the USA have noted that there are important gainers and losers. In transport deregulation the important losers have been those in small or rural communities who used to have linear direct routes with several major centres. The hub and spoke structure of delivery has often meant the complete disappearance of some services with the substitution of single route services to one major hub, albeit with greater frequency. In addition incumbent protected monopolists have seen their profitability challenged although there are often grounds for believing that they can and do see off potential entrants after deregulation where the absence of ongoing competition policy fails to eradicate the barriers to entry arising from established brand names, excess capacity, responsive pricing and network access. Gainers are customers experiencing efficiency improvements and taxpayers relieved of the requirement to fund public sector investment programmes. Measuring the precise efficiency gains can be problematical, although the Baumol and Bailey framework discussed earlier suggests somewhere to start. Unfortunately, as some of the empirical work has revealed, it is often very difficult to separate the endogenous efficiency gains from the exogenous price, income and other shocks impacting on the industry during and after the deregulation procedure. In brief the efficiency measurements require:

 (i) before and after comparison of input–output ratios and industry costs in measuring productive efficiency;
 (ii) before and after comparison of the range and diversity of processes, products and services in order to measure dynamic efficiency;
(iii) before and after comparison of the use of Ramsey pricing in order to measure allocative efficiency.

None of these factors is easily separated from the influence of exogenous variables, and some of them require very detailed and sophisticated specification of cost, demand and production functions. In addition it is an important finding of the deregulation models that the before and after comparison of market structure is a poor guide to the net benefits of deregulation. In any case it is difficult to separate the effectiveness of a single deregulation episode from the continuing need for an active competition policy so that it is impossible to be certain about the size of the gains from deregulation. It is fair to say however that only a minority of commentators have suggested that the deregulation exercises of the 1980s and early 1990s have been fruitless.

References

Bailey, E. E. and **Baumol, W. J.** (1984) Deregulation and the theory of contestable markets, *Yale Journal on Regulation*, 1, 111–37.

Baumol, W. J., Panzar, J. and **Willig, R.** (1982) *Contestable Markets and the Theory of Industry Structure*, New York, Harcourt, Brace, Jovanovich.

Baumol, W. J., Panzar, J. and **Willig, R.** (1986) On the theory of perfectly contestable markets, in Stiglitz, J. E. and Matthewson, F. (eds), *New Developments in the Analysis of Market Structure*, Cambridge, Mass., MIT Press.

Button, K. J. and **Swann, D.** (1991) Aviation policy in Europe, in Button, K. J. (ed.), *Airline Deregulation: International Experiences*, London, David Fulton Publishers.

Cave, M. (1989) The conduct of auctions for broadcast franchises, *Fiscal Studies*, 10, February, 18–31.

Davis, E. (1984) Express coaching since 1980: liberalisation in practice, *Fiscal Studies*, 5, February, 76–86.

Demsetz, H. (1968) Why regulate utilities?, *Journal of Law and Economics*, 11, 55–65.

Forsyth, P. (1983) Airline deregulation in the United States: the lessons for Europe, *Fiscal Studies*, 4, November, 7–22.

Gilbert, R. (1989) The role of potential competition in industrial organisation, *Journal of Economic Perspectives*, 3, summer, 107–27.

Jaffer, S. M. and **Thompson, D. J.** (1986) Deregulating express coaches: a reassessment, *Fiscal Studies*, 7, November, 45–68.

Joskow, P. L. and **Schmalensee, R.** (1983) *Markets for Power: an Analysis of Electrical Utility Deregulation*, Cambridge, Mass., MIT Press.

Leibenstein, H. (1966) Allocative efficiency vs X-efficiency, *American Economic Review*, 56, June, 392–415.

McCormick, R. E., Shughart, W. F. and **Tollison, R. D.** (1984) The disinterest in deregulation, *American Economic Review*, 78, December, 1075–9.

OECD (1985) *OECD Economic Surveys 1985/6: United States*, Paris, Organisation for Economic Cooperation and Development, 67–84 and 120–4.

OECD (1988) *OECD Economic Surveys 1987/8: United Kingdom*, Paris, Organisation for Economic Cooperation and evelopment, 68–72.

OECD (1991) *OECD Economic Surveys 1990/91: United Kingdom*, Paris, Organisation for Economic Cooperation and Development, 80–2.

Stalon, C. (1992) Restructuring the electric industry, *Resources and Energy*, special issue on 'The future of utility regulation: an agenda for the 1990s', 14, 1/2, April, 55–76.

Train, K. (1991) *Optimal Regulation: the Economic Theory of Natural Monopoly*, Cambridge, Mass., MIT Press.

Tullock, G. (1967) The welfare costs of tariffs, monopolies and theft *Western Economic Journal*, 5, June, 224–32.

Weyman-Jones, T. G. (1989) *Electricity Privatisation*, Aldershot, Avebury.

Williamson, O. (1975) Franchise bidding for natural monopolies – in general and with respect to CATV, *Bell Journal of Economics*, 7, 73–104.

CHAPTER 5

The new public sector management: surrogate competition and contracting out

Peter M. Jackson

Introduction

During the past fifteen years successive Conservative governments in the UK have experimented with the organisation, production and delivery of public services. This has included the introduction of competitive tendering to the National Health Service (NHS) and local government; devolved budgeting in Whitehall departments; the local management of schools; the establishment of internal markets for the NHS and some local authority services; and privatisation of the management of council estates. The underlying culture of public sector management, its value and belief system, has been challenged. Previous values based upon public administration and serving the public interest have been confronted by an emphasis upon market testing, serving individual customers and business planning.[1]

Some of these changes originate in the public choice literature, which views public service bureaucracies as being inherently x-inefficient (Tullock, 1965; Niskanen, 1968), and allocative inefficient (Jackson, 1982). Opening up public service bureaucracies to greater competition should improve efficiency and bring public expenditure under control (Flynn, 1989).

These changes in the organisation of public services reflect other changes taking place in society generally. Some have described these trends in terms of the emergence of a post-Fordist society,[2] which gives greater emphasis to flexible production, getting close to the customer, customisation of services, rapid response to changing needs, and the end of large-scale bureaucratic hierarchical organisation based upon command and control (Peters and Waterman, 1982; Kanter, 1985 and Peters, 1992). The new forms of organisation emphasise the efficiency gains of contracting out, networking, focusing on core competencies and satisfying customer needs.

One graphic account of the changes has been given by Kenneth Baker who, as Secretary of State for Education in the mid 1980s, was responsible for designing the devolution of management in schools. Baker suggests that what has happened is that central government has initially taken powers away from the rim of a wheel (local government) and brought them back to the hub of central government before redistributing them back to the rim. Dispute focuses on the new distribution of rights and entitlements and upon whether power was in effect devolved to the rim of the wheel after it was taken back to the centre. Structural change always involves a redistribution of power and rights which is a political and controversial act.

How can we make sense of these changes in the public sector? That is the aim of this chapter, which reviews the new public sector management, the use of internal markets, devolved budgeting and the contracting out of public services.

5.1   The new public sector management

The standard public administration model in which bureaucrats passively implement efficiently and effectively the policies of politicians has been challenged. First, the public choice school regard bureaucrats as endogenous non-passive agents who have their own personal agenda that will influence policy outcomes (Tullock, 1965; Niskanen, 1968; Jackson, 1982). Second, inactive 'administration' has given way to more active 'management' with a focus on the efficiency and the effectiveness of the bureaucratic machine.

The new public sector management model emphasises the importance of financial devolution, explicit standards of measuring performance, clear relationships between inputs and outputs; increased accountability, the superiority of private sector management practice and styles, the efficiency of competition and contracting out and efficiency and parsimony (Hoggett, 1991; Hood, 1991; Stewart and Walsh, 1992). These managerial changes can be thought of as part of a wide definition of privatisation – the greater use of market testing and the importation of private sector best managerial practice into the public services. They are responses to demands to cut back on public spending and the quest for improved value for money in the delivery of services including improvements in the quality of services. The new public sector management is idealised as a means of improving public sector efficiency. The number of NHS administrative staff, for example, grew by 23 per cent between 1987 and 1990.

This chapter will examine a number of these new managerial instruments. In particular the use of competitive tendering and forms of surrogate competition such as internal markets. The change from a public administration paradigm to the new public management paradigm is not, however, as innocuous and value-free as is often supposed. There is a strong presumption, which is seldom challenged or subjected to critical testing, that private sector management practice is better than public sector practices. Also, the values of private sector management are assumed to apply with equal force to the public services. Deep-seated issues of political legitimacy and rights are involved. Separation of the roles of purchaser and provider helps to diffuse blame if things don't work out according to expectation. Blame is diverted away from government. Instead of complaining to government, people direct their displeasure at suppliers.

5.2 Internal/quasi markets

In an attempt to improve the efficiency of public services simulated competitive market conditions have been introduced especially to the NHS and on a more limited scale, to local authorities in the UK. These are markets in the limited sense that they replace public service bureaucratic monopolies, in which decisions are made by administrative fiat, with competition between alternative suppliers for contracts to supplier customers/clients. The term used to describe these new surrogate competitive arrangements is internal or quasi markets. They are 'internal' in the sense that the transactions take place within some pre-determined institutional boundary and they are 'quasi' because they differ in important respects from conventional markets. They are not necessarily driven by the profit motive nor are the transactions exchanges of privately-owned entitlements. In such markets the consumer or final user of the service is not usually the purchaser. A third party, an agent such as the patient's GP, makes purchases on behalf of the final customer (Le Grand, 1991; Bartlett, 1991, Ferlie; 1992).

The advocates of internal markets emphasise the benefits of transactions through competitive markets. They regard the creation of such conditions within an organisation as the foundation for enhancing efficiency of service delivery; improving accountability and expanding choice. Greater efficiency will be achieved through price competition because contracts will be awarded to those agencies that supply the specified service at lowest cost.

Accountability, especially of monopolised professional suppliers of services, such as doctors and teachers, will be improved because the specification of a contract makes it easier to monitor their actions and their performance as measured in terms of outcomes. Choice is expanded because consumers of the services will have greater access to alternative sources of supply.

The benefits of markets do, however, depend crucially upon the coincidence of a number of special circumstances. In particular, there must be no externalities, consumers need to be perfectly informed, there must be no non-convexities in the production process such as economies of scale or economies of scope and the costs of transacting in markets must be zero. There must also be many alternative suppliers. That these conditions seldom exist in practice should come as no surprise. The problematic question which faces those who propose the use of internal markets is how serious are the departures from the idealised conditions of perfect competition?

Consider the number of alternative suppliers. Within the public sector this is usually small which could reduce the credibility of any threat of competition. Internal markets are, therefore, not seriously contested. Also, if providers are not only interested in profit maximisation but are, instead, also interested in pursuing public service objectives, then they are unlikely to respond simply to market signals.

Profit-maximising providers who supply to internal markets, can create problems of adverse selection (cream-skimming). That is, it is in their interests to reduce their costs. One way of achieving this is to discriminate against particular high cost users of their service. For example, low achieving pupils or expensive patients such as the very aged and chronically sick will not be taken on. Private sector residential homes for the elderly will compete for healthy high-income residents. This leaves the high-cost user as a problem for some other agency, usually the public sector, to pick up.

Information problems are another serious impediment that results in imperfection of internal markets. Will suppliers have sufficient information to enable them to set efficient prices for their services and will customers have sufficient information to monitor the service that they are receiving?

As will be demonstrated with reference to the services that are considered below, problems of internal market imperfection are only just beginning to be identified. The suppliers of services in quasi-markets are not necessarily driven by the objective of profit-maximisation, nor need they be privately owned. Ownership, incentive structures, and the objectives of the new institutions of supply are not clear. This makes it difficult to understand the likely behaviour of the new institutions and, therefore, their impact on resource allocation and distribution.

5.3 Managed competition : the NHS

As a response to rising health-care costs, governments around the world have sought solutions that involve administrative, managerial, budgetary, and structural reforms. The UK's National Health Service is no exception. As a result of the Griffiths Report (1983), general managers were introduced to manage NHS facilities and the 'hotel' support services of hospitals (i.e. catering, laundry and cleaning) were put out to competitive tendering, which was compulsory.

What were the effects of competitive tendering? A National Audit Office (NAO) study in 1987 examined differences in the value of the new contracts compared to the old. Changes in value were due to changes in wage rates; changes in the number of hours worked and the number of staff. No allowance was made for inflation. The NAO study found reductions in the value of contracts of between 20 and 30 per cent with cost savings being larger for domestic services than for catering. A similar study was carried out by Domberger, Meadowcroft and Thompson (1987). They found that it was the *threat* of competitive tendering which caused hospitals to reduce costs. The principal method used to reduce costs was not to fill vacancies, rather than changing wages and conditions of service because these were tied to nationally determined Whitley Council rates. These results were confirmed by Milne (1987) who found also that there was evidence of loss-leading by private sector contract cleaning and contract catering firms. One firm became tied into a loss-making contract and was taken over by another firm. Milne and McGee (1992) conclude that, 'when looked at in terms of the costs saved, particularly domestic services, but even for catering, it must be judged some success. Here was a source of efficiency savings to channel more funds for patient care, yet keep a lid on government spending. This conclusion stands, even when account is taken of the financial costs of setting up competitive tendering and the attendant costs of redundancies.'

Whether or not the introduction of competitive tendering had little impact on wages and conditions of service as Domberger, Meadowcroft and Thompson claim is disputed (see O'Connell Davidson, Chapter 7). A Treasury publication in 1986 pointed out that 'most savings from contracting arise because contractors offer poorer conditions of employment'.[3] The government rescinded the Fair Wages Resolution to coincide with the introduction of competitive tendering.

Competitive tendering was undoubtedly a catalyst to the introduction of cost savings. All was not, however, plain sailing. In the first contract round, the very short timetable for implementation meant that many contracts were poorly specified. Many private firms were not prepared to respond to the introduction of competitive tendering. Also the NHS was not regarded as a highly profitable market. The result was that few private sector firms contested the contracts. In Scotland, for example, very little interest was shown in NHS laundry services. Threat of new entrants will only result in cost savings provided the threat is credible. If public services learn that the private sector will not compete in these markets then the efficiency benefits of competitive tendering are minimised.

Fundamental and long-reaching changes to the character and structure of the NHS began in 1987 with the publication of the White Paper, *Promoting Better Health Care.* This was followed up in 1989 with a further White Paper, *Working for Patients,* and in 1990 with the NHS and Community Care Act. These changes, which introduced patient-focused care, are explained in greater detail in this volume by Robinson, Chapter 8. Among the 1990 reforms was the establishment of an internal market for health care and a redistribution of powers and responsibilities for patient care away from the Community Care Councils towards the District Health Authorities. The District Health Authority (DHA) which is now responsible for the health care needs of individuals living within its area, acts as if it were a customer making purchasing decisions on behalf of patients after carrying out a needs assessment.

Prior to these reforms, resources were allocated to hospitals through a series of bureaucratic procedures. Central government provided a budget to the District Health Authorities who in turn allocated a budget to each hospital in their areas in return for a range of services. Those who purchased the services (the DHAs) were also, in effect, responsible for providing them. This system provided no real incentives to improve efficiency. Hospitals did not compete with one another, or with other suppliers, for patients and, therefore, for revenue. There was very little information about treatment costs, quality of service, or the effectiveness of alternative forms of treatment. Consumers had no choice. There were no alternative sources of supply, except a limited amount of private medicine, which was too expensive for the average patient.

The reforms created a purchaser/provider split. Those who purchase health care services, on behalf of patients, are now separate from those who provide them. Purchasers act as the patients' agents. They assess health needs and purchase health care to meet these needs. This role is carried out by the DHAs, who receive a budget from central government. The providers are essentially the hospitals, who are no longer under the direct control of the DHAs. Hospitals compete with one another for contracts awarded by the purchasers.

The new relationship between purchaser and provider is designed to improve efficiency. Purchasers will seek providers who offer value for money and in order to remain in business, providers will need to organise supply efficiently.

Central to the reforms are the GPs. They are the first port of call for most patients who are referred by their GPs to specialist consultants for treatments. In 1948 when the NHS was established, GPs were independent contractors. The contract between the GP and the NHS established the relationship which would exist between the two parties, especially how GPs should be paid. Between 1948 and 1966, payment was on a per capita basis. This was changed in 1966 to a salaried service plus a complex capitation fee and fees for services provided such as cervical cytology, immunisations and night visits.

The nature of GP contracts is a sensitive issue because it is closely related to the old and vexed question of the status of GPs within the hierarchy of the medical profession. The new contract, introduced in 1990, specified more clearly for the first time the services which GPs were expected to provide. Emphasis is now given in the contract to preventive medicine, which is to be effected through screening and regular check-ups. GP and ancillary staff are required to offer all patients over 75 years a health check. Changes were also made to the way in which GPs are paid: more of their remuneration is now attached to capitation fees (60 per cent compared to an average of 47 per cent under the 1966 contract). The new contract now requires GPs to provide more information about the health care needs of their patients to the Family Practitioner Committees (FPCs) who will use it to monitor whether or not health care services are meeting local needs.[4]

Many GPs have misgivings about the new contracts. Some are suspicious about the new accountabilities that were introduced. They are sceptical about the medical value of screening. Few studies confirm the effectiveness of screening as a tool of preventive medicine. Moreover, there is a danger that the incentives, which the new contracts introduce, will result in GP behaviour which meets the requirements of the contract and which responds to the financial rewards of the contract, rather than offering an interpretation of what current medical practice has to provide to satisfy the needs of patients (Morrell, 1991).

Some GPs, whose practices are large (over 11,000 patients), were given the opportunity of becoming 'fundholders'. That is, they were given responsibility to manage budgets for staff, drugs and some elements of secondary care.

These changes, the introduction of an internal market and a set of new contracts for GPs, were made in the name of greater efficiency and cost-effectiveness. What, however, have been the implementation problems and have improvements in efficiency been achieved?

Markets, be they real or quasi, are not costless to run. (Coase, 1937; Alchian, 1950; Williamson, 1975). Transactions costs can be significant and can absorb any efficiency gains. Contracts have to be priced if they are to be exchanged. This is not done by some anthropomorphic entity called 'the market' (i.e. prices are set by markets). Rather hospitals require new and expensive management information systems that will inform pricing decisions. How much, for example, does it cost to treat a patient for medical problem X? The costs of transacting don't stop there. There are also the costs of billing many different purchasers; the monitoring costs of ensuring that invoices have indeed been paid and the opportunity costs of late receipt of revenues.

On the other side of the market those who are purchasing health care incur search and decision costs as they scan alternative sources of supply. It has been estimated that close to £1 billion has been spent on introducing new management information, accounting and control systems into the NHS. The opportunity cost of the investment in this new transactions technology is the welfare loss experienced by patients who would have been better off if the resources had been put directly into patient care. The gamble is that the long-run dynamic efficiency gains of the new administrative arrangements will outweigh short-run welfare losses.

Markets are not perfect. The capital of hospitals is indivisible, which can result in them charging District Health Authorities monopoly or imperfect prices. One means of solving this problem would be to give DHAs access to information about the costs of supply of each hospital. Whether that would be feasible or the information reliable is questionable. An alternative is to make the market in health care more contestable by forcing hospitals to compete with one another for business. The existence of economies of scope might, however, be significant and if these are to be obtained, then markets will become less contestable.

Economies of scope arise when it is less expensive to have a group of services or activities under one roof, for example, accident and emergency alongside acute specialities. Those economies can, however, be eroded if specialist hospitals (such as hospital trusts) or the private sector cream off the more profitable services. The same problem can arise if GPs, under their new contractual arrangements, refer their patients to their own clinics for minor operations. The outcome could, therefore, be that a DHA is left with a District General Hospital whose average costs are rising because its profitable business is being hived off. Not only do the average costs of the hospital rise, but the average costs of the whole system rise also, because economies of scope are not available to the new specialist units.

There is an overwhelming belief running through these reforms that the creation of surrogate competition through quasi markets will result in improvements in efficiency. The mechanisms through which this is to be achieved are never set out clearly. It is not obvious that the institutional changes that have been made will improve allocative efficiency by giving consumers of health services greater choice or voice. The DHAs do not face incentives that compel them to take notice of the needs of their consumers. Health care managers are not rewarded on the basis of meeting consumer/patients' needs nor are they sanctioned if they do not. The costs of finding out if treatments are effective are usually high and the performance monitoring of most medical interventions takes a considerable length of time.

There is only a weak form of accountability between a DHA and its patients/clients. Some patients could choose to go to a GP fundholder. This move would result in a loss of revenue to the DHA. There is, therefore, a threat from fundholders but it is weak because not all patients have access to a GP fundholder. Moreover, GP fundholders face incentives that encourage 'cream-skimming' and are, therefore, likely to turn away high-cost patients. Fundholders are paid on a per capita basis, not according to the severity of their patients' medical conditions, that is, they are paid according to an average notional cost and not marginal actual cost. Some have argued that this incentive structure could result in a two-tier health system. Healthier and low-cost patients will be accepted by fundholders and will have greater voice and choice while the less healthy and high-cost patients will be forced to accept whatever services the DHAs offer.

Hospitals, that is the suppliers (providers) of health care, are now categorised as NHS hospitals, NHS trusts and private hospitals. An NHS trust hospital has greater freedom to manage its affairs than an NHS hospital. The structure of incentives facing hospitals does not, despite the rhetoric of the reforms, give a strong encouragement for efficiency improvements. The pricing policy adopted by hospitals is constrained to charging average cost. Profits are not permitted nor is cross-subsidisation or price discrimination. This means that hospital managers will be denied market signals that would enable them to identify those activities which generate the highest marginal returns. Because NHS hospitals are budget constrained, risk-averse managers will make savings when and where they are offered by chance. This will result in an unbalanced service in the medium to long run and undermines management's responsibility to achieve strategic objectives. Any overspending will be reflected in the reduction and eventual closure of services. Trusts, on the other hand, are allowed to make a surplus and will, therefore, allocate resources to those services which maximise returns at the margin. Services which have lower marginal returns will be provided by NHS hospitals if they are to be provided at all. What this means is that NHS hospitals could become providers of last resort to high-cost patients. Any comparison of the relative performance of NHS hospitals and trusts would be a complete nonsense.

Figure 5.1 illustrates the different outcomes for NHS hospitals and trusts. An NHS hospital will spend up to its budget constraint, i.e. to Q, where total revenue (the budget) equals total cost. A profit maximising trust will produce up to Q_0 where marginal revenues equal marginal cost. At Q_0 the surplus, AB, is maximised. NHS hospitals, will, therefore, over-invest in capital and employees.

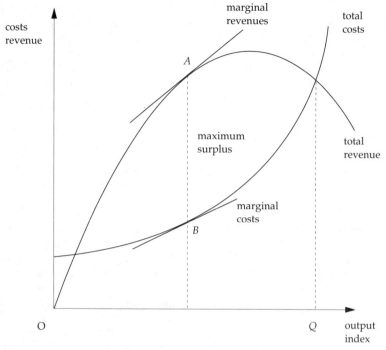

Figure 5.1

Principal-agent relationships in economics are characterised by an asymmetry of information. Those who provide health care have more information about costs and production conditions than those who purchase health care. Outcomes below those expected could be due to poor performance on the part of the supplier or chance. Without complex and expensive monitoring systems, which track the efforts and performance of suppliers, then purchasers are unable to account for any variance between expectations and outcomes. Health services are complex and heterogeneous unlike standard products sold on markets. Medical audit is, consequently, likely to be expensive. Contracts, therefore, need to be designed so that they are incentive compatible. That is, provider's (agents) incentives should encourage them to behave in a way that will serve the interests of purchasers (principals). This problem is referred to in the literature as the 'market for lemons' (Akerloff, 1970). Unless we can trust the reliability and quality of what is on offer, markets can degenerate, as in the case of the second-hand car market, to inefficient solutions where consumer needs are not adequately met.

If however, accounting systems become too complex, in an attempt to provide accurate management information for pricing decisions, then there is a greater chance of fraud. Patients could, for example, get assigned to diagnostic-related groups which are more financially rewarding. Auditing complex accounting systems is expensive especially in the face of asymmetric information. Trust is essential.

DHAs face the problem that they do not know whether they are getting value for money from providers. When demand greatly exceeds supply, which is the situation in many parts of the health sector, then the power of the purchaser is reduced relative to that of the provider. Local monopolies can arise so that DHAs are charged higher than average cost prices. There is no equivalent to the regulator in the NHS to safeguard the purchasers' interests and the capacity within the system to monitor contracts effectively is inadequate. At the same time the development of suitable quality and performance targets has been slow. The purchasing role has been given insufficient attention. There is no clear link between the assessment of health needs by a DHA and its purchasing strategy. Few DHAs have an overall model of the components of a purchasing strategy. Given this background, who is it that is shaping health services – purchasers or providers? A clear answer does not exist to this question.

The picture which emerges from the initial implementation of the health reforms is that it is not patient-focused care but budget-focused care which is being supplied. There is little local assessment of demand. Instead, there is central imposition of standards and targets set by central government politicians. Purchasers generally accept what is on offer. They do not appear to be able to stipulate what is to be provided or how it is to be provided. The professional autonomy of clinicians has been challenged and their performance is threatened by medical audits. Clinicians have become demoralised as the culture of managerialism, with its emphasis upon value for money and performance measurement, clashes with the older and more traditional values and ethics of the medical profession. Some clinicians have become involved in management either directly as unit managers or as clinical managers or indirectly by adopting the principles of the new managerialism.

5.4 Contracting out: local authority services

The incoming 1979 Conservative government had identified local authorities as a source of inefficiency and waste in public spending. The 'winter of discontent', which had led up to the 1979 general election, had given substance to Conservative perceptions that local authorities were out of control, unaccountable and a threat to political stability. Specifically, left-wing elected Labour councils were seen as a threat to a Conservative central government and the local authority public sector unions were regarded as having too much power. These sentiments were expressed some years later by Nicholas Ridley, one of the leading architects of Thatcherism, when he was Secretary of State for the Environment and in charge of local government, 'the grip which local government unions have over those services in many parts of the country . . .' (*Local Government Chronicle,* 4 April 1989, p. 1).

In order to reduce the countervailing power of local authorities complex rate-capping schemes with penalties for over-spending were introduced. The Community Charge (poll tax), which history will record as the most expensive tax reform fiasco, and which brought down a Prime Minister, was to be the ultimate means of bringing local authorities to account. Alongside these financial reforms the introduction of competitive tendering would 'smash that grip once and for all . . .' that local government unions had over local public services (Ridley, *op. cit.*).

Compulsory competitive tendering (CCT) had been introduced into local authorities in the 1980 Local Government Planning and Land Act and covered services such as highways, buildings and maintenance work. The Local Government Act, 1988, extended CCT to refuse collection; building cleaning; other cleaning; schools and welfare catering; other catering; grounds maintenance; and vehicle maintenance.

The 1988 Act 'requires local authorities . . . who wish to afford their own staff the opportunity of carrying out certain activities to expose the activities to competitive tendering'. Conditions were laid down by central government to ensure that competition was effective and that local authorities did not engage in anti-competitive practices. These conditions included; the local authority must advertise a call to tender; it must consider at least three tenders if more than three companies express an interest; and it must prepare its own written bid. Furthermore, the local authority must not, when awarding contracts, take into account non-commercial criteria such as, insisting on nationally agreed wage rates, insisting that the workforce is unionised, insisting on equal opportunities clauses. Financial efficiency, making a statutory minimum rate of return on capital of 5 per cent p.a., dominated all other considerations including democratic control of services and the wider social benefits of services.

Contracting out brought with it a number of organisational and managerial changes. As in the NHS, purchasers and providers were split. The consultative paper, *Competing for Quality*, had agreed 'the task of setting standards, specifying the work to be done and monitoring performance is done better if it is fully separated from the job of providing services'. Separate trading accounts were set up, new billing and invoicing systems were created and the administrative infrastructure of letting and monitoring contracts was established. These changes represent the transactions costs of operating the new system.

What has been the experience of contracting out of local authority services? Has efficiency improved? Have there been cost savings? How have costs been reduced? Is the market for local authority contracts competitive? Surveys have been produced by Parker (1990), Jackson (1992) and Szymanski and Wilkins (1992).[5]

The first round of contracts, following the 1988 Act, started in August 1989. Painter (1991) using a data set drawn from a variety of sources examined contracts awarded by 299 local authorities (out of a total of 514). Of the 438 services that had been put up for tender, 74 per cent of the contracts were won in-house. There was, however, a variation by service. Refuse collection and street cleaning was a favourite for competitive tendering, 72 per cent of the contracts were won in-house, 97 per cent of school and welfare catering went in-house, 57 per cent of building cleaning and 70 per cent of grounds maintenance contracts. Building cleaning is characterised by low entry barriers, low wages, casual labour, low unionisation rates, and excess private sector capacity. Compare this with catering which has higher entry barriers due to the need for specialist equipment and high volume output. It also has low profit margins. Competition is most intense in refuse collection, street cleaning and building cleaning.

Painter (1991) found that, 'a tiny minority of services covered by the survey were contracted out when the council was Labour controlled' (p. 201) The bulk of contracting out has occurred in Conservative-controlled Rural District Councils.

Some local authorities used the threat of competition to force their employees to accept a deterioration in their terms and conditions of employment. Cuts in hours of work and pay, reductions in conditions of service usually fall on women in part-time jobs (see O'Connell-Davidson, Chapter 7). The retainer paid to schools catering staff during the school holidays was reduced and in some cases eliminated.

The improvements in efficiency resulting from competitive tendering were examined by Domberger, Meadowcroft and Thompson (1986), (hereafter DMT). They found that the cost of refuse collection was 22 per cent lower in local authorities which contracted out and about 17 per cent lower in authorities which awarded the services in-house. DMT controlled for quality and found no reductions in quality following contracting out. The DMT study can, however, be criticised for its methodology. Choosing different functional forms for the cost function, for example, will give significantly different results and will wipe out efficiency gains. There needs to be an a priori reason for choosing one functional form compared to another. Another problem with the DMT study was that it had not made sufficient allowance for the different types of collection technologies used.

Ganley and Grahl (1988) found that the improvements in efficiency, as measured by reductions in refuse collection costs, were due mainly to reductions in wages, longer working hours and poorer working conditions.

The DMT study was reworked by Buck and Chaundy (1993) using a respecified cost function which was justified on analytical grounds and which made better provisions for incorporating quality variables. This study confirms the results of the DMT study as too does a follow up study by Szymanski and Wilkins (1992). They did, however, find that the efficiency gains from retaining services in-house were considerably smaller than those estimated by DMT. There were significant reductions in the number of employees for contracted-out services, which implies that productivity was higher in contracted-out services and that they were better organised. Efficiency gains in the Szymanski and Wilkins study did not show up as direct pay cuts. The productivity gains for in-house contractors were much smaller and not statistically significant.

The Audit Commission (1984) and Cubbin et al., (1987) found that the best private sector firms and the best local authorities are as efficient as one another. Walsh (1991) argued that compulsory competitive tendering resulted in explicit contracts with standards specified clearly. Prior to this local authorities found it difficult to monitor quality.

Why have so many contracts been won in-house? This has in part been due to a lack of interest by the private sector, a lack of capacity by the private sector, a failure by the private sector to take on the risks of local authority contracts and the low profit margins that local authority contracts offer. There are also barriers to entry deriving not only from the needs of specialist equipment but also the specialist knowledge that has been acquired by the incumbent local authority provider over the years.

Local authorities' own direct labour organisations (DLO) have won contracts despite the absence of a level playing field. DLOs are required by statute to achieve a minimum 5 per cent rate of return but of course, private sector contractors are not, and have the option of cross-subsidising their activities.

Competitive tendering has changed the organisation of local authority services, the managerial culture inside local authorities, and has resulted in efficiency gains. The studies which have measured the gains in efficiency have been confined to refuse collection, a reasonably easily measured service. Whether or not large efficiency gains are to be found in other services remains to be seen.

Some local authorities have not fully appreciated their role as clients under the Compulsory Competitive Tendering (CCT) system (Audit Commission, 1993). Since 1988, local authority services worth £2 billion have been put out to tender. There have, however, been a number of problems. First, some consumers (purchasers) have been dissatisfied. In a survey of 150 schools, 30 per cent expressed dissatisfaction with CCT services such as cleaning, catering and ground maintenance. Second, there are issues relating to poor contract management. The Audit Commission found that the client costs of managing contracted services varied from 1.4 per cent of total annual expenditure for education catering to 12.5 per cent for vehicle maintenance. This variance reflects a lack of understanding of the client role and a degree of inefficiency by local government administration. There is a need, the Audit Commission argues, to write contracts with clients' requirements in mind, to ensure that the conditions of all contracts are well defined and comprehensive, to make the contract-letting procedure as clear as possible, to involve both consumers and contractors in the monitoring and feedback system, and to ensure that the administration of the contract is as efficient as possible.

Despite the wave of CCT after 1988, the privatisation of local authority services has effectively been halted since 1993. This is because CCT might have been carried out in breach of EC law. The issue is focused on the 1977 EC Acquired Rights directive which was incorporated into British law by the 1981 Employment Act. Within the Act the Transfer of Undertakings (Protection of Employment) regulations (TUPE) implies that any staff transferring from public to private employment are entitled to keep the same pay and conditions of service as before. Advice given by the Department of Employment indicated that TUPE did not apply to the privatisation of services through CCT. However, this ruling is no longer certain and it could be that the TUPE regulations would need to be applied retrospectively to the 250,000 public employees who have either been made redundant or suffered a cut in their wage rates.

5.5 Local management of schools

The 1988 Education Reform Act introduced the concept of local management of schools (LMS). The objectives of the reforms were to decentralise down into the schools decision-making powers giving parents greater choice over which school their children might attend. It is a clear example of Kenneth Baker's analogy of redistributing new powers to the rim of the wheel. As will be shown, however, the outcomes were not altogether as intended and subsequent reforms have resulted in a greater concentration of powers over education policy at the level of central government. These changes have been carried out with the aim of improving the quality of education and giving greater value for money.

Under the provisions of the 1988 Act, powers were withdrawn from the LEAs and their responsibilities were redefined. LEAs were, from 1988, no longer responsible for their traditional role of controlling and administering local education. Previously they had set local education policy within broadly defined national guidelines. Now, instead, the LEAs were assigned the task of setting an education strategy and assuring quality. 'A providing authority was to give way to an "enabling" authority', (Ranson, 1992, p. 133). Central government was to determine a national curriculum, which all schools were obliged to follow.

Following the 1988 reforms, schools are now allocated a budget, which is centrally determined according to a formula that is based upon an assessment of their needs. LEAs had, prior to 1988, given each school a budget according to locally determined education policies and the LEA had been responsible for administering and controlling the budget. These responsibilities were, after 1988, transferred first to central government, which determined the budgets for each school, and second to the governors and headteachers of the schools who determined how the budget was to be allocated. The LEA was in effect bypassed. Powers were also devolved to schools which enabled them to decide upon their admissions policy. All of these changes were to be phased in with all schools having in excess of 200 pupils to have responsibility for managing their budgets by the end of 1993.

The new formula funding system essentially determines a school's budget according to the number and the age of the pupils on its roll. About 75 per cent of the needs-based formula funding is allocated on the basis of age-weighted pupil numbers. The remaining 25 per cent is allocated according to special education needs, the type of premises and the size of the school (DES Circular 7/88, p. 3). The LEA top-slices the total education budget, which it receives from central government, to finance core services provided by the LEA, such as inspection, central administration and the education psychology service.

These procedures result in a different allocation of resources when compared to the previous system of LEA school budget determination, which was not necessarily related to age-weighted pupil numbers. No studies, to date, have reported on the extent or consequences of the shift in resources.

The 1988 Act also enabled schools to 'opt out' by establishing themselves as grant-maintained schools. In this case, schools receive their grant directly from central government and not via the LEA.

Lying at the heart of LMS is the consistent philosophy of the 1980s that the devolution of decision-making in public services serves to enhance the accountability of those who deliver the services to those who use them. This is expressed clearly in DES Circular 7/88:

> Local management is concerned with far more than budgeting and accounting procedures. Effective schemes of local management will enable governing bodies and head-teachers to plan their use of resources – including their most valuable resource, their staff – to maximum effect with their own needs and priorities, and to make schools more responsive to their clients – parents, pupils, the local community and employers.

The 1988 reforms were advanced further in 1991 when Secretary of State for Education, Kenneth Clarke, announced that his intention was to encourage more schools to opt out of LEA governance by seeking grant-maintained status. This would, in effect, leave the LEA in the long run (about five years), once opting-out was complete, with only a residual role involving special education needs provision. Such a policy clearly emasculates the powers of the LEA but the policy was pursued without adequate public debate and with very limited consultation.

In an attempt to speed-up the opting-out process and the transition to a system of grant-maintained schools, a number of incentives were introduced by central government. In particular, grant maintained schools were given start-up grants and substantial capital grants. They were also awarded a 15 per cent supplement to their maintenance grant which was to be paid by the LEA in respect of the central services that the LEA would have provided to the school if it had not opted out. The grant-maintained school could then decide whether or not it wished to purchase these services from the LEA or from the private sector.

The most recent phase of eduction reform in Britain came with the publication of the July 1992 White Paper *Choice and Diversity*. The proposals in the White Paper further reduced the powers of the LEA but instead of redistributing and devolving them further down to schools and parents, they have been centralised in the Department for Education. Powers have been taken to the hub of the wheel but not redistributed to the rim. Responsibility for education is to be fragmented between different organisations. Decisions about education are to be centralised and will reside in the Secretary of State. This clearly reduces parental choice. A Funding Agency for Schools (FAS) will be established and will administer the grants to grant-maintained schools. For those LEAs which have a high proportion of grant-maintained schools, the FAS will take over from the LEA responsibility for planning the supply of school places, otherwise it will share that responsibility with the LEA. The Secretary of State for Education and the FAS will constrain the powers of the governors of grant-maintained and LEA schools. Finally, for those schools, which are failing to achieve acceptable standards, the Secretary of State will appoint an education association to take over the school.

What have been some of the initial consequences and problems of these reforms? The relationship between a school and its LEA has changed. Resource allocation decisions, which were once the province of the LEA, now reside in the school's board of governors and the headteacher. It is they who decide upon the allocation of resources between staff costs, heating, lighting, equipment and internal maintenance etc., which account for about 85 per cent of the previous LEA budget. Admission criteria to schools have changed. The school governors can increase pupil numbers, subject to an absolute capacity constraint imposed by school size, in an attempt to increase the size of the school's grant. A school's board of governors is no longer the agent of the LEA. It is independent and the school's headteacher is now the agent of the board of governors. These changes in principal–agent relationships are not without consequence for resource allocation and the determination of education policy outcomes but no studies have reported on these effects.

This situation differs sharply from the previous regime in which an LEA allocated resources to schools according to its local education policies and local assessment of educational needs, which were not necessarily based upon the number of pupils in a school or the age distribution of its pupils. When it comes to decisions about the allocation of resources at the margin, the differences between the two systems will have significant implications for the achievement of educational outcomes (results). A formula-based system allocates resources according to an assessment of 'average' needs. Different schools do, however, have pupils whose educational needs differ at the margin. For example, a school which has an above average number of pupils with learning difficulties will lose out under the new formula-based system. This, of course, assumes that the previous LEA resource allocation system picked up such problems and was able to target resources to those schools in greatest need.

Previously LEAs had the freedom to vire between budget heads within the local authority budget. They could control admissions and control staff appointments. Now the LEA can only set the total education budget. It can only plan education in its area with the consent of the schools' governing bodies. The LEA does, however, retain responsibility for the quality of education in its region, but this raises a number of difficult issues. Does the LEA have in place processes which will enable it to define objectives and to monitor and evaluate the financial and non-financial performance of the non-opted-out schools? If the LEA is to be held responsible for the quality of its education then it must have some degree of control over the resource decisions made in schools. This puts into focus the need to define more carefully the relationship between the LEA and the governing bodies which is currently a cloudy area. Two recent reports from the Audit Commission (1989a and 1989b) cast doubts about whether or not sufficient attention has been given to these issues.

Parental choice is highlighted in the *Parent's Charter,* which is incorporated into the Education (Schools) Act, 1992. 'Your choice of school directly affects that school's budget – every extra pupil means extra money for the school. So your right to choose will encourage schools to aim for the highest possible standards.' (DES, *Parent's Charter,* p. 14).

Enhanced choice requires relevant information to aid decision-making. To this end the government is to publish the results of examination and national curriculum tests (if they stand the test of time!) along with truancy rates and school leavers' destinations. While these will not be published as 'league tables', clearly the data can be presented in such a form.

Will such data inform decision-making and enhance choice? League tables give a snap-shot picture. For a variety of factors, including the school's resource base and pupil mix, the ranking of schools over a longer period of time is likely to be unstable. Someone choosing to enter a good quality school at the age of 12 years may exit from a lower quality school at age 18 years. League tables might be a clearer reflection of social deprivation and under-resourcing of schools relative to their educational needs rather than their performance. They give no information about the value added by a school nor do they (obviously) give information about the immeasurable dimensions of the education experience.

Even if choice is informed is it effective? When a school is full, the parents of those children who are not admitted do not have increased powers of choice. They are denied their choice. Indeed, many parents now feel disillusioned and cheated because the choices they thought they would have under the new system cannot be exercised. They are forced off their demand curve and experience a welfare loss. There is not a market in education and the pseudo-market which has been established is far from any ideal. New entrants, for example, cannot come into the market to satisfy excess demand. The capital expenditure for new schools needs local authority and central government approval which is unlikely to be given when neighbouring schools have excess capacity and the central government's macro-economic policy is to reduce public spending and the borrowing requirement.

When a school opts out from the LEA, it introduces selectivity. The school chooses the pupils rather than parents choosing the school. To maintain its excellence in terms of examination results, and hence, its position in the 'league tables', a school faces a strong incentive only to accept those pupils who are potentially high achievers. This is yet another example of the tendency towards 'cream-skimming' which is encouraged by the reforms.

Parental choice in Scotland over the past ten years is the subject of a recent report by Adler (1993) who concludes that parental choice led to an inefficient use of resources, widening disparities between schools, increased social segregation and threats to equality of educational opportunity. Parental preferences are shaped by a desire to send their children to schools that have an acceptable socio-economic background and which on average produce good results. Parents, however, have no information on the value added of schools. High performance schools, as defined by the league tables, do not necessarily add much value, therefore, parental decisions have a weak and ill-informed effect upon the child's educational attainment.

Schools in poor areas will tend to lose pupils to those schools in better areas. This not only results in relatively high per pupil costs (an apparent inefficiency indicator) but the loss of pupils means a loss of resources with the result that schools in deprived areas will not be able to provide a full range of educational opportunities. This is not to argue that all inner-city schools are condemned to low achievement. Rather, it applies to those schools in deprived areas with declining pupil numbers. It would seem that parental choice results in a negative sum game in which the gains obtained by some pupils are less than the losses experienced by others. Either the outcome of the negative sum game is accepted for the community as a whole or the community acting collectively seeks to redress the outcome in accordance with its sense of distributive justice. What is in conflict is the right of parents to exercise their choice on behalf of the interests of their children and the community's desire to promote the education opportunities of them collectively as a whole. By redistributing the responsibilities of the LEA, central government has created a negative sum game for education. The LEA can no longer redistribute resources to those areas of greatest need and to those areas that will add greatest value at the margin. By substituting local management for local governance, central government policies have probably reduced both allocative efficiency and equity while improving X-efficiency. Whether or not that was a price worth paying is not known.

The relationship between parent and child is one of principal and agent. Devices such as the *Parent's Charter* give emphasis to parental choice. This assumes, however, that parents act as perfect agents. This is not necessarily so and it is not clear that there are safeguards in the system to protect against this.

Enhancing choice is intended to improve allocative efficiency. It was argued that parental choice for many was not effective but even if it is, what options or alternatives do parents have to choose from – what is the nature of the education choice set; what menu is on offer? The answer is, there is little choice other than the school to which a child might be sent. Those who use education and those who supply it are constrained by the national curriculum, which now dominates the timetables of most schools. Parents cannot shop around different schools to choose that curriculum which they believe best serves the needs of their children. The national curriculum determines the teaching of core subjects such as Mathematics, English, Science and foundation subjects such as History, Geography, Technology, Art, Music, Physical Education and Modern Languages (at secondary school). These subjects are to be assessed through national unified tests. This means that there is now greater central government control of the curriculum and greater centralised direct control over the criteria of educational achievement. It is difficult to argue that this enhances choice and, therefore, allocative efficiency and welfare.

Those who supply education also face constraints which limit their choices of options over the most appropriate education production function. Not only does the national curriculum constrain the nature of the service that is to be produced and delivered, but also teachers' salaries, which account for 80 per cent of a school's costs, are determined, along with conditions of service at the national level. Local 'management' of schools is a poor choice of phrase to describe the realities of what goes on within a school. The headteacher, as a latent manager, has little choice and therefore, a narrow scope within which to make managerial decisions. Constrained from above and below, headteachers can end up as budget administrators.

Headteachers in those schools which are losing pupils, and hence, resources, will be faced with the problems of managing decline – struggling in the face of declining resources to maintain their ability to deliver the minimum national curriculum. In the absence of a mechanism to distribute resources to such schools, disadvantaged groups will remain disadvantaged.

The reforms have significant consequences for LEAs. As opting-out increases, many LEAs will become totally unviable. They will have no obvious role to play especially if schools choose their inspectors and other central services from the private sector instead of from the LEA. The big unknown is how many schools will, in fact, choose to opt out for grant-maintained status. This situation of uncertainty has had a significant impact on the morale of those who remain within the LEA. Under the arrangements of opting-out the strategic role of the LEA is minimal as too is its role of quality assurance. The role of the LEA is now that of a service agency and the local government of education is all but dead.

Education has many stakeholders and, therefore, a diversity of preferences and expectations to serve. It is a service with strong associated externalities. Those features of the service should guide the choice of the 'governance system' for education. Yet the system which has been chosen focuses upon a particular set of interests, i.e. current parents, current pupils and current employers. Who safeguards the interests of future generations? Are existing boards of governors sufficiently representative of the range of stakeholders' interests? These questions highlight the problems of managing education within a democratic system and yet, by denying the role of local politics, these issues are taken off the agenda and the appearance of a solution is portrayed. All decisions are now centralised with the Secretary of State for Education and the unselected and locally unaccountable funding agency. The choice facing a school is not simply whether or not to opt out to a remote, technocratic and centralised funding agency which has little knowledge of, and no interest in, local conditions.

What impact have these reforms had upon the effectiveness of the education system? Much of the emphasis of the reforms has been upon process. Little is said about output. Levacic (1990) in her studies of Solihull and Cambridgeshire's experiences with devolved budgeting and LMS concluded that the changes had resulted in a greater freedom for LEA staff to respond to local conditions. That study was completed prior to the publication of *Choice and Diversity*. No study has concluded that these changes will make the education system more effective. To do so requires a debate on the purpose and objectives of an education system which ranges beyond the needs to serve narrow economic interests. This debate is not taking place. Equally there is a great faith that the reforms will improve the efficiency and quality of education and yet this also requires a discussion of what the outputs and outcomes of education might be let alone what they should be. It is economic naivety to believe that it is possible simply to legislate a production function for a service as complex as education.

5.6 Decentralisation and contracting: central government

In an attempt to improve financial control over the spending of public money within central government departments, a system of devolved budgeting, which went under the heading of the Financial Management Initiative (FMI), was introduced in 1982. Devolving budgetary powers had been discussed as far back as 1969 in the Fulton Committee Report. It was not, however, until the publication of *Efficiency and Effectiveness in the Civil Service* (Cmnd 8616) in 1982 and the determination of the Prime Minister of the day, Margaret Thatcher, that a system of devolved budgeting was in fact implemented. Many previous experiments during the 1970s, including programme analysis and review (PAR) and output budgeting (OB) had failed because of a lack of commitment from the top. Mrs Thatcher's commitment not only to bring public expenditure under control, but also to deliver value for money from public funds gave an authority to the FMI, which no other system had enjoyed (Jackson, 1988; Metcalfe and Richards, 1984, 1990).

The objectives of the FMI were to establish for each major central government department a system which would:

(1) set clear objectives and performance measures;
(2) define clearly responsibility for making resource allocation decisions and scrutiny for determining value for money;
(3) provide a ministerial information system (MINIS) which would give information about unit costs, training needs, etc.

Senior civil servants (and Ministers) were to be held accountable and judged in terms of what had been achieved (outcomes or outputs) rather than what had been spent (inputs). This was a clear recognition that financial accountability (i.e. living within budgets) is a necessary but not sufficient definition of accountability.

The FMI was a generic term – it described a set of principles. Each department defined and negotiated its own logic and reality for the FMI. In practice, there was no single system and each department implemented its own variant of the FMI. The introduction of the FMI completely changed the incentive system which had previously existed in Whitehall. Budgetary systems are not neutral in their behaviourial impacts. Prior to the establishment of the FMI, departments had little (if any) relevant information about objectives; about how resources were allocated or about costs. The system of vote accounting had focused upon the costs of inputs and functions not the costs of outputs or activities. Also, those who made decisions about budgetary control were frequently different from those who managed the service. Given these implicit incentives those who provided the service did not regard themselves to be responsible for providing value for money. There was nothing to encourage the search for cost savings.

Devolved budgeting means giving financial responsibility to those who make decisions and who can influence activity and, therefore, costs.

Establishing cost centres/budget centres ensures that budget managers are charged for all of their expenditures. If managers have information that enables them to understand the activities that give rise to spending (the 'cost drivers'), they are in a better position to control costs. Local managers have a better chance of having local information and knowledge to search for improvements in efficiency and effectiveness.

If devolved budgeting is to deliver efficiency savings, then it is necessary to produce relevant cost information; to have in place adequate cost control systems and to have managers who are sufficiently well trained in interpreting these new information systems. Additional relevant information is not, however, sufficient. An appropriate incentive system must also exist. If local efficiency improvements and cost savings are syphoned off by the centre and reallocated to other departments, then this is equivalent to levying a 100 per cent tax, which clearly has disincentives. A balance has to be found which either allows all efficiency savings to be retained by the department to be allocated according to local definitions of spending needs, or allows a significant proportion to be retained. Finding the balance is a search for a Pareto efficient set of budgetary incentives.

Did the FMI deliver efficiency improvements? This question is difficult to answer. Given the intangible nature of most public services, it is possible to deliver cost reductions which appear to be improvements in efficiency but which are in fact, reductions in quality of service. However, weak evidence does exist to support the claim that improvements in X-efficiency did arise as a result of the FMI.

The use of performance indicators, another element of the FMI package, increases accountability by changing the incentives that managers face. An over-zealous and uncritical use of performance indicators can, however create disincentives that distort resource allocation decisions and thereby reduce rather than improve efficiency. For example, by their nature, performance measures concentrate on the quantifiable dimensions of activity. If improved performance is rewarded then the measurable can drive out the immeasurable with important consequences for the nature of the service which is provided, consumer satisfaction and hence, allocative efficiency. Performance measures can also cause managers to focus on the short term. Thus, long-run considerations of dynamic efficiency are ignored. Fear of the consequences of not performing adequately generally produces risk-averse or safety-first responses which can render managers impotent, especially when they face complex and uncertain environments (Jackson, 1988; Jackson and Palmer, 1992).

The philosophy of devolving budgets and decision-making within Whitehall departments was further extended in 1988 with the publication of the Ibbs report from the Efficiency Unit of the Cabinet Office, *Improving Management in Government: The Next Steps* (Cm 524). The report noted the following:

- the civil service is too big and too diverse to manage as a single entity;
- resource allocation is too centralised;
- the system is too prescriptive about how resources should be managed.

Ibbs' foundations are found in modern organisation theory, which emphasises the disintegration of organisations – as compared to the vertically and horizontally integrated large corporation – into small, focused, flat and flexible units (Chandler, 1977, 1990; Kanter, 1985; Peters, 1992). Smaller and more specialised organisations are found to be more efficient and more adaptable in unstable changing environments. The conclusions of Ibbs are also that decentralisation, following the implementation of the FMI, had been partial and incomplete. Not all departments had adopted the FMI with conviction. Also there remained too much centralised control over core services, which constrained the decisions of local departmental managers. Recruitment, dismissal, choice of staff, promotion, pay, hours of work, accommodation, grading, organisation of work and the purchase and use of IT equipment were all centrally determined and outside the control of individual managers. Things were 'structured to fit everything in general and nothing in particular'. The benefits of a centralised and unified civil service are outweighed by the costs of centralisation.

The recommendation of the Ibbs Report was to devolve further by decoupling many of the activities of central government departments by putting out, on an 'agency' basis, those departments which are involved in the delivery of services. Those departments which advise Ministers and formulate policy are kept in. The 'Next Steps Agencies' or Executive Agencies are given new freedoms which include the freedom to negotiate local wages, employment levels, conditions of service, IT policies, etc. Plans exist to set up 80 agencies employing 75 per cent of the current civil service. Examples of agencies include the Stationery Office, Employment Services, Passport Department, Vehicle Inspectorate, Met. Office, Companies Registration Office, Royal Parks, Historic Royal Palaces, Queen Elizabeth II Conference Centre, etc.

The creation of Next Steps Agencies is a form of contracting. Executive Agencies exist to carry out the executive functions of government within a policy framework set by a department. Each agency obtains a contract or a Framework Document from a central government department which specifies the services to be provided, performance targets, and of course, the budget. Performance reviews are carried out to monitor whether or not the terms of the contract are being honoured. The Chief Executives of the agencies are accountable to Parliament for the delivery of their services and the operation of their agencies.

The relationship between an Executive Agency and its parent department is one of 'contracting' rather than contracting out. That is, there is a contract which focuses service delivery objectives and, therefore, acts as a catalyst for efficiency improvements. The contract itself is not contestable in competitive markets as would be the case in contracting out when alternative suppliers bid for the award of the contract.

What have been the consequences of the Executive Agencies? It is far too early to identify substantive and sustainable changes in efficiency and effectiveness. That will only come about after tracking the activities of the agencies for a number of years. Nevertheless, the change in culture (values, beliefs and incentives) as the activities encompassed by the agencies leave the centralised civil service and are located within a clearly focused organisation, in which managers face real choices and have freedom to make decisions, does provide a more fertile basis for realising efficiency improvements. However, the absence of competitive forces and any weakness in the monitoring and regulation of agencies could easily result in increasing X-inefficiency. The moral hazard problem of all principal–agent relationships might simply have been exported and to the extent that agencies become remote from their parent departments then the probability of agencies engaging in opportunistic behaviour and pursuing their own sub-objectives is increased.

5.7 Problems within the PSM paradigm

The new public sector management (PSM) paradigm raises important issues of rights and legitimacy. Contracts give expression to who is entitled to receive a service. This can set into sharp relief the rights of individuals *qua* consumers against the concept of citizenship rights. The PSM model gives to managers the right to manage – politics is in large measure replaced by management and in turn management is replaced by inspectors and auditors. What is it that legitimates managerial action in the PSM model?

Richards (1992) has discussed some of these problems by comparing three distinct paradigms:

(a) The public administration paradigm. The model contains three principal groups, politicians and producers of public services with administrators existing between these two groups. Political action is legitimated via citizens voting in the ballot box while producers' legitimation resides in their professionalism and expertise.

The role of politicians is to give expression to the needs, preferences and demands of the electorate and citizens of the nation while the producers use their professional expertise to deliver the services. Administrators negotiate order between the politicians and producers. Those who emphasise the X-efficiency of bureaucracy would argue that this was in fact negotiated inefficiency.

(b) The efficiency paradigm. This replaces the administrator in the above paradigm with a 'manager' and epitomises the 'do it like the private sector' attitude. Emphasis is upon performance measures, standard setting and audit. Managers (in the NHS and local authorities, etc.) now challenge the received wisdom of the professionals who produce the service. Not only does this result in conflict and the need to allocate scarce managerial resources to contain the conflict, it also expresses two different sets of rights – the rights of professionals and the rights of managers. What is not clear is the source (if any) of the legitimacy of managerial rights. Are they agents of the politicians and do their rights fall within the shadow of the political rights? Or are they the agents of the consumers of public services and do consumer rights differ from citizenship rights? Active management results in the re-distribution of resources which has consequences for the distribution of welfare – the issue is what legitimises these resource allocation decisions?

(c) The public sector management paradigm. This model extends the efficiency model and collapses the managers and producers of public services into a single group. Between politicians and the producers of services there now exists the consumer. This paradigm gives greater emphasis to the problems emerging from the efficiency paradigm. The problem of potential conflict between managerial and producer (professional) rights remains. Emphasis on the consumer is manifest in the Citizen's Charter and the Patient's Charter but there is a great confusion of meaning – 'citizenship' as used in the context of the charter really means 'consumer'. The Citizen's Charter is about public service consumers' rights. Citizenship, however, is different from the more narrow notion of consumer.

Changes to patterns of rights, legitimation, and the distribution of power in society are quietly taking place without much public discussion. Systems of social and political democracy are being dismantled without recognition that this is what is happening. Post-war history is one of struggle to get different forms of participation in the decision-making processes of society legitimised and yet the quiet managerial revolution taking place throughout the public sector is eroding this with the signing of each new contract. Questions such as who has the right to design, to write and to enforce the new contracts are simply not being answered. Who has the right to set the rules of the game? Who is the guardian of the public good?

Advocates of the new public sector management, such as Osborne and Gaebler (1992), tend to overemphasise the importance of reorganisation as the driver of change. As Chandler (1977) and Galbraith (1973) have emphasised, structure follows strategy. Changes in structure are necessary but not sufficient for improvements in performance. Without a strong guiding strategy most structural change is ineffective. Public sector management is more than simply ensuring the efficient provision of services to individuals. There is also the matter of meeting highly valued social goals. The consumer/client individualism of the new public sector management ignores or forgets about these objectives. Issues relating to the distribution of benefits from public services, who wins and who loses as a consequence of the new institutions of contracting out, quasi markets, etc., are sidelined. Individuals in their role as citizens have a strong sense of altruism. When one citizen cannot afford health care, for example, other citizens rally round.

Political issues, such as delivering services which *citizens* value, are sensitively dealt with by Barzelay (1992) who emphasises the change in incentives created by greater decentralisation, especially its motivating influence. Beyond the hype, 'getting close to the customer' requires public sector managers to give careful consideration to who their customers and clients are and if customers are to be treated equally. The role of public sector managers needs to be given greater thought. Public sector managers are not simply the dead hands of bureaucracy. It is through them that social change takes place. They play an important role in the design and implementation of social change. Unless they face appropriate incentives public policies will fall short of expectations.

Conclusion

Public sector reforms based upon an exaltation of the efficiency properties of markets, the introduction of surrogate competition, changes in the culture of public sector managers, the use of competitive tendering and contracting-out have so far had limited success. The dream was that the problem of financing the growing demands for public services can be solved by the search for improved efficiency.

Few countries have come close to solving the problem of delivering efficient and effective public services. Outputs and outcomes are complex, multidimensional and difficult to measure. It is difficult to achieve agreement on what the outcomes should be. Such debates are too often shrouded in ideological mists and political rhetoric. Objectivity rapidly dissolves. Central issues such as the purpose of health care, education, social services, and so on, do not disappear by exporting the provision of the services to the private sector or some arm's length agency. Reductions in smoking and increased spending on nutrition are generally agreed to be more cost-effective in improving health outcomes. These policies are not attractive and are difficult to implement. How can we get people to eat and drink sensibly and to stop smoking? The pay-offs from such policies are time inconsistent; they are long term and lie outside of normal electoral cycles. Moreover, they are expensive to the Treasury – they involve increases in public spending and reductions in tax revenues.

The efficient operation of internal markets and competitive tendering requires a great deal of information on the definition of outputs, transactions, costs and performance. These costs are much greater than is often supposed.

Notes

1. See Ascher, 1987; Day and Klein, 1983; Griffiths, 1988; Department of Health, 1989; HMSO, 1989; Department of Education and Science, 1988.
2. For a fuller discussion of post-Fordism, see Chapter 1 of this volume.
3. Her Majesty's Treasury (1986) *Using Private Enterprise in Government: Report of a Multi-Departmental Review of Competitive Tendering and Contracting for Services in Government Departments,* London: HMSO.
4. The FPCs were transformed into Family Health Care Service Authorities, FHSAs.
5. The Local Government Bill (1991) and the consultative paper *Competing for Quality,* proposed an extension of competitive tendering of local authority services. This built upon provisions which has already been made in the Local Government Acts, 1980 and 1988, the Environmental Protection Act, 1990, the Education Reform Act, 1988 and the National Health Service and Community Care Act, 1990.

References

Ackerloff, G. (1970) The market for lemons: quality uncertainty and the market mechanism, *Quality Journal of Economics,* vol. 84, pp. 488–500.

Adler, M. (1993) *An Alternative Approach to Parental Choice*, London: National Commission on Education.

Alchian, A. (1950) Uncertainty, evolution and economic theory, *Journal of Political Economy*, vol. 58, pp. 211–21.

Ascher, K. (1987) *The Politics of Privatization: Contracting out Public Services*, Basingstoke: Macmillan.

Audit Commission (1984) *Securing Further Improvements in Refuse Collection*, London: HMSO.

Audit Commission (1989a) *Assuming Quality in Education*, London: HMSO.

Audit Commission (1989b) *Losing an Empire: Finding a Role*, London: HMSO.

Audit Commission (1993) *Realising The Benefits of Competition: The Client Role for Contracted Services*, London: HMSO.

Bartlett, W. W. (1991) *Quasi-markets and construct: a market and hierarchies perspective on NHS reform*, School of Advanced Urban Studies, Bristol.

Barzelay, M. (1992) *Breaking Through Bureaucracy*, University of California Press.

Buck, D. and **Chaundy, D.** (1993) Competitive tendering and efficiency in refuse collection revisited, mimeo.

Chandler, A. D. (1977) *The Visible Hand: The Managerial Revolution in American Business*, Cambridge, Mass.: Harvard University Press.

Chandler, A. D. (1990) *Scale and Scope: The Dynamics of Industrial Capitalism*, Harvard/Belknap: Harvard University Press.

Coase, R. H. (1937) The nature of the firm, *Economica* (NS), pp. 386–405.

Cubbin, J., Domberger, S. and **Meadowcroft, S.** (1987) Competitive tendering and refuse collection: identifying the source of the efficiency gains, *Fiscal Studies*, vol. 8, no. 3, pp. 49–58.

Day, P. and **Klein, R.** (1983) The mobilisation of consent versus the management of conflict: decoding the Griffiths Report, *British Medical Journal*, vol. 287.

Department of Education and Science (1988) *Education Reform Act: Local Management of Schools*, London: HMSO.

Department of Education and Science (1988) *Top-Up Loans for Students*, Cm 520, London: HMSO.

Department of Health (1987) *Promoting Better Health*, London: HMSO.

Department of Health (1989) *Working for Patients: The Right Approach*, Cm 555, London: HMSO.

Department of Health (1990) *National Health Service and Community Care Act*, London: HMSO.

Domberger, S., Meadowcroft, S. and **Thompson, D.** (1986) Competitive tendering and efficiency: the case of refuse collection, *Fiscal Studies*, vol. 7, no. 4, pp. 69–87.

Domberger, S., Meadowcroft, S. and **Thompson D.** (1987) The impact of competitive tendering on the costs of hospital domestic services, *Fiscal Studies*, vol. 8, no. 4, pp. 39–54.

Ferlie, E. (1992) The creation and evaluation of quasi markets in the public sector: a problem for strategic management, *Strategic Management Journal*, vol. 13, pp. 79–97.

Flynn, N. (1989) The new right and social policy, *Policy and Politics*, vol. 17, no. 2, pp. 97–110.

Galbraith, J. (1973) *Designing Complex Organisations*, Addison-Wesley.

Ganley, J. and **Grahl, J.** (1988) Competition and efficiency in refuse collection: a critical comment, *Fiscal Studies*, vol. 9, pp. 81–5.

Griffiths, R. (1988) *Community Care: Agenda for Action*, London: HMSO.

Griffiths Report (1983) *NHS Management Inquiry*, Department of Health and Social Security, London: HMSO.

HM Treasury (1986) *Using Private Enterprise in Government*, London; HMSO.

HMSO (1989) *Caring for People: Community Care in The Next Decade and Beyond*, London: HMSO.

Hoggett, P. (1991) A new management in the public sector?, *Policy and Politics*, vol. A, no. 4, pp. 243-56.

Hood, C. (1991) A public management for all seasons?, *Public Administration*, vol. 69, no. 1, pp. 2–19.

Jackson, P. M. (1982) *The Political Economy of Bureaucracy*, Oxford: Philip Allan.

Jackson, P. M. (1988) The management of performance in the public sector, *Public Money and Management*, vol. 8, pp. 11–16.

Jackson, P. M. (1988) Management techniques in the UK public sector, *International Review of Administrative Sciences*, vol. 54, pp. 247–66.

Jackson, P. M. (1992) Competitive tendering for local government services: recent British experience, paper presented to European Conference on New Methods of Delivering Local Services, University of Paris, Dauphine, October – forthcoming in conference proceedings.

Jackson, P. M. and **Palmer. B.** (1992) *Developing Performance Measurement in Public Sector Organisations*, Leicester University Management Centre.

Kanter, R. M. (1985) *The Change Masters: Corporate Entrepreneurs at Work,* Counterpoint, London: Unwin Paperbacks.

Le Grand, J. (1991) Quasi-markets and social policy, *Economic Journal,* 101, September, pp. 1256–67.

Levacic, R. (1990) Evaluating local management in schools, *Financial Accounting and Management,* vol. 6, no. 3, pp. 209–27.

Metcalfe, L. and **Richards S.** (1984) Raynersim and efficiency in government, in Hopwood, A. and Tompkins, C. (eds) *Issues in Public Sector Accounting,* Oxford: Philip Allan.

Metcalfe, L. and **Richards, S.** (1990) *Improving Public Management,* London: Sage.

Milne, R. G. (1987) Competitive tendering in the NHS: an economic analysis of the early implementation of HC(83)18, *Public Administration,* 65, 2, 145–60.

Milne, R. and **McGee, M.** (1992) Compulsory competitive tendering in the NHS: a new look at some old estimates, Institute for Fiscal Studies, vol. 13, no. 3, August, pp. 96–111.

Morrell (1991) The role of research in development of organisation and structure of general practice, *British Medical Journal,* vol. 302, pp. 1313–16.

National Audit Office (1987) Competitive tendering for support services in the National Health Service, Session 1986–87, HC 318, London: HMSO.

Niskanen, W. A. (1968) Non-market decision-making: the peculiar economics of bureaucracy. *American Economic Review,* May, vol. 58, pp. 293–305.

Osborne, D. and **Gaebler T.** (1992) *Reinventing Government,* Reading, Mass.: Addison Wesley.

Painter, J. (1991) Compulsory competitive tendering in local government, *Public Administration,* vol. 69, no. 2, pp. 191–210.

Parker, D. (1990) The 1988 Local Government Act and compulsory competitive tendering, *Urban Studies,* vol. 27, pp. 653–67.

Peters, T. (1992) *Liberation Management,* London: Macmillan.

Peters, T. and **Waterman, R.** (1982) *In Search of Excellence: Lessons from America's Best Run Companies,* New York: Harper and Row.

Ranson, S. (1992) Education, in F. Terry and P. M. Jackson (eds), *Public Domain 1992,* London: Public Finance Foundation.

Richards, S. (1992) Who defines the public good?, Public Management Foundation Working Paper.

Stewart, J. and **Walsh, K.** (1992) Change in the management of public services, *Public Administration,* vol. 70, Winter, pp. 499–578.

Szymanski, S. and **Wilkins, S.** (1992) Competitive tendering: lessons from the public sector, *Business Strategy Review*, Autumn, pp. 101–13.

Tullock, G. (1965) *The Politics of Bureaucracy*, Public Affairs Press, Washington, DC.

Walsh, K. (1991) *Competitive Tendering for Local Authority Services: Initial Experiences*, London: HMSO.

Williamson, O. E. (1975) *Markets and Hierarchies: Analysis and Antitrust Implications*, New York: Free Press.

CHAPTER 6

Nationalisation, privatisation, and agency status within government: testing for the importance of ownership

David Parker

Introduction

The word 'privatisation' was not commonly used until the early 1980s. Within a decade, however, not only was it an accepted part of the language in most Western countries, more surprisingly it featured in the headlines of newspapers in Warsaw, Prague, Budapest and even Moscow. The policy of privatisation is now a worldwide phenomenon affecting both the traditional capitalist countries and the former communist bloc alike. The programmes introduced by governments differ in detail and intensity; nevertheless they are all driven by a belief that by transferring assets from public ownership to private ownership efficiency will improve. The policy of privatisation is the product of a growing disillusionment with state production during the post-war period.

In Britain, where a large privatisation programme was pursued in the 1980s, disillusionment took the shape of growing criticism of the nationalised industries. These giant industrial organisations had been created mainly by the 1945–51 Attlee governments but had proved difficult to manage effectively during the 1960s and 1970s. However, once selling state enterprises appeared to win wide public support, attention also turned to the civil service and difficult-to-privatise welfare services, notably education and health. In April 1988 the Conservative government introduced its 'Next Steps' initiative intended eventually to reduce the size of the central bureaucracy from 550,000 to less than 100,000 (HMSO, 1988). This is to be achieved by transferring personnel to quasi-governmental 'agencies' which will run former activities on more commercial lines and perhaps with new senior management brought in from the private sector. The same government also tackled what it considered to be the disincentive effect of 'red tape' in education and health by providing independent budgets for schools and contracting for health care between fundholding GPs and self-governing hospitals. Just as head-teachers could now be 'budget holders' freed from total dependence on local authority education departments, so GPs could operate their own finances buying 'best care' for their patients. The 'Next Steps' initiative, along with the sale of state industries and reforms in education and health, were intended to result in a more efficient use of scarce resources.

Unfortunately, however, assessing the value of privatisation and 'agency' initiatives is hampered by a lack of empirical study of public versus private efficiency. Where studies have been undertaken their usefulness is often restricted by the problem of making like-with-like comparisons. State activities are often monopolies or much larger in scale than their private counterparts. Hence there are very few industries where direct comparison can be made. Moreover, surveys of the studies which have been undertaken have reported mixed results (e.g. De Alessi, 1980; Borcherding, et al., 1982; Millward and Parker, 1983). In particular, in addition to ownership, product market competition and the degree of continued state regulation of enterprises are identified as significant factors determining managerial behaviour.

Turning specifically to the UK, there have been very few comparative studies, largely because nationalisation created monopolies. Pryke (1971, 1981) argues, in one such comparison of the private and nationalised sectors, that state industry outperformed private industry in the 1950s and 1960s in terms of the growth in labour and total factor productivity but performed much less well in the 1970s, when performance was 'third rate, though with some evidence here and there of first-class standards' (Pryke, 1981, p. 257). However, recent data from the Treasury (Table 6.1) suggests that the nationalised industries improved their performance dramatically

Table 6.1 Performance of nationalised industries

	Labour productivity (annual % change)		
	Nationalised industries	Whole economy	Manufacturing
1979/80	0.1	0.7	0.9
1980/81	−0.5	−3.8	−5.3
1981/82	6.5	3.5	6.9
1982/83	2.4	4.0	6.4
1983/84	7.2	4.0	8.3
1984/85	6.0	2.9	4.8
1985/86	9.6	1.1	2.4
1986/87	6.2	3.6	4.8

Source: Treasury, Economic Progress Report, No. 193, December 1987, p.5.

in the mid-1980s and may have again performed better than the economy in general in terms of labour productivity growth. It is difficult to see what general conclusion can be drawn from this record. A more recent study of the early effects of the 1980s privatisations, by Bishop and Kay (1988), is equally enigmatic. While government Ministers, the popular press and many economists have praised the success of the privatisation programme in raising efficiency, Bishop and Kay conclude:

> The overall picture to emerge . . . is one of substantial change. Output and profits have grown, margins have increased, employment has declined. But the relationship of these changes to the fact of privatization is not immediately

apparent from the data. The privatized industries have tended to be faster growing and more profitable, but it seems that the causation runs from growth and profitability to privatization, rather than the other way round (pp. 40–1)

There is, therefore, a clear need for more empirical study of the effects of privatisation and, equally, the results of related reforms which have created quasi-independent agencies to take over traditional state activities.

The remainder of this chapter is concerned, firstly, with assessing the a priori arguments for privatisation and then, secondly, with reporting the main results of a recent research programme into ownership and performance. This research measured the extent to which performance changed in a number of organisations in the UK which crossed between the public and private sectors or underwent a status change within government.[1] In the main, only organisations which experienced relevant ownership changes before 1982 were included so that the 'longer-term' effects of the change could be assessed (the exception is British Airways which was included for reasons explained later). This meant that while most of the privatisations of the 1980s could not be included, the research avoided the criticism that it is still too soon to assess the full effects of recent privatisations. Also, although these ownership changes are not included, the results are still relevant to an assessment of the likely effects of the privatisation, 'Next Steps' and other related government programmes both in the UK and elsewhere.

6.1 The case for privatisation

The case for privatisation cannot be safely made simply on the basis of the existing knowledge of public versus private efficiency provided by empirical studies. Instead, the main intellectual force has come from a priori or deductive reasoning centred on 'public choice' and property rights theories. These theories have been popularised through the publications of free market pressure groups such as the Institute of Economic Affairs and the Adam Smith Institute in the UK and the Pacific Research Institute and the Cato Institute in the USA. Hence they are now well known and the briefest of summaries will suffice here.

Public choice theory is concerned with the nature of decision-taking within government. Rejecting the Weberian notion of disinterested officials actioning democratic decisions, public choice theorists (e.g. Niskanen, 1971; Buchanan, 1978; Mitchell, 1988) argue that government officials are just as inclined to pursue their own ends as other individuals. Drawing from the neoclassical model of the utility-maximising economic man, they conclude that government policy is likely to be shaped to maximise the utility of public sector employees rather than the public at large. Moreover, they further argue that politicians, whose role is to lay down policy and monitor the performance of state officials, are also likely to pursue their own utility in terms of maximising the chances of re-election. In this environment the power of pressure groups, such as public sector trade unions, is increased to the point where public services are run in the interests of the employees and other special interests rather than the public. The result is an over-bloated or inefficient public sector.

Property rights theory complements public choice economics. In this theory the source of inefficiency in state organisations lies in the attenuation of property rights. In the archetypal capitalist firm the entrepreneur has a direct interest in the most efficient use of the firm's resources because his or her income is the residual after revenues are deducted from production costs. In joint stock companies, which now dominate in capitalist economies, property rights are less obvious and ownership and control of the business are divorced. The business is ultimately owned by the shareholders but the use of resources is controlled by the directors. The shareholders' wealth, both in terms of dividends and capital growth, depends on profits, while managers may earn all or the bulk of their income in the form of fixed salaries. Nevertheless, property rights theorists (e.g. Alchian, 1965; Furubotn and Pejovich, 1974) argue that the ability of shareholders to trade their shares means that managers cannot afford to lose sight of the need to manage efficiently and pursue high profits. Where shareholders are disappointed by the performance of their management, shares will be sold leading to a fall in the share price. This in turn will make the company more vulnerable to a takeover bid by alternative management.

This view of the operation of the private capital market is simplistic, perhaps naive, but it does contain a germ of truth even if the takeover threat is not reliable (Grossman and Hart, 1980; Lawriwsky, 1984). Certainly in the public sector there are no shares to trade and there is no threat of a hostile takeover bid. In addition, financing does not require an approach to the banks or the equity market through a rights issue. The Exchequer, and hence the taxpayer, underwrite all debts of state enterprises.

Although the public choice and property rights theories have different nuances, they obviously complement each other. Together they suggest that economic activity undertaken in the public sector will be performed with less productive (cost) efficiency than the same activity in the private sector. Also, as public sector activities may not charge market prices (e.g. education and health), or where market prices are set they are set by large monopolies, the public sector is associated with less allocative efficiency.

State enterprises tend to be protected from competition. For example, under the Coal Industry Nationalisation Act, British Coal has rights to mine coal in Great Britain 'to the exclusion (save as in this Act provided) of any other person', and imports of coal were restricted. Similarly, before deregulation of local bus services by the 1985 Transport Act, public sector bus services in Britain faced only limited competition from private bus operations. It has been a leading tenet of economic theory since Adam Smith that competition is generally superior to monopoly. Under competition prices are related more closely to marginal supply costs leading to allocative efficiency and survival in the competitive market requires production costs to be minimised.

From this brief discussion it should be clear that there are two broad forces identified in economic theory which lead to high allocative and productive efficiency – the capital market and the product market. In the remainder of this chapter we are primarily concerned with productive efficiency. In Figure 6.1 these two forces are represented by the capital market on the horizontal axis and the product market on the vertical axis. Point A represents the position of a firm which is directly controlled by a government department. It is politically controlled and there are no tradeable shares, hence we would expect from the public choice and property rights theories that efficiency will be low. Point B represents an activity undertaken by a government agency which has some, if limited, autonomy from the political process. Examples include the trading funds set up with their own finances under the 1973 Trading Fund Act and the more recent agencies established under the 'Next Steps' initiative. Public corporations (nationalised industries) can be placed at point C. They have more autonomy than quasi-governmental agencies and were designed in the immediate post-war period to act at 'arm's length' from government. Their chairmen may be drawn from the private sector, commercial style accounts are published and employees are not civil servants. At the same time, however, government Ministers intervene in long-term strategy and sometimes in day-to-day management decisions. Also, government acts as ultimate guarantor of the industry's finances.

Points D, E and F correspond to forms of ownership in the private sector. Point D includes those private sector firms which are close to the public sector because of state funding or a reliance on state contracts. This might diminish incentives to be efficient. Point E is the joint stock company; while point F represents private ownership where property rights are least attenuated – notably the owner-managed firm.

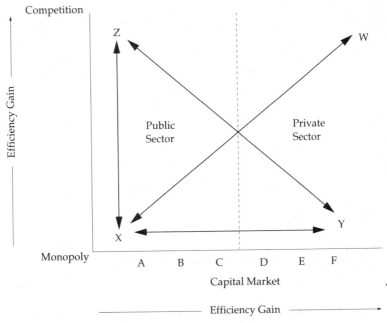

Figure 6.1 Mapping for efficiency improvements

Turning to the vertical axis, movements upwards correspond to a shift away from monopoly towards competition and hence greater product market pressure to be efficient. In summary, therefore, Figure 6.1 provides a mapping of the expected relationship between ownership and performance, drawn from the theories outlined earlier, and competition and performance. Although for convenience discrete points on the horizontal axis have been identified A to F, both ownership and the product market are best viewed as continuous dimensions. The schema implies the following:

- Changes in ownership involving movements away from political control towards private ownership, but with no change in competition, will be associated with improved efficiency due to a change in the capital market.
- Increased competition in the absence of a change in ownership will be associated with improved efficiency due to a change in the product market.
- Changes in ownership involving a movement away from private ownership towards public ownership will be associated with reduced efficiency due to a change in the capital market.
- less competition, even where there is no change in ownership, will lead to a reduction in efficiency.[2]

In Figure 6.1 these movements are illustrated as X to Y, X to Z, Y to X and Z to X respectively. The largest efficiency gains are likely to be associated with movements from X to W, that is towards private ownership and more competition; while a movement from W to X, involving political control and less competition, is likely to lead to a significant deterioration in efficiency. Movements either way between positions Z and Y imply an ambiguous result because the changes in the product and capital market constraints on managerial behaviour conflict.

From this discussion the following central hypothesis can be derived: changes in ownership away from political control and towards private ownership, especially when also associated with increased competition, will lead to appreciable improvements in efficiency.[3] It is, of course, precisely this view which underpinned the policy of privatisation in the UK in the 1980s and which currently drives the policy in Eastern Europe. The emphasis given to promoting competition also has implications for current discussion of the role of regulation of privatised public utilities (Parker, 1989). The property rights and public choice theories suggest that privatisation of monopolies will lead to some efficiency gains (though these gains may mean higher profits rather than lower prices), but the largest efficiency gains will occur where privatisation is associated with more competition. Where 'natural monopoly' prevents efficient competition, the regulatory structure should create managerial incentives similar to those which exist under competition.

6.2   The organisations studied and the performance measures used

To test the central hypothesis that ownership affects economic performance, ten organisations were selected covering a number of possible moves between the public and private sector (nationalisation and privatisation) and within the public sector (from government department to trading fund or public corporation status). Two of the organisations underwent two ownership changes in the period studied, hence twelve relevant status changes were studied. The ten organisations, their status changes with the relevant dates, and the predicted effect on performance are summarised in Table 6.2.

Table 6.2   Organisational status changes

Type of change	Organisation	Date	Prediction from central hypothesis of change in performance
Government department to trading fund	Royal Ordnance Factories	July 1974	Improvement
	Royal Mint	April 1975	Improvement
	HMSO	April 1980	Improvement
Government department to public corporation	Post Office Postal	April 1969	Improvement
	Post Office Telecommunications	April 1969	Improvement
Public corporation to (local) government department	London Transport	Jan 1970	Deterioration
Local government department to public corporation	London Transport	June 1984	Improvement
Change of ownership:			
(a) Public limited company to public ownership	Rolls-Royce	Feb 1971	Deterioration
	British Aerospace	April 1977	Deterioration
(b) Public corporation to public limited company	British Aerospace	Feb 1981	Improvement
	National Freight	Feb 1982	Improvement
(c) Anticipation effects – public corporation to public limited company	British Airways	1980–87	Improvement

Four nationalisation/privatisation cases were included – British Aerospace, Rolls-Royce, British Airways and the National Freight Corporation (NFC). British Aerospace was created on the nationalisation of the UK's two largest aerospace companies – the British Aircraft Corporation, Hawker Siddeley (Aviation and Dynamics) – and the smaller Scottish Aviation in 1977. Four years later the corporation was privatised.[4] Rolls-Royce was bought by the state in February 1971 following a financial crash associated with major cost over-runs in the development of the RB211 engine. The company was privatised in 1987, though this event came too late to be included in the study. The decision to privatise British Airways was made in 1980 but had to be postponed until 1987, mainly because of legal disputes in the USA relating to the collapse of Laker Airways (British Airways along with Pan Am and TWA was accused of anti-competitive practices), and later because of the need to renegotiate the Bermuda II agreement which regulates traffic on the vital Atlantic routes. However, because the management were aware that privatisation was imminent, we might expect to find a large growth in efficiency between 1980 and 1987. Lastly, the National Freight Corporation was established as a state holding company for the nationalised freight and related undertakings in 1969. It was privatised in February 1982 in a celebrated worker and management buy-out.

The movements within the public sector which were studied included the Royal Mint, HMSO (the government's stationery office), the Royal Ordnance Factories, London Transport and the Post Office. The Royal Ordnance factories, the Royal Mint and HMSO had for a long time been run within government departments, but with a view to making them operate more commercially were given trading fund status in 1974, 1975 and 1980 respectively. Under trading fund status, management are still accountable to the Minister and the employees remain civil servants. The organisation, however, has its own accounts and is financed by trading receipts instead of parliamentary votes. This provides for a greater degree of financial autonomy and managerial independence than exists when activities are directly run by government departments.

London Transport, which manages the capital's bus and underground services, was one of Britain's first public corporations when established in 1933. In the post-war years it had a chequered history of ownership though it always remained a public corporation. From 1963 it was responsible to central government but in 1970 it became accountable to the Greater London Council which had been established five years earlier. This change resulted in 14 years of periodic and extensive political intervention in the management of London Transport, notably in relation to pricing policy. Following the decision to abolish the GLC, the corporation once again became accountable to central government in 1984 and its management were expected to operate more commercially. Given the extent of political intervention in London Transport during the GLC years, we would expect performance to have deteriorated after 1970 and improved again after 1984. Lastly, the Post Office postal and telecommunications businesses were separately studied. The Post Office moved from being a government department to public corporation status in 1969, again with a view to raising efficiency.

Performance changes were measured using three sets of measures. The reason for using different measures was to check for 'measurement bias', i.e. the possibility that performance might have improved using one measure but not using another (something found to be true for many of the organisations studied).

The three sets of performance measures were:

- Labour and total factor productivity. Four-year averages were used for before and after the dates of the status change to capture 'lead and lag' effects. There is always the possibility that performance might have improved ahead of the date of the status change or that there might have been a delay caused by reorganisation costs before performance responded. Longer periods were not used because these might have reflected performance changes unrelated to the ownership change. To control for the effects on performance caused by general changes in the macro-economy, notably the business cycle, changes in the organisation's productivity were compared with changes in productivity in the same periods for the whole of the UK economy, public corporations and, in the case of manufacturing organisations, UK manufacturing industry.

Labour productivity was measured by the relationship between a weighted index of physical quantities of output and the volume of labour input. In the absence of reliable information on average hours worked, the average number of employees was used as the labour input. Where no adequate physical output measure was available, this was approximated by deflating the value of output by price deflators, including an own industry deflator. Using more than one price deflator provided a test of the sensitivity of the results to the precise deflator used.

Total factor productivity was defined as:

$$\text{TFP} = \frac{\text{Weighted index of physical quantities of output}}{\text{Total expenditure on inputs/Weighted index of input prices}}$$

Again, where there was an absence of quantity data physical output was approximated by applying relevant price deflators to value of output figures.

- Employment functions. Various employment functions were tried though the Ball and St Cyr (1966) function usually gave the best fit and had the added advantage of simplicity. Employment functions relate the amount of employment to a series of independent variables and in the Ball and St Cyr function the relationship is expressed in general form as:

$$N = f(q,t,N_{t-1})$$

where N is employment, q is output, t is a time trend and N_{t-1} is a lagged dependent variable from which the speed of adjustment of employment to its optimal level can be calculated. The equation is expressed in natural logarithms.

By introducing a binary (dummy) variable for the ownership change, it was possible to test whether ownership had a statistically significant effect on the employment relationship. The binary variable was applied in both shift and slope forms so that the relationship tested was:

$$Ni = a + b_i V_i + cXV_i + D + m_i$$

where V_i is a vector of variables, notably output, the time trend and the lagged dependent variable, X is a slope shift dummy variable for status change applied to V, D is an intercept shift dummy, and m_i is the usual stochastic error term.

Where employment efficiency rose following the status change the sign on the dummy variable will be negative suggesting less employment to output; the sign will be positive if employment efficiency fell. The use of an employment function permitted an assessment of the longer-term effects of organisational status changes on the relationship between employment and output than provided by the labour productivity calculations. It also permitted the introduction of other factors which might have impacted on the relationship.

- Financial ratios. A series of standard financial ratios were calculated for each organisation. Appropriate adjustments were made to the reported accounting figures to create a consistent series over time where there had been changes in accounting practice. The following ratios were calculated:

  - rate of return before interest and tax on net assets (profitability);[5]
  - debts to turnover and stock to turnover (use of working capital);
  - sales to net fixed assets (use of capital stock);
  - labour's share in expenditure and value added per employee (use of labour).

  Profitability is usually taken to be the key financial ratio to which the others contribute. However, using profitability alone is unsatisfactory when considering organisations which spent some or all of their time in the public sector. In the public sector goals other than profitability are often considered as, or more, important. Performance measured simply in terms of the rate of return on net assets could, therefore, simply reflect changes in objectives.

  The ratios were calculated using four-year averages for before and after the status change and were tested using a simple covariance model which took the form:

  $$V_{it} = a + bt_i + bXt_i + D + m_i$$

  where V_{it} is a vector of financial ratios and once again t is a time trend, X is a binary variable in slope form and D in shift form to capture the effect of the ownership change. Other factors affecting financial performance are reflected in the time trend, t.

Returning to the organisations studied, only three – HMSO, British Aerospace (nationalisation) and London Transport (post-1984) had appreciable changes in their competitive environment at around the time of the status change which might have impacted on performance. In 1982 HMSO lost its monopoly of stationery and other supplies to government departments. The nationalisation of three airframe manufacturers to create British Aerospace reduced competition; while in the case of London Transport, from 1984 an increasing number of London bus routes were subjected to competitive tender.

6.3 Results

Space precludes the inclusion of all of the statistical results, but the main ones are reported in Tables 6.3, 6.4 and 6.5 (for fuller details see Parker and Hartley, 1991a and 1991b, and Hartley, *et al.*, 1991). Table 6.3 provides a selection of results from the employment function tests; Table 6.4 includes the figures on labour and total factor productivity adjusted for changes in productivity in the whole economy, public corporations and the manufacturing sector; while Table 6.5 is a summary of the results of the significance tests on the financial ratios. In all cases dates refer to accounting year ends. For example, for HMSO 1977–80 refers to the accounting years year ending 31 March 1977 to 31 March 1980.

Table 6.3   The employment function results

	a	$\log Q$	$\log N_{t-1}$	t	D_1	D_2	X_1	X_1	R^2
HMSO	6.22* (2.29)	+0.20# (2.08)	+0.36# (2.16)	−0.02x (1.59)	−0.19** (3.95)				0.99
Royal Mint	3.44x (1.82)	+0.21* (2.42)		+0.01 (0.24)	−3.25* (2.32)		−0.41* (2.17)	+0.43* (2.30)	0.69
Royal Ordnance Factories	1.91# (1.82)	+0.18* (2.78)	+0.88** (8.20)	−0.02** (4.94)	+0.11** (3.61)				0.87
PO Postal	7.04** (3.50)	+0.10* (2.15)	+0.35* (1.97)	+0.01* (2.23)	−0.01 (0.55)				0.72
PO Telecom	10.76** (46.03)	+0.74** (3.69)		−0.05* (2.76)	−0.12** (3.12)				0.78
London Transport	−2.04 (1.72)	−0.38** (4.33)	+1.38** (13.59)	−0.01 (0.87)	−0.01 (0.50)	−0.04# (1.86)			0.96
Rolls-Royce	4.65** (3.23)	+0.12* (2.20)	+0.51** (4.20)	+0.01 (0.03)	−0.13** (4.32)				0.92
British Aerospace	6.65** (3.36)	+0.80* (2.79)		−0.02* (2.50)	+4.73* (2.16)	+5.19* (2.36)	−0.66# (2.15)	−0.71* (2.32)	0.53
National Freight	21.48** (4.41)	−0.25 (1.03)	−0.26 (1.22)	−0.09** (4.12)	−7.46** (3.27)		+1.46** (3.24)		0.99
British Airways	0.91 (0.71)	+0.79** (5.38)	+0.51** (4.85)	−0.03** (3.95)	−0.07# (2.14)				0.97

Notes

(1) R^2 is adjusted for degrees of freedom; **indicates significant at the 1% level, * at the 5% level, # at the 10% level using 2 tail tests, x indicates significant at the 10% level using a 1 tail test only. Figures in brackets are t ratios. There was no evidence of significant first-order autocorrelation.

(2) Q = output; N_{t-1} = lagged employment; t = time trend; D = binary variable; $X_1 = D_1 \times \log Q$ except for Royal Mint where = real wages; $X_2 = D_2 \times \log Q$.

(3) For HMSO the dummy variable is lagged to 1982. See discussion in text.

Source: Parker and Hartley, 1991a, Table 3, p. 412.

Table 6.4   The labour and total factor productivity results

Organisation	Whole economy		Public corporations		UK manufacturing	
	LP	TFP	LP	TFP	LP	TFP
Trading funds						
HMSO						
1977–80	0.5	–2.4	–1.3	–0.8	1.1	2.5
1981–84	0.2	–5.0	–3.3	–1.0	–2.8	–9.4
1982–85	7.1	–3.5	3.8	–3.2	4.1	–7.7
Royal Mint						
1972–75	–6.3	–3.6	–8.5	–6.9	–8.1	–7.0
1976–79	6.2	1.7	2.3	4.2	6.6	5.7
Royal Ordnance Factories						
1971–74	9.6	2.5	8.9	1.8	7.6	–1.2
1975–78	6.3	1.2	3.4	1.3	6.6	4.5
Public corporations						
Post Office Postal						
1966–69	–4.0	–4.4	–8.1	–5.6	n.a.	n.a.
1970–73	–1.5	–4.8	–0.4	–3.6		
Post Office Telecommunications						
1966–69	2.2	–0.4	–2.0	–1.6	n.a.	n.a.
1970–73	8.6	–1.0	9.7	0.2		
London Transport						
1966–69	–0.6	–1.5	–3.8	–2.7	n.a.	n.a.
1970–73	–0.1	–4.4	–1.3	–3.2		
1980–83	–0.5	–4.9	–5.7	–3.8		
1984–87	7.2	4.8	*	*		
Ownership changes						
Rolls-Royce						
1967–70	–10.4	–5.6	–13.6	–6.9	–11.1	–6.0
1971–74	10.6	2.5	9.9	1.8	8.6	–1.2
British Aerospace						
1973–76	4.0	0.1	–0.9	–3.2	2.4	–2.0
1977–80	–1.2	–3.0	–4.0	–1.3	0.1	1.9
1981–84	4.0	–1.8	0.5	2.2	0.9	–6.2
National Freight Consortium						
1977–80	–0.7	–0.6	–3.5	1.0	n.a.	n.a.
1980–83	5.0	0.3	–0.2	1.4		
1983–86	5.8	0.4	0.3[a]	1.2		
British Airways						
1976–79	3.7	1.0	–0.3	3.5	n.a.	n.a.
1980–83	5.7	3.6	0.5	4.7		
1981–84	5.3	1.1	1.8	5.1		

Source: Hartley, Parker and Martin, 1991, Table 3, p. 56

Notes:

*   Privatisation distorts public corporation figures in this period, therefore results not reported.

(1)   Figures show difference, in percentage points, between an organisation's average annual productivity growth and the corresponding national average figure (organisation - UK).

(2)   LP = average annual growth in labour productivity (%).
      TFP = average annual growth in total factor productivity (%).

(3)   Figures based upon output deflated by each organisation's nearest own price deflator or a physical output series where available.

a   1983–85 only.

n.a.   not applicable, service industry.

Inevitably, using a number of financial ratios meant that not all of them pointed in the same direction. To provide a guide, albeit crude, to the overall impact, each of the financial ratios was weighted equally to derive the 'net total' column. An improvement in any ratio was given a value of 1; where it deteriorated a value of –1. A net total greater than zero means that more financial ratios improved rather than deteriorated; and vice versa for a negative total. Changes in the stocks and debtors ratios need to be treated with special care as the direction of change associated with an improvement in performance is not certain. Lower stocks and debtors ratios may not always be desirable. Too few stocks might mean an inability to meet new orders. Fewer debtors could result from pestering customers to pay to the point where future sales are lost. An alternative view is to interpret any change in these ratios, in whatever direction, as evidence of improved performance. The final column in Table 6.4 adopts this approach. It is important to stress that either 'net total' is merely a crude illustrative guide implying an equal weighting of the ratios and, therefore, the figures must be interpreted with care. It can be argued that profitability is the key ratio, though as already explained there is a problem in using profitability alone when measuring changes in performance for organisations which spent at least some of their time in the public sector. Nevertheless, it is interesting to note that in five of the cases profitability rose following the status change (though for Rolls-Royce contrary to expectation) and for none of the organisations did it decline.

In the cases of British Airways and the National Freight Corporation the performance measures showed evidence of improvement. The anticipation of privatisation and actual privatisation respectively seem to have had the desired effect. The British Airways results are unambiguous. In terms of the employment equation for the NFC, the inclusion of a slope dummy on output indicates that before privatisation the output coefficient was insignificant but became significant following privatisation. Along with the expected negative and significant shift dummy, this implies that privatisation was associated with a large increase in employment efficiency. In Table 6.4, three time periods are reported for the NFC with the period 1980 to 1983 reflecting the 'anticipation effect' of impending privatisation in 1980–81 and the company's first nineteen months in the private sector. The financial ratio results for the NFC are also supportive of the view that privatisation improved efficiency if it is accepted that any changes in the stocks and debtors ratios suggest a performance change.

Turning to British Aerospace, the Ball and St Cyr employment function provided a poor fit and instead a function based on the Treasury employment function is reported (for more on this see Parker and Hartley, 1991a, p. 413). The shift dummies proved to be positive as expected for nationalisation but contrary to expectation for privatisation. However, the interaction terms on output suggest an improvement in employment efficiency, especially after privatisation in 1981. In other words, the coefficient on output was somewhat higher during the period of nationalisation implying a greater increase in employment was needed to produce any given increase in output. This result is also borne out by the figures for labour and to a lesser extent total factor productivity in Table

6.4. Labour productivity growth was worse during the four years of nationalisation than in the earlier or following periods of private ownership. The total factor productivity results are more mixed, but the slight improvement in relation to the performance of public corporations and UK manufacturing during the period of nationalisation is a feature of the very poor productivity record of public corporations and manufacturing in these years. Similarly, the sharp recovery in UK manufacturing productivity in the early 1980s accounts for the deterioration in relative total factor productivity performance after 1981. The financial ratio results, however, do not confirm that nationalisation lowered performance and an assessment of the effects of privatisation depends upon the interpretation placed on the deterioration in the stocks ratio.

Owing to lack of reliable data, for the Royal Mint financial ratios could not be calculated. But in terms of labour and total factor productivity growth the Mint's transfer from government department control to trading fund status seems to have produced the anticipated efficiency gains. A Peel and Walker (1978) formulation of the employment function, which includes real wages as an independent variable, proved more satisfactory than the Ball and St Cyr equation, though there was evidence of multicollinearity between output and the lagged dependent variable so the latter was omitted. The results suggest that the movement to trading fund status led to an improvement in efficiency as reflected in the negative sign on the shift dummy, though this was partially offset by an increase in the coefficient on output, implying a one-off efficiency gain at the time of the status change.

In the case of the Royal Ordnance Factories, contrary to expectation labour productivity growth seems to have declined following the granting of trading fund status and, with the exception of the comparison with trends in UK manufacturing, total productivity growth also appears to have deteriorated. Again because the mid- to late 1970s was a period of very poor growth in manufacturing total factor productivity in the UK, this may explain why the performance of the Royal Ordnance Factories looks more respectable when contrasted with this index. There was also no sign of the expected improvement in efficiency as measured by the employment function results, where the coefficient of the shift dummy is positive rather than negative. Only using the financial ratios could a performance improvement be identified (Table 6.5).

Turning to the HMSO, immediately after becoming a trading fund the performance in terms of comparative labour and total factor productivity seems to have worsened. Taking the period after 1982, however, when the HMSO faced competition for government contracts, labour productivity seems to have recovered though the performance in terms of total factor productivity remained disappointing. With regard to the financial ratios, there was either no evident change in performance or a slightly improved performance depending on the interpretation placed on the deterioration in the debtors ratio. The employment function result reported takes 1982 as the date of the status change and the result suggests improved performance.

Table 6.5 Summary of the financial ratio tests

Organisation	Date of status change	Stocks ratio	Debtors ratio	Wages ratio	Fixed assets ratio	Profitability ratio	Value added ratio	Net total	Net total*
London Transport	1970	Improved	No change	No change	No change	No change	No change	1	1
London Transport	1984	Improved	Deteriorated	No change	Improved	No change	No change	1	3
HMSO	1980	Improved	Deteriorated	Deteriorated	No change	Improved	n/a	0	2
National Freight	1982	Deteriorated	No change	Improved	Deteriorated	Improved	No change	0	2
Post Office (telecommunications)	1969	n/a	Deteriorated	Improved	No change	No change	No change	0	2
Post Office (postal)	1969	Improved	n/a	Improved	Deteriorated	No change	No change	1	1
British Airways	1980	Improved	No change	No change	No change	Improved	Improved	3	3
Rolls-Royce	1971	Improved	Improved	Improved	No change	Improved	Improved	5	5
Royal Ordnance	1974	Improved	n/a	No change	Improved	Improved	Improved	4	4
British Aerospace	1977	No change	n/a	Improved	No change	No change	No change	1	1
British Aerospace	1981	Deteriorated	No change	No change	No change	No change	No change	-1	1

n/a: not available

Source: Parker and Hartley, 1991b, Table 5, p. 640.

Notes

*treating any change in the stocks and debtors ratios as improvements.

163

The results relating to the public corporations were also mixed. The nationalisation of British Aerospace has already been discussed. The transfer of the postal and telecommunications businesses from government department control to a public corporation in 1969 led to improvements in labour productivity and perhaps also to some improvement in terms of the financial ratios (though once again, for telecommunications this depends on the interpretation placed on the higher debtors ratio), but the results using the other measures were more confused. For telecommunications, the Ball and St Cyr employment function provided a poor fit, therefore the lagged dependent variable was omitted, in which case longer-term employment efficiency did seem to improve after the introduction of public corporation status (but see Parker and Hartley, 1991a, p. 413 for reservations). For the postal service, the status change dummy variable in the employment function was statistically insignificant at the 10 per cent level or better.

At first blush perhaps the most surprising results were those for Rolls-Royce. Instead of performance deteriorating as expected following the state takeover, it actually improved irrespective of which measure is used. It is interesting to note, however, that labour productivity, in particular, actually fell in the mid-1970s. Between 1975 and 1978, for instance, the decline was between 1.4 and 3.7 per cent per annum depending on the precise measure used (Parker and Hartley, 1991a, p. 410). This may mean that the 1971 financial crash acted as a short-term stimulus to reorganise and cut waste, but that within a few years state ownership was having the expected deleterious effect on performance.

Lastly, London Transport remained a public corporation throughout the period studied but was subjected to more political intervention during its years under GLC control between 1970 and 1984. The expectation was that performance would have deteriorated after 1970 and improved from 1984. Our study suggests that the establishment of GLC control did not lead to an immediate performance deterioration except in terms of total factor productivity. However, the transfer from GLC control in 1984 *did* lead to the expected efficiency improvements. This result may be explained by the fact that political intervention in London Transport by the GLC intensified in the late 1970s and early 1980s.

Conclusions

The research reported in this chapter was concerned with testing a central hypothesis derived from the public choice and property rights literatures that changes in ownership status away from political control towards private ownership, especially when also associated with increased product market competition, lead to improved performance. This was tested by studying ten organisations which underwent 12 relevant status changes either within the public sector or involving movements between the public and private sectors.

The results were mixed and often varied depending on the precise performance measure used. Table 6.6 provides an overall summary of the results with the organisations listed according to the extent to which the results supported the central hypothesis. The following are the main conclusions.[6]

Table 6.6 Ownership status and performance – did performance change as expected?

Organisation	Labour productivity	Total factor productivity	Employment function	Financial ratios
British Airways	Yes	Yes	Yes	Yes
London Transport (1984 change)	Yes	Yes	Yes	Yes
NFC	Yes	Yes	Yes	Yes?
Royal Mint	Yes	Yes	Yes?	N/A
British Aerospace (privatisation)	Yes	Yes?	Yes?	Yes?
HMSO	Yes	No	Yes	Yes?
Post Office Telecommunications	Yes	Unclear	Yes?	Yes?
Post Office Postal	Yes	Unclear	No	Yes
British Aerospace Nationalisation	Yes	Unclear	Yes?	No
Royal Ordnance Factories	No	No?	No	Yes
London Transport (1970 change)	No	Yes	No	No
Rolls-Royce	No	No	No	No

Notes

(1) A question mark after the answer indicates that the result was not entirely clear. In the labour and total factor productivity columns it indicates that the majority of results were supportive of the conclusion. In the financial ratios column it indicates that performance changed as expected only if the final 'net total' column in Table 6.5 is used. For the significance of the question mark in relation to the employment function results, see the discussion of the results in the main text.

(2) N/A = no data available.

● Three cases of privatisation were studied involving British Airways, the NFC and British Aerospace. The results for British Airways and the NFC were strongly supportive of the central hypothesis, while those for British Aerospace were only slightly less supportive. In other words, privatisation seems to have led to the expected performance improvement.

- The results for those organisations which changed status within government were more confused. In the case of the trading funds, the performance of the Royal Mint and, on the whole, the HMSO improved, but the results for the Royal Ordnance Factories were disappointing. The granting of public corporation status to the Post Office in 1969 may have led to some improvement in labour productivity in both the postal and telecommunication businesses, and perhaps a marginal improvement in terms of the financial ratios, but in terms of total factor productivity the result was unclear.
- The results for the nationalisation cases were perhaps the most surprising. There was some evidence of a worsening in the performance of British Aerospace after 1977 in terms of the use of labour but not necessarily in terms of the other performance measures. In the case of Rolls-Royce, initially state ownership led to an improvement in performance, though performance deteriorated later. The experience of London Transport following the abolition of the GLC and the imposition of a clearer commercial objective, supports the view that political control reduces efficiency.
- In three cases, the HMSO, London Transport after 1984 and the nationalisation of British Aerospace there was a change in ownership status and an apparent change in product market competition. The HMSO and London Transport faced more competition, while the merger of three aerospace companies within the UK to form British Aerospace reduced domestic competition. According to the schema in Figure 6.1, the coupling of a change in ownership with a change in the competitive environment should lead to significant changes in performance and this was broadly confirmed in two of the cases. The HMSO's performance improved more noticeably after 1982 when it lost its monopoly of public sector supplies and London Transport registered a clear improvement in performance after 1984. The British Aerospace results were less obvious, but there was no overwhelming evidence of a deterioration in performance. This might, however, be explained by the fact that the corporation worked in an industry heavily dependent on state aid and government contracts so that even before 1977 there was only limited competition between the constituent companies of British Aerospace.

It is always dangerous to draw firm conclusions from what was clearly a small sample. However, the results do not contradict the view that privatisation improves performance and they provide some support for the argument that political intervention in an organisation's operations damages efficiency. They seem to bear out Stephen Littlechild's warning some years ago in relation to organisations which retain some government ownership, that 'as long as ultimate control lies with government, one cannot realistically hope to avoid all the problems.' (Littlechild, 1983, p. 14). The introduction of trading fund or public corporation status within government had a less reliable effect on performance than outright privatisation in the cases studied.

The schema in Figure 6.1 performed well. Longer movements along the horizontal axis (public to private ownership) did seem to be associated with more noticeable performance changes. Also, the independent effect of product market competition on efficiency seems to have been borne out. This conclusion has obvious implications for programmes which introduce agency status within government, such as the 'Next Steps' initiative, as well as for the ongoing debate about the merits of public and private ownership, especially where there is continuing state regulation.

Notes

1. The research was funded by the ESRC (Project number E 0925006) as part of its Management in Government Initiative. I would like to acknowledge the contribution of my co-researchers, Professors Keith Hartley and Andrew Dunsire, and the statistical assistance provided by Bob Lavers and Stephen Martin. As far as the contents of this chapter are concerned, the usual disclaimer applies.
2. This, of course, may not be true where there are appreciable scale or scope economies. However, for the purposes of the remainder of this chapter this need not detain us.
3. Figure 6.1 and the reasoning on which it is based also implies that movements *within* the private sector (e.g. D to F or F to D) will be associated with changes in efficiency. However, this chapter is concerned only with agency status within government and movements across the public–private boundary.
4. Although the government retained 48.4 per cent of the shares until May 1985, 1981 can be taken as the date of privatisation because from that date the government ceased to intervene in the affairs of the company.
5. Calculating profitability before interest charges removes the effect of different types of financing. In particular, public sector activities have no equity, hence privatisation, by substituting equity for loan stock, reduces the interest charge and increases post-interest profitability. Taking post-interest figures would introduce a bias in favour of the profitability results after privatisation or before nationalisation.
6. In interpreting the results it would be useful to know more about the history of the organisations and their internal management with a view to explaining why it is in some cases performance changed as expected but in other cases it did not. This might permit answers to an important question. What are the internal organisational changes that lead to improved efficiency? In other words, what are the critical factors for success when ownership changes? Clearly, changing ownership cannot in itself change performance, something must change within the organisation, but what is it?. This issue is addressed elsewhere (Parker, 1992).

References

Alchian, A. A. (1965) Some economics of property rights, *II Politico*, vol. 30, pp. 816–29.

Ball, R. J. and **St Cyr, E. B. A.** (1966) Short-run employment functions in British manufacturing industry, *Review of Economic Studies*, vol. 33, pp. 178–207.

Bishop, M. and **Kay, J.** (1988) *Does Privatization Work? Lessons from the UK*, Centre for Business Strategy, London Business School, London.

Borcherding, T., Pommerehne, W. and **Schneider, F.** (1982) Comparing the efficiency of private and public production: the evidence from five countries, *Zeitschrift für Nationalökonomie*, vol. 42, supplement 2.

Buchanan, J. M., *et al.* (1978) *The Economics of Politics,* Institute of Economic Affairs Readings, 18, London.

De Alessi, L. (1980) The economics of property rights: a review of the evidence, *Research in Law and Economics,* vol. 2, pp. 1–47.

Furubotn, E. G. and **Pejovich, S.** (1974) *Economics of Property Rights,* Ballinger, Cambridge, Mass.

Grossman, S. J. and **Hart, O.** (1980) Take-over bids, the free rider problem and the theory of corporations, *Bell Journal of Economics,* vol. 11, pp. 42–64.

Hartley, K., Parker, D. and **Martin, S.** (1991) Organisational status, ownership and productivity, *Fiscal Studies,* vol. 12, no. 2, May, pp. 46–60.

HMSO (1988) *Civil Service Management Reform: the Next Steps,* Cmnd. 524, London.

Lawriwsky, M. L. (1984) *Corporate Structure and Performance: the Role of Owners, Managers and Markets,* Croom Helm, London.

Littlechild, S. C. (1983) *Regulation of British Telecommunications' Profitability,* London: HMSO.

Millward, R. and **Parker, D.** (1983), Public and private enterprise: comparative behaviour and relative efficiency, in R. Millward, D. Parker, L. Rosenthal, M. T. Sumner and N. Topham (eds), *Public Sector Economics,* Longman, London.

Mitchell, W. C. (1988) *Government as It Is,* Hobart Paper 109, Institute of Economic Affairs, London.

Niskanen, W. A. (1971) *Bureaucracy and Representative Government,* Aldine-Atherton, New York.

Parker, D. (1989) Public control of natural monopoly in the UK: is regulation the answer?, in M. Campbell, M. Hardy and N. Healey (eds), *Controversy in Applied Economics,* Harvester-Wheatsheaf, London.

Parker, D. (1992) Ownership, organisational changes and performance, in T. Clarke and C. Pitelis (eds), *The Political Economy of Privatisation,* Routledge, London.

Parker, D. and **Hartley, K.** (1991a) Organisational status and performance: the effects on employment, *Applied Economics,* vol. 23, no. 2, February, pp. 403–16.

Parker, D. and **Hartley, K.** (1991b) Do changes in organisational status affect financial performance?, *Strategic Management Journal,* vol. 12, no. 8, November, pp. 631–41.

Peel, D. A. and **Walker, I.** (1978) Short-run employment functions, excess supply and the speed of adjustment: a note, *Economica,* vol. 45, pp. 195–202.

Pryke, R. (1971) *Public Enterprise in Practice,* MacGibbon and Kee, London.

Pryke, R. (1981) *The Nationalised Industries,* Martin Robertson, Oxford.

CHAPTER 7

Metamorphosis? Privatisation and the restructuring of management and labour

Julia O'Connell Davidson

Introduction

The British privatisation programme did not start out with a coherent set of clearly specified aims and objectives,[1] but as Abromeit (1988: 72) has noted, over time government members have 'made it their business in various speeches to equip the *de facto* policy, after the event, with a more or less consistent philosophy'. This philosophy is a form of liberal anti-pluralism, and the case for privatisation is basically a microcosm of the New Right's case for 'rolling back the frontiers of the State'. The New Right holds that it was the excessive state intervention associated with Keynesian economic policy in the post-war years which led to the British economic crisis of the mid-1970s (slowing economic growth and rising unemployment coupled with rising inflation). It is argued that in pursuit of the 'unnatural' goal of full employment, governments borrowed, bureaucratised and taxed excessively, creating a 'nanny state' which stifled real wealth creation and economic growth and nurtured 'the cancer of inflation'.

For New Right thinkers, the nationalised industries epitomised the evils of state intervention and were symbolic of the political strength of organised labour in the post-war years. Insulated from the discipline of market forces, these public sector organisations were characterised by their critics as bureaucratic, inflexible, inefficient and unresponsive to customer demands. The government's privatisation programme has therefore been enthusiastically received by those on the New Right, and the rhetoric surrounding privatisation is often almost euphoric. Not only is privatisation welcomed because it reduces state involvement in the economy (which is seen as an end in itself since 'the business of government is not the government of business' – Nigel Lawson, 1987), it is further claimed to usher in a brave new world of efficiency and consumer responsiveness. Once freed from 'the cobwebs of the State' and exposed to the fair winds of the market, people and institutions will flourish. Managers will be restored their potency as they regain the 'freedom to manage', while once moribund and sterile organisations will become efficient producers. Privatisation is also seen to be of wider political significance. It is celebrated as standing alongside events in Eastern Europe as part of a worldwide rejection of socialist values and practice, and even seen as a means of vanquishing 'brutality, ignorance, poverty, corruption and waste' (Clarke, 1987).

Government ministers and civil servants may use more measured tones, but they preach the same basic message. Privatisation is held to be 'a remedy for some of the ills that have beset UK industrial performance in recent years' (John Moore MP, 1983) and a 'new economic creed' (John Redwood MP, 1988). More importantly for the purposes of this chapter, it has been argued that privatisation is good for employees; 'privatisation benefits customers, employees and the economy as a whole . . . Employees benefit from working in a company with clear objectives and the means to achieve them, and from higher salaries and bonuses earned by the possibilities of higher productivity' (HM Treasury, 1990: 5). Employees are said to benefit from the opportunity to become shareholders in their privatised companies, and it is further asserted that job satisfaction will be enhanced since employees' efforts will no longer be lost in an impersonal, inefficient, bureaucratic machine. In short, workers are claimed to accrue both material and psychological benefits from working in dynamic, innovative and efficient private firms.

Two central ideas lie at the heart of this rhetoric. First, there is the notion that market forces and hierarchical, bureaucratic control constitute two different and diametrically opposed ways of regulating economic institutions. Regulation by market forces is good. It encourages competition, which in turn forces organisations to provide high quality goods or services efficiently, or else go bust. Hierarchical bureaucratic control is bad. It insulates the organisation from vital information, both about customer preferences and about waste and inefficiency. Instead of the organisation being guided by the 'invisible hand' (through which the interests of the mass of individuals in society are co-ordinated), it is controlled by a handful of 'faceless' persons who, at best, are fallible and have only partial access to information, and, at worst, may abuse their position to advance their own status and power. Second, the rhetoric implies a necessary link between profitability and efficiency. It is assumed that privatisation will make organisations more profitable by stimulating greater efficiency, and that it therefore carries benefits for employees and consumers as well as for the Treasury and for investors. This idea that efficiency gains are the sole route to increased profitability is vital to the New Right's moral defence of privatisation – an open commitment to providing profits for shareholders at the expense of an industry's customers and workers would appear cynical, to say the least.

When the rhetoric is held up against events in the real world, however, problems with both of these key ideas begin to emerge. The dualism between the regulation of economic activity by markets and by bureaucratic hierarchies which lies at the centre of the philosophical justification for privatisation is over-simplistic. It exaggerates the differences and downplays the similarities between nationalised and private sector industries, and so far as the utilities are concerned, privatisation cannot spell an end to government influence over economic activity. This is because, as Price points out, there are limits to the degree of competition which can be introduced into the utilities. The government has therefore been forced to introduce 'regulation . . . designed to mimic market forces where market failure meant that they could not be relied on directly to perform these functions' (Price, this volume, Chapter 3). Meanwhile, the notion that these simulated market forces encourage management to find ways of increasing efficiency rather than merely profitability and that privatisation therefore augurs well for labour is less than convincing when recent changes to work organisation, employment practices and industrial relations within the privatised utilities are considered.

This chapter aims to illustrate these points by describing developments in two privatised utilities (which will be referred to as 'Albion Water' and 'National Utility').² It examines the effects of privatisation upon employment practices, work organisation and industrial relations in these organisations and so provides an opportunity to compare the political rhetoric against the experience of workers in the real world. Changes to management structures, especially those which supposedly mark a break with traditional, hierarchical organisation, are also explored and parallels between the government's attempt to design a regulatory framework which mimics market forces and management's attempts to simulate market forces within these two utilities are considered. The chapter argues that the simulation of market forces within these companies has played an important role in facilitating changes to employment relations, work organisation and industrial relations; changes which have, in turn, helped to raise profit margins. The idea that this greater profitability reflects greater efficiency is highly questionable, however.

7.1 *Privatisation and restructuring: an overview*

Employment practices, work organisation and industrial relations at both Albion Water and NU have undergone rapid and extensive change in preparation for and subsequent to privatisation. However, it is important to note that none of the changes described below (cuts to direct labour levels, increased resort to subcontract, workplace 'flexibility', increased intensity of working and so on) are peculiar to privatised concerns. Instead, they appear to mirror developments in other sectors of the economy. In practice, there is nothing new about the utilities sharing a great deal of common ground with private sector concerns. To begin with, like all nationalised industries, the utilities were increasingly cash-limited and under pressure to finance their capital investment out of operating profits by governments struggling to contain or reduce the PSBR from the mid 1960s on. The effects of this on public sector management priorities and practice were similar to the effects of recession and the profit squeeze upon private sector concerns. Moreover, although New Right thinkers like to portray nationalised industries as non-commercial organisations, inspired by socialist principles and pursuing socialist goals, in reality these organisations could hardly be said to depart from the private sector model. The main nationalisations carried out by the Attlee administration in 1945–51 set the precedent for future nationalisations, and were heavily influenced by Herbert Morrison who held that 'the best business brains' should be left to run public industry efficiently. As Schott (1983: 354) observes: 'Various industries were nationalized, but they were to operate on hierarchical lines like private firms with recognized business talent in charge . . . Consultation between management and workers at various levels within these nationalized industries was envisaged, but the structures for it were not particularly influential.'

Of course, the nationalised industries differed from privately owned companies in the sense that they did not have to compete in the capital market, and that governments could interfere in certain decisions, but management's right to manage the workforce was not questioned and the boards of nationalised industries were typically dominated by people with a strong commitment to the business ethos. The idea that they were run along totally different lines to private sector organisations is something of a fiction, as those who had hoped that nationalisation would constitute a step towards worker democracy soon discovered. It is true that the utilities were, until recently, very much engineering-led, technocratic organisations, but again this was not unique to the public sector. Much of the private sector was also modelled on these lines until the late 1970s or early 1980s, when the lieutenants who generated the white heat of the technological revolution were increasingly squeezed out by a new breed of 'intrapreneurial' and upwardly mobile accountants and lawyers.

The public utilities did, however, have three really singular features. First, they were monopolies. Second, virtually every industry and every household was dependent upon their products and services. Third, governments were in a position to shape industrial relations in the nationalised industries far more directly than could be achieved in the private sector, and industrial relations in the utilities of the 1960s and 1970s certainly bore the stamp of the broader political commitment to some form of corporatism. (It is also significant that, so far as the utilities were concerned, it was widely believed that any serious industrial relations problem would carry equally serious electoral consequences for the government of the day, a view supported by experience in 1974.) These last two features gave the utilities their distinctive character. On the one hand, employees' awareness of the social usefulness of their product led to the development a very strong public service ethos within the utilities (workers traditionally took pride in their safety record, in the quality and impartiality of advice offered to consumers, and in a number of socially responsible activities such as free servicing of old age pensioners' appliances – see O'Connell Davidson 1992 and 1993). On the other hand, government involvement meant that the utilities were characterised by constitutionalist and fairly harmonious industrial relations. They were densely unionised, with well established national bargaining machinery through which relatively good packages of job security, working conditions and employment benefits (if not high wages) were negotiated.

It was in this context that the notion of the state as a 'model employer' emerged.

However, privatisation and the restructuring of the public sector through the 1980s has, as Fairbrother (1991:71) notes, given 'an entirely new meaning . . . to [the idea of] the state as a model employer to be emulated by other sectors'. It can be argued that in terms of dismantling the industrial relations machinery and practice of the post-war era, and of pursuing workplace flexibility and labour intensification, the state has led the way not only through legislation and its own practice as an employer, but also through its privatisation programme. This is well illustrated by a description of events at Albion Water and NU.

The restructuring of work and employment at Albion Water and National Utility

One of the most visible consequences of the Government's privatisation programme has been a rapid and dramatic contraction in direct employment. Between 1979 and 1989, the number of public sector employees fell by over 1.2 million (Labour Research Department 1990: 25), and SCAT (1990) estimates that more than 70,000 jobs were destroyed as a direct result of privatisation and compulsory competitive tendering in the 1980s. If jobs lost during pre-privatisation 'efficiency' drives were taken into account, the figure would be far higher. These cuts are the more

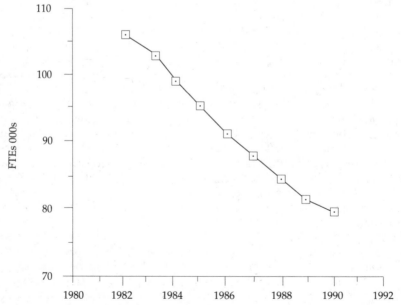

Figure 7.1   National Utility direct labour levels 1982–1990.
Source: National Utility Annual Reports and Accounts.

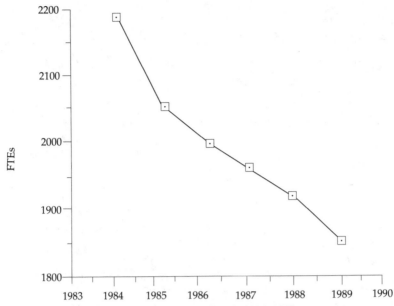

Figure 7.2   Albion Water direct labour levels 1984–1989.

significant given that public sector workers have been central to the post-1966 growth in trade union membership. They 'represent an attack on one of the fastest-growing parts of the organised labour movement' (Massey 1984: 183). Like other privatised and about to be privatised concerns, Albion Water and National Utility (NU) savagely cut direct labour levels in the 1980s (see Figures 7.1 and 7.2).

Both companies claim that reductions to direct labour levels have been supported by productivity improvements and increased efficiency but it seems likely that these cuts have also been facilitated by changes to employment patterns, in particular, by increased resort to various forms of subcontract. In itself, there is nothing new about the use of contract labour in either of these utilities.

However, during the 1980s contract labour has been introduced into areas such as catering, cleaning and grounds maintenance which were previously staffed solely by direct employees (see O'Connell Davidson 1991), and the ratio of contract labour to direct labour is increasing in those areas which have always used contract labour. For example, in 1982, NU employed the services of an average of 43 thousand direct manual employees, and 12 thousand contract workers. By 1990, the number of direct manual employees had fallen to a mere 28 thousand, whilst the number of contract workers had risen to over 13 thousand. In other words, over an eight-year period, contract workers went from representing around 22 per cent to 32 per cent of the manual labour force. Managers, workers and union officials report the same trend at Albion Water. Accounting practices make it difficult to obtain precise figures, but some indication of the degree of change can be obtained by presenting the cost

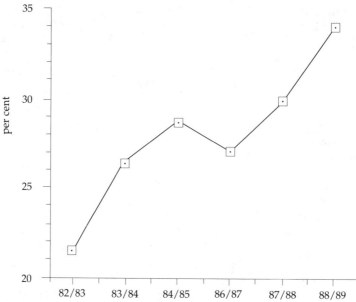

Figure 7.3 Albion Water: cost of hired and contracted services as a percentage of expenditure on all labour since 1983.
Source: Albion Water Annual Reports and Accounts.
Note: Figures for 1985–86 not available.

of hired and contracted services as a percentage of employment costs plus expenditure on hired and contracted services (see Figure 7.3).

These contract workers offer precisely the same degree of skill as that offered by direct labour, and in both companies, contract labour is used to undertake virtually identical tasks to those performed by direct labour. However, the two groups of workers enjoy very different terms and conditions of employment. Direct employees are not especially well paid, but they are densely unionised and enjoy a relatively high degree of job security (cuts to direct labour levels have been achieved through 'natural wastage' and voluntary retirements, rather than forced redundancies) and a relatively good package of fringe benefits. Contract workers are totally non-unionised, have minimal employment security and no rights to any non-statutory sickness or pension benefits. Indeed, there is a growing trend among firms of contractors to take on workers on a self-employed basis, rather than as direct employees, and thus both Albion and NU are increasingly using the labour of workers who are not even entitled to statutory benefits. Contract labour is thus extremely vulnerable. Indeed, it is precisely their insecurity which makes contract workers attractive to both companies. As an NU manager explains:

> With our own chaps, we have to pay them while they're on holiday; we have to pay when they take their statutory sick days, which they always do; when they have their obligatory accident, which they always manufacture once a year. To know you've got 48 weeks of one man's labour you have to keep two gangs of direct employees going. With the contractor you just pay for the 48 weeks of

labour. Also, you only pay for what you want. We're not under any obligation to find work for contractors during slack periods, whereas we can't just get rid of our own chaps.

The shift towards greater reliance upon non-unionised contract workers with minimal rights to employment benefits is of some significance. It not only undermines the achievements of public sector unions in these industries, it also means that both NU and Albion Water are increasingly replacing their own direct employees with cheaper, more vulnerable workers. This means that even if the privatised utilities were to remain 'model employers' to their own direct labour, conditions in the industries as a whole would deteriorate as the role of direct employer is subcontracted out to smaller, less scrupulous and less profitable firms (for a more detailed description of employment practices and working conditions within firms of subcontractors, see O'Connell Davidson 1993 and Fevre 1987). But the question of whether either NU or Albion can still be characterised as 'model employers' to their own direct labour is open to debate. The pattern of employment relations within these companies is not simply changing as a consequence of increased resort to contract labour. Relationships with direct employees are also being transformed.

In the past, both Albion and NU were characterised by a certain uniformity of employment relations (with all direct employees from canteen staff through to managers enjoying the same degree of employment security, similar rights to fringe benefits, seniority rather than performance-based progression through grades, and so on). Privatisation has stimulated diversification, making the pattern of employment relations more varied. In both companies, there has been a growth in 'non-standard' direct employment such as temporary and part-time contracts. The sum effect of these changes is to divide the labour upon which these companies rely horizontally (into 'standard' direct employees, temporary staff, part-time employees, free-lance workers, contract workers, self-employed workers) as well as vertically by occupational status and grade. This change is of enormous significance for industrial relations. As will be seen later, it affects union density and makes the task of organisation far more problematic.

Furthermore, work organisation at NU and Albion has undergone extensive change throughout the 1980s, as various forms of work 'flexibility' have been introduced. For example, many craft workers at Albion Water are now being asked to provide multiple skills instead of specialising in one particular trade. The aim is to move towards work being undertaken on a one-job-one-man basis, which cuts down 'idle time' (time lost as one craftsman waits for a co-worker to finish his or her portion of the work). The effect of this is to speed up working and pare down rest periods. It also has safety implications since the pace of work is more relentless, which increases stress and fatigue. This kind of job enlargement is also evident at NU, especially for clerical workers (manual unions have, thus far, resisted such change more effectively). There is no room here for a detailed account of changes to working practices, but the overall impact of restructuring has been to increase the pace and intensity of working (see O'Connell Davidson, 1990a, b).

A survey of Albion Water and NU employees[3] found that more than half of the 442 respondents reported that they now worked harder than they had four years previously, and that their performance was now more closely monitored by management. Over 60 per cent said that pressure at work had increased since privatisation while only around 11 per cent reported increased job satisfaction. A large majority of those surveyed further said that privatisation had not affected their pay one way or the other. In contrast to the predictions of government ministers, improved productivity was not leading to 'higher salaries and bonuses'. It is also worth noting that although employees believed themselves to be working harder and under greater pressure as a consequence of privatisation, they did not generally endorse the New Right view that privatisation improves efficiency. Less than a third of manual and clerical employees agreed that privatisation had made their company more vigorous and efficient, and perhaps more surprisingly, only 53 per cent of managers could be mustered to endorse this view. The fact that employees at Albion and NU have less faith than their political masters in the virtues of private enterprise was also evidenced by answers to another set of questions. Only 22 per cent of the sample (including managers) believed that private firms are more likely than public sector organisations to protect the interests of the consumer; only 12 per cent thought that private concerns were more likely to be concerned with health and safety issues; and only 10 per cent thought private firms were more likely to protect the environment.

The real point, however, is that privatisation can hardly be said to have enhanced pay, prospects or conditions for direct employees in these utilities, nor to have increased job satisfaction as proponents of privatisation would predict.

The impact of privatisation on industrial relations

The government claimed that privatisation would enhance industrial relations in the utilities in a number of ways. The White Paper for the privatisation of the water industry states that as a consequence of privatisation, 'employees will benefit from shareholdings, closer identification with their businesses, greater job satisfaction, better motivation, and the prospects of the rewards that enterprise has brought to those who work for other industries that have been privatised' (Cmnd 9734, 1986: Paragraph 7). This is in line with government's more general claims about the virtues of privatisation, which is said to eradicate 'old fashioned distinctions between workers and owners' (HM Treasury 1990: 4-5) and allow employees to share in the success of their employer. In general then, privatisation is supposed to lead to more 'co-operative' industrial relations. However, as Nichols (1986: 176) points out, though New Right politicians use the rhetoric of co-operation, their 'achievements' in terms of changing shop-floor behaviour owe more to reducing trades unions' powers to protect their members and to fostering fear and anxiety, than to nurturing 'co-operative' sentiments among the workforce. The public sector has been an arena in which successive Conservative governments have been most anxious, and most directly able, to refashion industrial relations. As Heald and Morris observe 'the "good employer" tradition has died and the official promotion of public sector trade unionism as one of the bases for sound industrial relations [has been] abruptly reversed' (1984: 32).

Aside from the fact that public sector unions played a key role in the downfall of governments in both 1974 and 1979, government Ministers in the early 1980s were hostile to them because of their rapid growth and success. Thus, John Moore MP argued in 1986 that 'Public sector trade unions have been extraordinarily successful in gaining advantages for themselves in the pay hierarchy by exploiting their monopoly collective bargaining position' (1986: 78). Public sector unions have been attacked not just through the comprehensive legislative assault on unions in general, but also by the privatisation programme (Ascher, 1987: 101) which reduces the power of public sector unions: 'by removing access to Exchequer funds, thus making management more cost conscious in responding to trade union claims, [and] by providing opportunities to dismantle national agreements. The latter are seen as a strategic factor underpinning trade union bargaining power in the Public Sector.' (Ogden, 1990: 4).

In virtually all the industries and services which have been privatised, or which are subject to privatisation plans, there has been a movement away from national level negotiating, away from a 'constitutionalist' approach towards industrial relations. Beynon et. al. (1991) and Winterton (1990) discuss this trend in the coal industry, Upham (1990) describes the same pattern in British Steel, Ascher (1987) in the NHS, Ferner (1987) in British Rail. The experience of the water industry was no exception. In 1986, Thames Water gave notice to withdraw from the national pay bargaining machinery. Northumbria Water soon followed suit, and in August 1988 the other eight Regional Water Authorities collectively gave the unions twelve months' notice of their intention to end national negotiations on both pay and conditions (Financial Times, 26.8.88; Ogden, 1990). The electricity unions were successful in persuading the government to include a clause in the legislation which prevented companies from withdrawing from national agreements until after flotation, and in obtaining a 'gentlemen's agreement' that no company would give the statutory twelve months' notice to leave the national machinery until after all the electricity companies had been floated (Ferner, 1990), but the water unions did not enjoy the same degree of power and influence.

Since, as Fairbrother and Waddington (1990: 40) observe, 'state sector unions have traditionally been highly centralised with workplace organisations centrally sponsored and controlled', the trend away from national bargaining alone poses very real organisational problems for most unions (see also Fairbrother, 1991). Add this problem to those created by successive Thatcher Governments' legislative assaults on trade union powers in general, and to the fact that the increasing substitution of contract labour for direct labour in many privatised or about to be privatised industries reduces union membership and control in the workplace, and it becomes clear that unions face enormous difficulties in this sector.

Government policy has directly affected the unions' position in Albion Water and NU in three main ways. First, tighter financial control through the 1970s and in the run-up to privatisation forced both organisations to shed labour, and this clearly impacts on the unions. Union density has always been greatest among manual workers, and certainly so far as Albion is concerned, it is the manual work-force that has been hardest hit by the policy. The more extensive use of contract labour described above means that both companies are partially replacing a well unionised work-force with totally non-unionised labour. Manual unions have made unsuccessful attempts to recruit contract labour, and given that the firms of civil engineering contractors Albion and NU use refuse to recognise any union, it is unlikely that such attempts will prove effective in the short term.

Second, privatisation has forced regional level union officials to deal with new issues. So far as Albion Water goes, the dismantling of national bargaining machinery means that unions must now enter into negotiations over pay with Albion management directly. This does open up certain possibilities previously denied to local and regional level unions, and may ultimately encourage the development of more active workplace union structures (see Fairbrother, 1991), but it must also be borne in mind that the unions are now dealing with a far more hostile employer. Albion managers explicitly state that team-briefings have been introduced in an attempt to by-pass collective representation, for example. Furthermore, both NU and Albion management are exploring ways of shifting from a seniority-based system of promotion and progression through grades to a performance-based system. Once again, this changes the terrain upon which the unions must attempt to protect their members.

Finally, privatisation has impacted on industrial relations by encouraging both NU and Albion management to make changes to patterns of employment relations. As noted above, there is greater use of temporary and part-time workers, as well as self-employed individuals. At Albion, certain work units modelled on the lines of Direct Labour Organisations, which means that their workers, though still direct employees, have their working practices and bonus payments determined at the level of the work-unit rather than the company as a whole. All this means that instead of organising a large, relatively homogeneous direct labour force, unions are facing an increasingly fragmented work-force. As well as organising 'standard' direct employees, they are faced by contract labour, self-employed workers, part-time employees, temporary employees and direct employees whose pay and conditions are linked to the performance of their particular work unit. To organise such a disparate body of workers is obviously a far more difficult task than that faced in the past. As one regional GMBATU official observed:

> This is our dilemma in the public sector. Every water authority, every local authority, every district council, they're all doing it every day, breaking the work-force down into smaller and smaller groups, putting out more and more services. We need to be everywhere at the same time. Every deal with every worker is different, there is nothing corporate about it, it's all fragmented. This is the unions' problem. How do you monitor all that, how do you keep it together?

All these problems are exacerbated by the wider political context in which they are set. Recent legislation has undermined the unions' ability to protect members, and privatisation itself changes the nature of industrial relations in the utilities. Price (Chapter 3) notes that in the post-war years it was assumed that nationalised industries would operate in the public interest, and this involved an expectation that nationalised concerns would 'act fairly as employers'. This meant that, as one union official put it: 'In the past, we [the unions and the employers] did have common interests.' Now this has changed: 'With privatisation, of course, there is a conflict of interests. We are looking to protect our members' job security and wages and conditions, management is looking to put money into the hands of the shareholders . . . They've got to make a profit however they can, no matter what the cost to the consumer or those employed in the industry.'

The changes to employment practices, work organisation and industrial relations described in this section have gone alongside equally drastic changes to management and organisational structures. These are set out below, and they not only raise the question of whether there is a relationship between the devolution of management and changes to employment relations and work organisation, but also raise some broader questions about the government's role in these developments.

7.2   Privatisation and organisational structures

When the first two major utilities were privatised in the early to mid-1980s, the government liberalised the markets for appliance retailing and servicing, but left their monopoly status in terms of utility supply intact. Neither did the government act to alter the existing organisational structure of these utilities. They were basically transformed from publicly owned bureaucratic, monolithic monopolies (in the language of their critics) into privately owned ones. This is hardly consistent with the aims now attributed to privatisation (i.e., exposing organisations to the discipline of the market, and so transforming massive, cumbersome bureaucratic institutions into vibrant, entrepreneurial, efficiency-maximising firms). The privatisation of massive monopolies attracted criticism not only from the political Left, but also from some of the government's most ardent admirers. For example, Clarke (1987: 80) remarks 'It would be easier and better for the self respect of privatisation if competition were opened up.' In response to such criticisms, the government acted to open up at least a portion of the utility supply markets. It also sought ways to deflect similar criticisms of the proposed electricity and water privatisations. This section is concerned with changes to management structures in Albion and NU which represent an attempt to break down the traditional bureaucratic, hierarchical structure of these organisations.

Devolved management at Albion Water

Injecting competitive pressures into the water industry was not an easy task. Even Margaret Thatcher described water as 'a natural monopoly'. But unless water companies were exposed to market forces, it would be difficult to see where the pressure to shift away from traditional, bureaucratic managerial control would come from. The government attempted to get round these problems in two ways. First, it has adopted a form of economic regulation which is claimed to prevent abuse of monopoly power through a price limitation formula, and which is supposed to simulate competition. The Regulator states: 'Because of the limited scope for direct competition, I will compare the performance of the appointed companies . . . [in terms of] their costs, their efficiency and their return on capital . . . In competitive markets, competition brings prices down to those of efficient firms. In the case of water I must set the charges limit to have a similar effect.' (Prospectus for Sale of Water plcs, 1989: 45)

Second, the government intervened far more directly than it had in previous privatisations in terms of giving the Regional Water Authorities advice on how to restructure in preparation for privatisation. Albion Water was advised by the government to make substantial changes to its organisational structure by introducing a variant of profit-centre management, much the same model as that which the government has imposed upon the civil service, the universities and former polytechnics. This model treats individual functions or departments as autonomous entities, which must enter into commercial transactions with other departments within the organisation. The basic idea behind this form of profit centre management is to dismantle 'monolithic bureaucracies' and replace them with a number of semi- or wholly autonomous business units which must enter into commercial transactions with each other, as well as with outside firms (see Jackson, this volume). Vertical bureaucratic management structures are superseded by 'flatter' horizontal structures, and managers face one another across internal markets instead of occupying positions in a hierarchy. In essence, this model of profit centre management is an accounting exercise designed to provide a variety of incentives and penalties for managers which will force them to adopt a commercial, private sector style of management.

As a water authority, Albion had been organised as a number of functions accountable to the board. The proposed economic regulation of the water industry prompted Albion Water to make substantial changes to its organisational structure. The Regulator's price limitation formula is designed to control the level of profit that can be extracted from the core activities of the Water plcs, supply and recovery. Non-core activities are not subject to economic regulation and this makes diversification an attractive option. From 1988 on, Albion began to diversify into areas such as plumbing, waste disposal and international construction contracting, and these new ventures are organised by separate subsidiary firms. Albion Water plc is now a holding company with a number of subsidiaries, only one of which (Albion Water Services Ltd) is involved in the core activities of water supply and sewerage. At present, the subsidiary firms account for only a minute percentage of turnover, but the board is committed to changing this situation.

Within Albion Water Services Ltd there is further organizational change and devolution of management. Various activities have been separated out and turned into independently accountable 'profit centres' which must 'buy' and 'sell' services from and to other departments or profit centres within the organisation, and engage in commercial ventures outside the firm. The board plans to further separate some of the 'profit-centres' in future, turning them into subsidiaries if they prove successful, but at present, they work as follows.

Each profit centre is supposed to act as if it were an independent firm. It therefore has to draw up a business plan, taking into account its income from charges or sales and outlining its proposed revenue and capital expenditure for the year, and submit this to the board. The board then allocates the profit centre a budget (the term 'budget' smacks of traditional bureaucratic control, however, and so a new jargon has been coined by Albion managers – the profit centre's budget is referred to as a 'pot of gold', or 'pot' for short). Having been allocated its budget, each profit centre is instructed to behave as if it were a small firm, operating a profit and loss account and pursuing output and profitability specified in its business plan. The profits generated by individual profit centres are ploughed back into the corporate whole. However, there are a range of rewards which are supposed to act as an incentive to profit centre managers, including profit related bonus payments, company cars, expansion of successful profit centres and so on. Sanctions for failing to meet profit and performance targets are also directed at the individual managers. They can be financially penalised, and ultimately face demotion or dismissal if they consistently fail to meet the targets agreed in the business plan.

This form of profit centre management clearly bears the hallmark of Thatcherite economic thinking. It is supposed to equal good management for the following reasons. First, the profit centre managers' 'pots' are like the 'housewife's kitty' – they know how much their 'pot' contains, and good sense dictates that they will not spend more than is available. Second, because other departments are charging for their services, the profit centre manager's voracious appetite for the organization's resources is curbed. The system ensures that these managers use their 'pots' wisely. Third, because they have to make a profit by 'selling' their services either to other departments or profit centres, or to outside firms, who may choose to go elsewhere if the service is shoddy or overpriced, the system forces them to keep costs to a minimum and standards at their highest. Finally, because profit centre managers have been given both 'freedom to manage' and personal responsibility for outcomes, there is great pressure on individual managers to perform effectively. They must, as the Americans put it, 'either shit or get off the pot'.

Profit centre management is thus supposed to stimulate and reward an entrepreneurial efficiency-maximising style of management by simulating market forces *within* the organisation. However, if profit centres are considered in relation to the whole organization, rather than to individual managers, they appear to have rather less potential as a radical, efficiency-maximising force. The idea is that when departments face each other across markets, instead of enjoying a hierarchical relationship, competitive pressures are injected into the firm and efficiency will improve. Yet in reality, most departments are monopoly suppliers to other departments, because no profit centre or department is given absolute freedom to choose its suppliers. The notion that a profit centre (for instance Operations) could decide that the finance department provided an inefficient and costly service and go to a cheaper outside firm for payrolling instead is fanciful since it would slash the volume of work for Albion's payrolling unit by about 40 per cent. Likewise, if Operations found that it could save money by going outside for vehicles instead of going to Transport (another profit centre), the cost to Albion as a company would again be high. An Albion Finance Manager comments: 'There is this conflict between the profit centre and the corporate whole, but that is very much the responsibility of the corporate whole to make sure that profit centres . . . do toe the line of the corporate good.'

In other words, the board would not allow a profit centre to make such decisions. Without freedom to choose between suppliers, the notion of a market between different units is a fiction. Profit centres are not disciplined by competitive forces if there is no real likelihood of losing custom, and so in reality it is still the board which must exert pressure for cost-cutting and greater efficiency. Profit centres do not only lack independence in terms of their choice of supplier. They are closely controlled by the board in other ways. Although profit centres are exhorted to think and act like independent firms and to conceive of other departments and profit centres as their 'customers', in practice they have virtually no autonomy at all. Their business plan must conform to criteria set out by the board, and must be negotiated with the board; capital and revenue expenditure is set by the board; their overheads, manning levels and employment practices are imposed from above; performance and profit targets are set by the board; and finally, they are constrained by the board in their choices of suppliers and customers. What is there left for market forces to act upon? Under the old regime, departments were bureaucratically allocated budgets, and their efficiency and profitability was determined by decisions taken by the board. Under the new system, budgets are replaced by 'pots', but the profit centre's efficiency and profitability is still crucially determined by the board's decisions.

Profit centre management has not entailed any decentralisation of power or authority, nor has it genuinely created market forces within the organisation. What function does it serve? At Albion Water, profit centre status is used by managers to justify cost-cutting exercises, changes in working practices and demands for increased productivity. It is here that an answer to the question posed earlier (namely, after the board has set performance and profit targets, direct labour levels, overheads and employment practices and so on, what is there left for market forces to act upon?) may be found. Labour is all that remains to be disciplined, and this is effected through the new forms of employment relations and work organisation and above all, through the labour intensification, which were described in the previous section.

Though the internal market is almost entirely fictional, Albion's senior managers make much of the notion of competition, and continually emphasise the need to cut costs and improve efficiency in order to 'win' work from other departments or profit centres. Workers in the new, independent profit centres have been asked to accept cuts to direct labour levels, elongation of the working day, cuts to bonus payments, the introduction of multi-tasking, pared down rest periods, and more, in order that their profit centre remains viable. They are exhorted to think of Albion, not as their employer, but as their 'customer', and this commercialisation of the employment relation has eliminated the old, tacit understandings about employment security, linking their continuity of employment explicitly not to the success of the firm which employs them, but to the success of their particular profit centre.

In short, profit centre management has sought to commercialise relationships between different units and departments within Albion, and these departments and units have, in turn, sought to commercialise their relationships with employees. The new accounting practices are used to provide incentives and sanctions for managers, and as a way of intensifying the pressure for changes to working and employment practices. They also make it easier to reduce the amount of activities which fall under the control of the Regulator. Profit centre management may have been recommended by government advisers for essentially ideological reasons, but Albion management has made very practical use of it.

Decentralising authority and centralising control at National Utility

The government did not intervene directly to reshape NU in preparation for privatisation as it did with the electricity and water industries. However privatisation and legislation which liberalised first the appliance market and subsequently part of the supply market, led to changes in top management priorities. Its prime concerns became first, how to make profits (diversification was seen to play a key role in this); and second, how to do this in the context of the economic regulation imposed by government. In the late 1980s NU began splitting the organisation into a number of independent business units, only one of which was involved in supplying the utility to domestic and industrial customers. This business unit remains a giant in relation to the other business units however (see Table 7.1) and will probably be split further into its constituent parts.

Table 7.1 National Utility business units by size, 1991

	Employees (000s)	Operating profit £m	Turnover £m
National Utility	76.2	1,310	8,675
Subsidiary 1	0.8	264	978
Subsidiary 2	0.4	68	378
Other Activities	2.6	13	87

Source: National Utility Annual Report, 1991

After restructuring NU was still dominated by one business unit which generated 86 per cent of the corporation's turnover, 79 per cent of its profits and 92 per cent of employment. This unit is organised as a number of regions, each of which is further subdivided into a number of operational districts, answerable to a regional board. Until recently, management structures within the regions remained very much as they had done prior to privatisation. Top management is now turning its attention to restructuring within the regions, and this restructuring takes the form of a decentralisation of authority, with districts being transformed into independently accountable profit centres. This devolving of management structures is, however, accompanied by a strengthening and centralising of senior management control over the region, just as devolved management at Albion appears to have consolidated the board's control. This is well illustrated by a description of how one region has recently restructured clerical work.

Around 90 per cent of NU's clerical workforce undertakes work arising from appliance retailing, servicing and repair, and sudden exposure to competition (alongside the general pressure to increase the return on capital for shareholders following privatisation) provided management with a strong incentive to cut costs and raise the productivity of clerical labour. Management sought to achieve this end by computerising clerical work (through the New Office Systems Strategy or NOSS) and introducing multi-functional team working (referred to as the Beta Structure). NOSS not only impacts upon employees in the very direct sense of changing the work they undertake, it also affects the relationship between district and regional management. It is thus part of the more fundamental restructuring of NU, shifting the pattern of control within the organisation.

In the past, there was a certain amount of variation between districts in terms of structure and work organisation. For example, some districts would be very much led by, and organised around, the distribution and engineering function, while others were more marketing-led. Similarly, the extent of computerisation varied from district to district, and clerical procedures associated with exactly the same activity could be performed in quite different ways in different districts. Thus, while regional management provided an overall framework in the form of various blanket policies and directives, the region had little direct control over the detailed, day-to-day activities within the districts. NOSS Beta is designed to change all this. It imposes a standard form of multi-functional team work upon all districts, and the new computer systems standardise clerical procedures across the entire region. A personnel manager explains: 'NOSS rationalises the control systems . . . one of its perceived advantages was that it . . . makes people work much more on prescribed procedures and follow prescribed methods.'

In this sense, control over clerical work is being centralised, but paradoxically, regional management claim to be devolving power down to the districts as part of their effort to break away from the 'rigidly hierarchical structure' NU developed as a nationalised industry. The Personnel Manager comments: 'NOSS and a lot of the other changes going on at the moment are all part of the move away from the massive bureaucracy . . . a move from that into a structure which is more reactive, which is about taking initiatives, being innovative, allowing people to be entrepreneurial even.'

This is management's spoken objective in transforming districts into independently accountable profit centres. Senior managers claim that this represents a devolution of power to the districts, which will in turn stimulate a more entrepreneurial style of management. These managers, like senior managers at Albion, are well versed in the ideas and language of contemporary management gurus. A regional personnel manager explained:

> If you read the sort of Tom Peters ideas about moving administration and decision making closer to the customers, there are a lot of advantages. At the moment we tend to take decisions here, in the regional office, and they are then imposed on the districts. I think the idea of allowing districts to make decisions locally, in response to local conditions, will make the districts more reactive and more innovative.

New accounting practices and a move to performance-related pay for district managers are tangible enough changes. What is questionable, as with Albion Water's profit centre management, is how much real autonomy is being devolved. As noted above, the region is actually centralising control over clerical procedures and organisation, imposing a common structure and common computer systems across the region. Again, the profit centre manager has no control over the allocation of central overheads, no choice over whether to 'buy' services such as pay-rolling and transport from NU or from an outside agency, no power to negotiate pay levels or employment policies, and is set targets for 'staff savings' as well as for costs and profits. What kind of decisions can district managers make? The same personnel manager continues: 'Clearly in a business like ours, we can't give people carte blanche. There are very basic things like safety and legal procedures, and our policy towards employees. These are fairly bedrock things that we wouldn't want changed.'

Yet he insists that profit centre management constitutes a decentralisation of power, and that there will now be room for 'entrepreneurial thinking'. The only actual example of this new freedom he could come up with, however, was the freedom for district managers to give interviews on local radio without first seeking permission from regional management. In practice then, this form of profit centre management does not appear to devolve much real power down to the districts. Market forces are again more symbolic than material. The prime objective is to make district managers more accountable. Once again, the value of the strategy to senior management is that district managers are thereby presented with a strong incentive to push through changes to work organisation and employment practices which cut labour costs. Meanwhile, the new accounting practices make it easier to convince employees that such rationalisations are necessary to ensure the viability of the profit centre in which they work. Again, as in Albion Water, changes to the relationships between different departments and/or units of the organisation are mirrored in changes to employment relations. The emphasis on accountability is being extended right down to the individual clerk. A district administration manager explains that 'the idea is to produce accounts for each clerical team, each geographical area, so you'll be able to see exactly how they compare, and that will lead to greater accountability'. 'Accountability' here means producing accounting information about smaller units, and: 'This means you can set teams financial targets . . . so you can assess their performance against financial targets and use that as an incentive to improve performance, rather than their efforts being lost in this huge, functional structure.'

At NU, the production of accounting information for each individual work group has been introduced in conjunction with requests to staff to identify themselves by name to customers, and with new technology that records every stroke of the keyboard each clerk makes and that allows every telephone conversation the clerk has to be monitored by the supervisor. These moves makes the individual clerk's performance far more visible than ever before, and thereby facilitates the shift away from seniority-based progression through grades towards performance-based progression, which is one of NU management's spoken objectives. It has also been used to justify replacing full-time with part-time posts and the reduction of staffing levels. In other words, for NU's clerical workers, the employment relation is being individualised. It has not, as yet, been explicitly commercialised. Unlike many groups of Albion employees, clerical workers at NU have not been told that their employment security rests on their team's profitability. However, these changes mark a clear break with the past, where the individual clerk's employment, pay and promotion was negotiated nationally and on the basis of the company's performance.

Managers use the language of personal development, personal accountability, rewards for the individual, and so on, to describe these changes to the employment relation, just as the shift to profit centre management is framed in terms of devolved power, greater autonomy for district managers and rewards for innovative, entrepreneurial management. In reality, both sets of changes appear to represent the centralisation of control within the organisation. A personnel manager illustrated this contradiction when he said first, that: 'Giving power to the districts means managers and staff can respond more flexibly to the local conditions . . . this complements the flexibility of the NOSS. It gives employees real opportunities for personal development and responsibility.'

During the same interview, he continued:

> The thing about the NOSS is that it standardises the way people work, and that does mean that within the region, we have more control at the centre . . . It does take away some of the individual self-expression in the work, but we needed to do it . . . It makes it far easier for us [Regional Management] to control staffing levels and costs and to achieve flexibility in terms of deploying staff.

In summary, devolved management structures were not imposed on NU upon privatisation as they were imposed on Albion Water, but NU management is now keen to move in the same direction.[4] In both organisations, the effect of devolution has been to further centralise control within the organisation, and to facilitate changes to employment relations and the intensification of labour.

7.3 Markets, profits and efficiency

As private concerns answerable to shareholders, the utilities must now make and maintain a return on capital. In the case of National Utility, this has to be achieved in a climate of increased competition. In the case of water companies, it has to be achieved in the context of tighter EEC legislation on water quality and poor climatic conditions. Yet, as can be seen in Figures 7.4 and 7.5, both companies appear to be fulfilling their obligations to shareholders magnificently.

Proponents of privatisation might take these climbing profits as evidence of the 'success of privatisation', and certainly few shareholders would disagree. However, as was noted in the introduction, the case for privatisation rests on the assumption that market forces and hierarchical, bureaucratic control are two clearly differentiated methods of regulating economic institutions, and that market regulation promotes greater efficiency by disciplining organisations that are wasteful, encouraging innovation and rewarding firms which provide the best service at the lowest price. Competition is supposed to drive firms to find the form of production organisation which most efficiently serves the existing market,

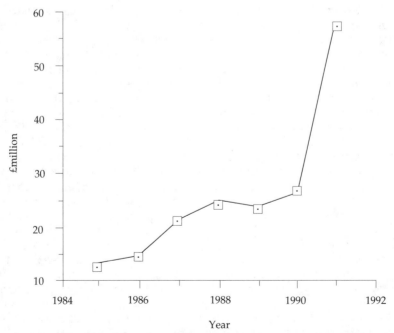

Figure 7.4 Albion Water operating profits 1985 to 1991. *Source:* Albion Water Annual Reports and Accounts.

189

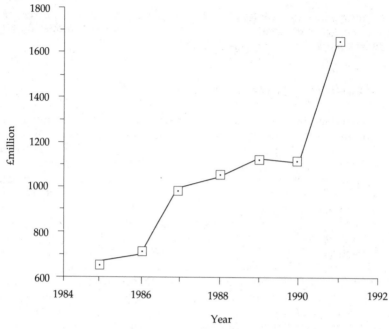

Figure 7.5 NU operating profits 1985 to 1991. *Source:* National Utility
Annual Reports and Accounts.

and when a firm reaps the rewards from so doing, it is argued that
employees as well as shareholders will feel the benefit. This chapter has
attempted to show that such views are problematic.

To begin with, the opposition between market and hierarchical control
is over-simplistic. Privatisation does not, and cannot, shift the utilities into
some kind of free-market Utopia with numerous different capitals
competing to provide the sovereign consumer with the best possible
service. Because of the near-monopoly qualities of the utilities, as well as
their strategic importance to the rest of the economy and to the health and
well-being of the entire population, it is incumbent on government to
provide economic regulation (and environmental regulation in the case of
water). There is no room here to consider whether economic regulation is
affording the consumer adequate protection, but it should at least be
noted that there is a large question mark over the extent to which
shareholders are benefiting at the expense of captive consumers. Take the
case of water. A recent Mori poll found that around 35 per cent of
consumers thought water charges either fairly or very unreasonable
(*Financial Times* 2.6.92), perhaps because water charges had risen by 15.2
per cent over the previous two years, three times faster than the European
average (SCAT, 1991). Benefits may also be being transferred from
consumers to shareholders through the erosion of standards of service;
water disconnections rose by 177 per cent between 1991 and 1992, while
complaints against water companies rose by 130 per cent during the same
period (SCAT, 1992).

For the purposes of this chapter, however, the point is that the form of economic regulation designed for each utility and the degree of zeal with which the regulatory agencies perform their duties will continue to exert an influence on management structures and strategies, work organisation and industrial relations within the utilities. In this sense, then, government ministers, civil servants, and quasi-governmental agencies must still make it their business to govern the activities of these businesses. The close relationship between politicians and managers in these privatised utilities also manifests itself in other ways. The form of profit centre management adopted by Albion Water bears the hallmark of Thatcherite economic thinking, and is very similar to the model of profit centre management that has been imposed on other public sector institutions. Moreover, the political Right is represented on the boards of privatised concerns.[5] In short, just as the nationalised industries were not controlled solely by politicians with no regard for economic and business exigencies, neither are the privatised utilities subject only to the free play of market forces. At this macro level, then, the notion of a sharp opposition between market and hierarchical control does not hold good.

Much the same can be said of control within the organisations. The shift towards devolved management structures at Albion and NU is claimed to represent a change in the control structures within the companies, from hierarchies to markets. As one NU manager put it: 'This is a move away from the massive bureaucracy . . . into a structure which is more reactive, which is about taking initiatives, allowing people to be innovative . . . a more decentralised structure where managers can be more like entrepreneurs, rather than being good bureaucrats.'

Yet as has been seen, though responsibility and accountability have been devolved, many of the changes to management structures actually appear to actually centralise control within the organisations. Again, the distinction between market and bureaucratic control is maintained far better at the level of rhetoric than it is in the real world.

It might be argued that all this is mere sophistry, and that in practical terms NU's and Albion's staggering profits demonstrate that the benefits of privatisation have indeed extended 'beyond our dreams' (Clarke 1987: 90). Inasmuch as profit centre management has facilitated cuts to labour costs, it would appear that the simulation of market forces within NU and Albion may have helped to increase profit margins in the short term. However, the effects of this restructuring on long-term profitability are open to question, as is the idea that it will encourage innovation and a more entrepreneurial style of management. Profit centre management makes short-term profitability the main criterion against which the profit centre's performance is evaluated, and the profit centre manager is held personally responsible for outcomes. Yet, as was noted above, it is the board's not the profit centre manager's decisions that crucially affect the profitability of each profit centre. Such an arrangement is likely to encourage profit centre managers to focus on keeping costs down, rather than to innovate, since the penalty for failure is high. Moreover, profit centre management generates a great deal of conflict over the allocation of central overheads, and negotiations can be time-consuming and costly. For these reasons, it is not given an unreserved welcome by managers themselves, indeed, many profit centre managers find their position intolerable. As one of NU's district managers put it, 'we are being given responsibility without authority'. Unless managers at the sharp end of the system give it their backing, it is unlikely to transcend its inherent problems and contradictions.

Even more important, so far as the New Right's moral defence of privatisation goes, is the issue of *how* profit margins are being raised. New right theorists and government Ministers have argued that regulation by market forces (whether real or simulated) enhances efficiency, and it is this increased efficiency which is rewarded with higher profits. Of course, labour costs are only one factor affecting profit levels, but for both Albion and NU, they are a significant factor.[6] It is therefore important to ask whether labour costs are falling because production is more efficiently organised now that the organisations are exposed to 'market' forces. 'Efficiency' is, as Turk (1983: 192) points out, a rather more complex concept than is often assumed in the economics literature, but if we simply take 'efficient' production organisation to be that which yields a larger output for the same, or less, input of labour, then it is by no means certain that either NU or Albion's soaring profits are a reflection of heightened efficiency.

Labour costs in both organisations have been reduced primarily through changes to employment relations and work organisation; changes which involve replacing sections of the direct labour force with cheaper labour, and squeezing more effort out of direct employees in return for a similar, or sometimes slightly worse, package of wages and fringe benefits. There is evidence to suggest that similar stratagems to cut labour costs are being adopted by other privatised and about to be privatised concerns. Fevre (1986) describes how large numbers of British Steel's manual workers were made redundant, then rehired by contractors to undertake exactly the same jobs under far worse conditions of employment and for less pay. Ancillary workers in the NHS have suffered the same fate (see Cousins, 1990). Meanwhile, the 1991 Coal Industry Bill, which prepares the ground for privatisation of the coal industry, proposed to give 'the Government the power to change miners' working hours from the 7.5 hour daily underground maximum set by the Coal Mines Regulations Act of 1908' (SCAT, 1991), allowing miners to work up to 13 hours underground.

Moreover, plans to contract out local authority and central government white collar work have recently been thrown into disarray by new regulations, stemming from a European Community directive, which protect workers' pay and conditions when they transfer to the private sector (Milton 1992). Although the full implications of these regulations are as yet unclear, it would be interesting to see whether privatisation remained an attractive option were employers to be legally prevented from improving 'efficiency' by slashing the wages, job security and employment benefits of the workforce.

The real point is that labour costs in privatised and about to be privatised organisations appear to have been cut largely by the simple expedient of dismantling the package of employment rights and benefits secured by organised labour in these industries in the post-war years. In this sense, there has been no real increase in output per unit of labour input, merely a reduction in cost for the company.

The fact that employers can improve profit margins by cutting costs in this particular way is unsurprising, but it can only be described as increasing 'efficiency' if the term is used in its most abstract sense. If getting workers to exert more effort for the same, or lower wages, or replacing secure, well unionised labour with disposable, non-unionised workers, and thereby reducing the employer's liability to fund pensions and sick pay is taken to constitute increasing 'efficiency', then it could be argued that the ills of the British economy would be cured by a return to the Masters and Servants Act of the nineteenth century. After all, labour costs could be further reduced if the arbitrary and sweeping powers enjoyed by nineteenth-century employers were reintroduced, or indeed, if employers rounded up workers at gunpoint and forced them to work for less than even their own subsistence, as was the case under forced labour regimes in colonial Africa (see Nzula *et al.* 1979).[7] In practice, what increases in profits that derive from such changes to work organisation and employment practices represent is a form of redistribution, away from workers in the industry and towards shareholders, rather than an increase in productive efficiency.[8] It may be that this too mirrors changes at a macro level. As Riley points out, one of the Government's reasons for privatisation was to buoy up the UK stock market with equities which would pay high and growing dividends.

> The achievements of these designer equities have been well up to specification
> ... Utilities now pay out 13 per cent of the dividends distributed by the 655 All-Share constituents and they account for 18 per cent of the total earnings. Given that, say, 40 per cent of profits are earned abroad, utility profits represent about 30 per cent of all the domestic earnings of British quoted companies (Riley 1992: XXIV).

This means that the selling-off of publicly owned assets not only helps to make the British economy look as if it is faring better than it otherwise would, and perhaps attracts overseas capital, it also helps to satisfy the needs of investment institutions and to fatten up the income of individual shareholders. In this sense, the privatisation programme could be said to funnel wealth that was once commonly owned by the nation towards the richer sections of society, just as within the utilities themselves, workers are being forced to relinquish rights and benefits so that shareholders and top executives may reap greater rewards. If this is so, the final irony about the New Right's emphasis on the opposition between markets and hierarchies may be that the more the economic activities of the utilities are regulated by real and imaginary market forces, the more the traditional hierarchies of wealth and social class in Britain are reinforced.

Acknowledgements

The support of the Economic and Social Research Council is gratefully acknowledged. This chapter is based upon research in two utilities which was conducted between 1988 and 1990 in the Department of Sociology, Bristol University (ESRC award number: R000231466). Much of the above material has already been presented in journals and books, and at conferences, and I am grateful to all those who have commented upon it, but above all to Theo Nichols. I would also like to thank Catherine Price and Peter Jackson for their comments on drafts of this chapter.

Notes

1. Proponents of privatisation can still reel off numerous, often somewhat disconnected, justifications for privatising. Letwin (1988: 28), for example, lists nine different 'central reasons' for privatisation, ranging from the need to attract overseas capital to the desire to transform the 'social and political landscape'.
2. At the request of management, neither company is identified by name. The research took place between 1988 and 1991, and involved both extensive fieldwork and a survey of 442 employees in Albion Water and National Utility.
3. 257 National Utility employees were surveyed in September and October of 1990, and 185 Albion Water employees were surveyed between December 1990 and February 1991. The sample included managerial, clerical and manual employees. The questionnaire sought their views on public and private sector organisations, privatisation, employee share ownership, work organisation and trade unions. For a full account of the results see O'Connell Davidson *et al.* (1991).
4. The way profit centre management worked at Albion was described to an NU manager, and he was asked whether the same thing was happening at NU. He replied, 'Just watch this space! We'll be into that before very long.'
5. For example, Norman Tebbit is a British Telecom non-executive director, Peter Walker is a British Gas non-executive director.
6. At NU in 1984, payroll costs constituted 20.7 per cent of operating costs. Had they remained at this level instead of falling by 3 per cent, it would have added an extra £235m to operating costs in 1991, which would imply a 15 per cent drop in profits. At Albion Water, employment costs represented 34.6 per cent of operating costs in 1985. Again, had they remained at this level, it would have added £7.1m to operating costs in 1989, which would have involved profits falling by almost 31 per cent.
7. This underlines more general problem with discussions about the relative efficiency of markets and hierarchies in the economics literature (particularly the new institutional economics literature – see Williamson and Ouchi, 1983, Williamson, 1985 and 1990). It is all very well to talk about the efficiency properties of these different modes of economic regulation in a *ceteris paribus* world, but in the real world, all things are not equal. Governments and employers make their choices between market and hierarchical regulation in a particular economic, political and institutional context. In the present climate of economic recession, with organised labour at its weakest point in post-war history, with high mortgage interest rates and the spectre of unemployment looming large, a shift towards market regulation may allow employers to introduce changes to employment relations, work organisation and industrial relations which serve to increase profits. If labour markets tighten up and organised labour strengthens its position, employers will once again be faced with problems of labour recruitment and retention, and in this context, hierarchical regulation may once again appear an 'efficient' mode of organisation. 'Efficiency' cannot be readily separated from 'power

considerations' in the analysis of organisational structure.
8. It might be objected that since employees are now often shareholders their loss is not significant. However, less than 4 per cent of share capital in either company is actually held by employees, and of this, the bulk is owned by managerial employees, rather than clerical or manual workers.

References

Abromeit, H. (1988) British privatisation policy, *Parliamentary Affairs*, Oxford University Press.

Ascher, K. (1987) *The Politics of Privatisation*, Houndmills: Macmillan Educational Ltd.

Beynon, H., Hudson, R. and **Sadler, D.** (1991) *A Tale of Two Industries*, Milton Keynes: Open University Press.

Clarke, P. (1987) The argument for privatization, in J. Neuberger (ed.), *Privatization: Fair Shares for All or Selling the Family Silver?*, London: Papermac.

Cousins, C. (1990) The contracting out of ancillary services in the NHS, in G. Jenkins and M. Poole (eds), *New Forms of Ownership*, London: Routledge.

Fairbrother, P. (1991) In a state of change: flexibility in the civil service in A. Pollert (ed.), *Farewell to Flexibility?*, Oxford: Basil Blackwell.

Fairbrother, P. and **Waddington, J.** (1990) The politics of trade unionism: evidence, policy and theory, *Capital & Class*, 41, Summer, pp. 15–56.

Ferner, A. (1987) Public enterprise and the politics of commercialism: changing industrial relations in British and Spanish railways, *Work, Employment and Society*, vol. 1, no. 2, pp. 179–203.

Ferner, A. (1990) The changing influence of the personnel function: privatisation and organizational politics in electricity generation, *Human Resource Management Journal*, Autumn.

Fevre, R. (1986) Contract work in the recession, in K. Purcell, S. Wood, S. Walby, A. Waton and S. Allen (eds), *The Changing Experience of Employment: Restructuring and Recession*, London: Macmillan.

Fevre, R. (1987) Subcontracting in Steel, Work, Employment and Society, Vol.1, No. 4.

Heald, D. and **Morris, G.** (1984) Why public sector unions are on the defensive, *Personnel Management*, May, pp. 30–4.

Labour Research Department, (1990) *Privatisation and Cuts: The Government Record*, LRD, 78 Blackfriars Road, London SE1 8HF.

Lawson, N. (1987) Closing the great divide, Special Report on Privatisation, *The Observer*, 25.10.87.

Letwin, O. (1988) *Privatising the World: A Study of International Privatisation in Theory and Practice,* Cassell Educational Ltd.

Massey, D. (1984) *Spatial Divisions of Labour,* London: Macmillan Education Ltd.

Milton, C. (1992) FO Will Suspend Contracting-out, *Financial Times,* November 14/15.

Moore, J. (1983) *Why Privatise?,* Conservative Political Centre, London.

Moore, J. (1986) The Success of Privatisation, in J. Kay, C. Mayer and D. Thompson (eds), *Privatisation and Regulation: the UK Experience,* Oxford: Clarendon Press.

Nichols, T. (1986) *The British Worker Question,* London: Routledge & Kegan Paul.

Nzula, A., Potekhin, I. and **Zusmanovich, A.** (1979) Forced Labour in Colonial Africa, London: Zed Press.

O'Connell Davidson, J. (1990a) The commercialisation of employment relations: the case of the water industry, *Work, Employment and Society,* vol. 4, no. 4, pp. 531–49.

O'Connell Davidson, J. (1990b) The road to functional flexibility: white collar work and employment relations in a privatised utility, *Sociological Review,* vol. 38, no. 4, pp. 689–711.

O'Connell Davidson, J. (1991) Subcontract, flexibility and changing employment relations in the water industry, in P. Blyton and J. Morris (eds) *A Flexible Future?,* Berlin: Walter de Gruyter.

O'Connell Davidson, J., Nichols, T. and **Sun, W.** (1991) *Employee Attitudes in Two Privatised Utilities,* unpublished survey report, University of Leicester, LE1 7RH.

O'Connell Davidson, J. (1992) The sources and limits of resistance in a privatised utility, in Resistance and Power in Organizations, J. Jermier, W. Nord, D. Knights, C. Smith and H. Willmott (eds), Routledge (forthcoming).

O'Connell Davidson, J. (1993) Privatization and Employment Relations: The Case of the Water Industry, London: Mansell (forthcoming).

Ogden, S. (1990) *The Impact of Privatisation on Industrial Relations in the Water Industry,* Cardiff Business School Annual Conference.

SCAT (1990) Privatisation and tendering take their toll, *Public Service Action,* no. 43, August.

SCAT (1991) Water company profits, *Public Service Action,* no. 45, November/

SCAT (1992) Water disconnections rise dramatically, *Public Service Action,* no. 47, July.

Redwood, J. (1988) Introduction to O. Letwin, *op. cit.*

Riley, B. (1992) No recession here, thank you, *Financial Times,* Weekend June 13/14.

Schott, K. (1983) The rise of Keynesian economics: Britain 1940–64, in D. Held (ed.) *States and Societies,* Oxford: Basil Blackwell.

HM Treasury (1990) Privatisation, *Economic Briefing,* no. 1, December.

Turk, J. (1983) Power, efficiency and institutions: some implications of the debate for the scope of economics, in A. Francis, J. Turk and P. Willman (eds), *Power, Efficiency and Institutions,* London: Heinemann.

Upham, M. (1990) Passages on the path to privatisation: the experience of British Steel, *Industrial Relations Journal,* vol. 21, no. 2, Summer, pp. 87-97.

Williamson, O. (1985) *The Economic Institutions of Capitalism,* New York: Free Press.

Williamson, O. (1990) The firm as a nexus of treaties: an introduction, in M. Aoki, B. Gustafsson and O. Williamson (eds), *The Firm as a Nexus of Treaties,* London: Sage.

Williamson, O. and **Ouchi, W.** (1983) The markets and hierarchies programme of research: origins, implications, prospects, in A. Francis, J. Turk and P. Willman (eds), *Power, Efficiency and Institutions,* London: Heinemann.

Winterton, J. (1990) Private power and public relations: the effects of privatization upon industrial relations in the coal industry, in G. Jenkins and M. Poole (eds), *New Forms of Ownership,* London: Routledge.

CHAPTER 8

Markets in health care

Ray Robinson

Introduction

A constant theme of the UK government's micro-economic policy during the 1980s was a belief in the superior efficiency of the private sector. A central component of this belief was that it is the competitive market environment within which private sector firms operate that provides the necessary incentive structure for the promotion of efficiency. This environment was often contrasted with the monopoly position of many public sector organisations and provided a major rationale for successive privatisation programmes in different sectors of the economy.

For most of the decade, however, the National Health Service (NHS) was not greatly affected by these policies. Despite the introduction in 1984 of a general management system based upon private sector principles (Griffiths, 1983), the basic structure of the service remained remarkably similar to the one first introduced in 1948. No doubt the government felt wary about challenging the underlying principles of an institution which successive public opinion polls showed continued to command deep and widespread support (Jowell *et al.*, 1987). As a result, incursions of competition and other market-based practices into the NHS were confined largely to tendering for the ancillary services of laundry, catering and cleaning (Ascher, 1987).

Towards the end of the decade, however, this situation changed quite markedly. Following a Prime Ministerial review of the NHS, a White Paper, *Working for Patients* (DoH, 1989a), was published in January 1989. This White Paper outlined the most radical set of reforms ever to be applied to the service. Most of these were subsequently embodied in the NHS and Community Care Act, 1990 and introduced on 1 April 1991. A striking feature of the reforms has been the introduction of a quasi-market into the NHS, involving trade in clinical services through a so-called 'internal market'.

This chapter examines the NHS internal market. It starts with a brief review of the economic reasons for public sector intervention in health care; of the forms that this intervention can take; and of the shortcomings of the type of government intervention represented by the traditional NHS which led to the 1990 reforms. This is followed by a description of the structure of the new style health market in which the key agencies on the demand and supply side of the market are identified. The next section examines the way in which the market can be expected to perform in terms of four main objectives; namely, efficiency, patient choice, service quality and equity in the distribution of health care.

At the outset, however, it is necessary to point out that, because the NHS reforms involve such a complex set of changes, it has not been possible to deal with all aspects of them in this chapter. Space limitations have meant that consideration is restricted primarily to the short-stay or acute hospital sector. Issues affecting primary care (i.e. GP services) are dealt with only in so far as they represent part of the market for hospital services. Long-term and community care, although the subject of market-based changes themselves, are not dealt with in this chapter.

8.1 Market failure and government intervention

It is a well-known prediction of economic theory that, under certain conditions, a competitive market will bring about an efficient allocation of resources. However, in health care markets, these conditions are rarely met. Market failures arising from uncertainty of demand, the existence of monopoly, and external costs and benefits will all prevent a market system from achieving an efficient allocation (McGuire *et al.*, 1988). In addition to its efficiency failings, there is no reason to suppose that a market system will produce a fair or equitable distribution of resources. This is likely to be an important shortcoming, given that equity is usually accorded a high priority in the case of health care.

In the light of the expected incidence of inefficiency and equity in a market system, it should come as no surprise to anyone to learn that there is widespread government intervention in health care in all developed countries.

This intervention can take a number of different forms. In most countries, governments intervene on the finance (demand) side to try to make sure that no-one is denied access to health care because of insufficient income or because of being such a bad risk that they are uninsurable. In some countries, this intervention is on a 'safety net' basis. In the United States, for example, federal and state governments offer assistance to low income and/or high risk groups who would find it difficult to get adequate private insurance. Thus, the Medicaid and Medicare programmes cover a large part of the health costs incurred by poor families and elderly people. These mean that, even in a system that places a high priority on the private market, approximately 40 per cent of the cost of health care is financed through public expenditure (Robinson, 1990).

In other countries, such as France, Germany and the Netherlands, governments adopt a more universalist approach to public funding. In both of these countries, the majority of the population have their health care costs covered in return for income-related payments into a social insurance scheme.

In all of these countries, however, government intervention is concentrated on the demand side. On the supply side, most hospitals are privately owned, and the majority of doctors and nurses are self-employed or employees in the private sector. In only a few countries does government intervention extend to the ownership of hospitals and to the direct employment of medical staff. Sweden is one of them. And so, of course, is the UK. In Britain, the public sector owns the overwhelming majority of health care assets, and most professional workers are either directly employed by the NHS or have a close contractual relationship with it. It is this monopoly of state finance and provision that critics argued had led to inefficiency.

Most of the empirical evidence relating to inefficiency in the NHS concentrates on X-inefficiency; that is, the failure to achieve productive efficiency by using resources optimally so that the minimum cost for each level of service provision is achieved. In 1983, for example, the Ceri Davies Report, which was commissioned and published by the Department of Health and Social Security (DHSS), highlighted the waste of valuable resources resulting from the under-use of space and the unnecessary retention of surplus capacity (Davies, 1983). By 1987, a National Audit Office report suggested that savings of between £300 and £500 million per year were achievable through the better use of NHS estate (NAO, 1988). Another study, also carried out by the National Audit Office, revealed serious under-use of operating theatre capacity (NAO, 1987). It showed that, in the five district health authorities which were investigated, only 50 to 60 per cent of daytime, weekday operating theatre sessions were actually used. Among the factors leading to under-utilisation were the failure of clinicians to use all of their scheduled sessions, non-availability of operating theatre staff and a shortage of vacant hospital beds. Reporting on these findings and the DHSS's response to them, the House of Commons Committee of Public Accounts commented:

> We acknowledge that the management of hospital resources is a complex task and that the use of operating theatres cannot be seen in isolation. However, we consider that the difficulty of achieving an exact balance between theatres, beds and staffing should not be used as a justification for failure to make best use of resources which are available and an excuse for low utilisation of theatres (Committee of Public Accounts, 1988, p. vii).

Failure to make maximum use of operating theatres, beds and staff time was also identified by Yates (1987) as one of the principal sources of excessive waiting times for hospital admission. And, in this connection, the Audit Commission (1990) has maintained that waiting times could be cut by one-third if all district health authorities (DHAs) used day surgery to the same extent as it is used in the 25 per cent of districts which use it most.

Apart from X-inefficiency, there is also some doubt about whether the size distribution of hospitals within the NHS is efficient. Although there have been surprisingly few econometric studies of hospital cost functions, those which have been carried out suggest a U-shaped function with minimum costs reached at 430 beds or more (Wagstaff, 1989). At the moment, however, less than 25 per cent of hospitals in Britain have 250 beds or more (DoH, 1988).

This evidence certainly suggests that there is scope for greater efficiency within the NHS. Indeed, in any organisation spending over £25 billion per year and employing over one million people, it would be surprising if this was not the case. The crucial question is, however: what incentive structure is likely to improve NHS performance?

8.2 *The new-style NHS health market*

Commenting on the traditional NHS, the US health policy expert, Alain Enthoven, noted that it: 'relies on dedication and idealism. It is propelled by the clash of interests of different provider groups. But it offers few positive incentives to do a better job for patients, and it has some perverse ones.' (Enthoven, 1985, p. 18).

Enthoven's suggested solution to this problem was to propose the introduction of an internal market within the NHS in which providers of services would compete with each other for funds. This, he argued, would act as a spur to efficiency. Despite a number of modifications and additions, the reforms contained in the 1990 National Health Service and Community Care Act bear the clear imprint of Enthoven's ideas. In particular, they

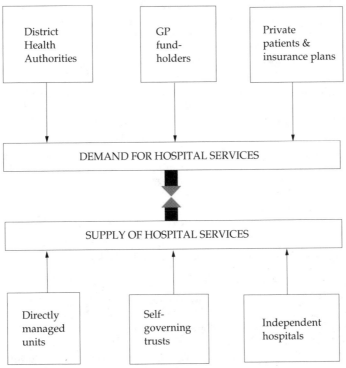

Figure 8.1. The new health market

involve separation between the responsibility for the purchase of services (demand) from their delivery (supply). The main organisations that will carry out these functions are depicted in Figure 8.1.

The purchasing arrangements involve three main categories of budget-holders. The major one is the district health authority (DHA). At present, there are approximately 190 DHAs in England. An average district contains a population of 250,000 people, although there is a good deal of variation around this average, with individual DHAs ranging from 100,000 to over 800,000 people. Since the introduction of the reforms, however, a number of districts have merged. This is a trend that can be expected to continue as districts concentrate on their purchasing function and are freed from provider responsibilities (see below).

In all cases, however, districts receive an annual cash allocation based upon their population size and its characteristics and are responsible for entering into contractual arrangements with providers for the delivery of services for their residents. Assessing their resident population's health care needs, ensuring that an appropriate service mix is provided and monitoring its quality are all part of districts' new responsibilities.

The second category of budget-holder comprises those GPs who have opted to become fundholders. By April 1993, over 1,000 practices had been given the opportunity to manage their own budgets. With these budgets, they are able to purchase a range of services directly for their patients. These services include diagnostic tests, out-patient services and a defined group of in-patient and day cases, such as hip replacement and cataract removals. As in the case of DHAs, fundholding GPs are free to take out service contracts with hospitals of their choosing, and are also able to substitute their own services for existing hospital ones where it is deemed appropriate (e.g. removal of minor lumps and bumps).

The third group on the demand side of the market comprises private patients and insurance plans. Although it is still small in relation to the NHS, the private health care sector has grown rapidly in recent years. By 1988, it was estimated that around 10 per cent of the population was covered by some form of private health insurance and that total private expenditure amounted to over £1 billion (Propper and Maynard, 1990). Private finance tends to be highest in those clinical areas where NHS waiting times are longest, i.e. minor elective surgery. As such, its growth in the future can be expected to depend, to a large extent, on the adequacy of NHS funding in these areas.

On the supply side of the new health care market, there are at present three main types of provider of hospital services. At the moment, many hospitals are constituted as directly managed units (DMUs) and are under the overall control of district health authorities. However, the purchaser/provider split means that greater responsibility for operational functions has been delegated to individual hospitals.

In the longer term, it is expected that practically all provider units will become self-governing trusts within the NHS. These play a key role in the new health care market as they are outside of DHA control and, therefore, represent a genuine separation of purchaser and provider functions. Trusts have greater freedom over capital expenditure and employment policies than DMUs, including the power to employ their own consultants directly instead of having their contracts held at the regional health authority level as at present. By April 1993, there were nearly 300 trusts and ministers have made it clear that they represent the preferred form of ownership structure for all units in the future.

Finally, on the supply side, there is the independent sector, comprising private, voluntary and charitable hospitals. As well as providing services directly, these may be expected increasingly to engage in joint ventures with the NHS, especially as the NHS starts to increase its sale of clinical services to private patients.

8.3 Objectives and performance in the new health market

Referring to its plans for introducing an internal market into the NHS, the government argued that: 'a funding system in which successful hospitals can flourish . . . will encourage greater competition. All this in turn will ensure a better deal for the public, improving the choice and quality of services offered and the efficiency with which these services are delivered.' (DoH, 1989b, p. 22).

This statement provides a convenient summary of the three main objectives of the internal market: namely, increased efficiency, more consumer choice and improved quality of service. To this list, however, a fourth objective should be added; namely, ensuring that equity is not jeopardised. This last condition is important because, as we argued at the beginning of this paper, achieving equity in the distribution of health care is a major reason for government intervention in this sector in the first place.

In this section, we shall examine these objectives and the way the new style NHS is likely to perform in relation to each of them. This examination will reveal the form and extent of government regulation that will be necessary in order to make sure that an acceptable balance is struck between sometimes conflicting objectives.

Efficiency

The case for expecting an internal market to increase efficiency rests on the assumption that supply-side competition between hospitals competing for service contracts will provide an incentive for them to use resources more efficiently. Those hospitals which fail to do so will incur higher costs and will thereby be placed at a competitive disadvantage. There are, however, a number of caveats which should be entered regarding the applicability of this model to NHS hospitals. Three of the most important ones centre on hospitals' objectives, hospital market structure, and the role of the price system.

A major difficulty in using the conventional market model as a basis for predicting hospitals' behaviour arises because they are far more complex organisations than most commercial firms and pursue multiple objectives, many of them non-financial (McGuire *et al.*, 1988, Ch. 11). In most firms, managers specify objectives in terms of profits, sales revenues, rates of growth and other financial variables. However, hospitals are non-profit-making organisations with a wide range of social obligations. Moreover, the division of professional functions within a hospital, especially the presence of doctors with clinical responsibilities, makes it far less easy to ensure that everyone works towards a common financial objective.

One solution to this problem is to place more authority with hospital managers. After all, they are responsible for winning service contracts from purchasers by offering cost-effective packages of care. Hospital funding depends upon their success in carrying out this task. But, while managers may have overall responsibility for financial performance, doctors make clinical decisions which determine how money is actually spent. They also have the ultimate responsibility for meeting any changes in workloads, either upwards or downwards.

It has been a recognition of doctors' pivotal role in committing expenditure that has led to successive attempts to include them formally in management decisions about the use of resources. The 'resource management initiative' (RMI) is the latest government-led attempt to involve doctors in the management process. However, despite considerable enthusiasm displayed by some of the participants at the RMI experimental sites, one recent study concluded that the general experience of including clinicians in budgetary decisions was disappointing: neither managers nor doctors had shown much enthusiasm for it (Pollitt *et al.*, 1988). Subsequently, a formal evaluation of RMI has concluded that it is still not possible to provide a definitive assessment of it as a working process for hospital management (Packwood *et al.*, 1991). Without an effective mechanism for ensuring that clinical activities within a hospital respond to the demands placed upon them by service contracts obtained by managers – whether this is achieved through tighter contractual control over doctors, through personal financial incentives, by budgetary incentives offered to specialist teams of clinicians, or by other means – it is difficult to see how competition between hospitals can be harnessed to increase overall efficiency.

The second reservation about the applicability of predictions based upon the competitive market model arises because many hospitals have monopoly power in their local markets. Outside of major urban conurbations, many hospitals face limited competition for their services within their patient catchment areas.

As is well known, economic theory predicts that a monopolist will restrict output and set prices above those of a competitive firm with the same cost conditions. While hospitals are unlikely to behave as profit-maximising firms, the existence of monopoly does suggest the need for some form of external regulation. In particular, there is a need to pay attention to the relationship between actual costs and minimum achievable costs (i.e. X-inefficiency) as hospitals facing limited competition will be under less pressure to adopt least-cost methods of production.

Recognising the limits to competition posed by the existence of monopoly power, the Department of Health (DoH) has argued that, for efficiency to be increased, it is not necessary for hospitals to face actual competitors, only that they face potential competitors. That is, markets should be contestable (Baumol, *et al.*, 1988). However, for a market to be contestable, certain conditions need to apply. In particular, it is necessary for there to be costless entry to and exit from the industry. This does not mean that there can be no set-up cost for new entrants; but it does mean that there can be no persistent cost advantage enjoyed by incumbent firms. In the case of hospitals, the considerable sunk costs represented by their past investments may well bestow just such an advantage on existing hospitals. One possible way of overcoming this obstacle is to view contestability in terms of the 'managements' of particular hospitals. In this case, it would not be the threat of a new hospital entering the market which forced existing hospitals to adopt efficient methods; rather, it would be the threat of a new management team taking over. This could be achieved through direct imposition from the DoH or, alternatively, through periodic competitive bidding for franchises to manage hospitals (Culyer and Posnett, 1990).

The third area of concern about efficiency in the internal market centres on the role that will be given to prices. In a market system, prices play a crucial role in bringing about an efficient allocation of resources. They act as signals indicating the relative opportunity costs of the commodity provided. However, in the case of health care, the need to meet certain social objectives means that many prices will be set administratively, often involving implicit subsidies which obscure the real costs of particular courses of action. The treatment of capital costs provides an example.

As part of the NHS reforms, a system of capital charges has been introduced for the first time. All hospitals are now responsible for meeting the interest and depreciation costs of their existing assets and new investments. This change means that capital assets can no longer be viewed as a free good. Instead, a pricing system is being used to encourage the more efficient use of resources. As a result, more attention will be focused upon the use made of the substantial NHS holdings of estate and capital equipment. This can be expected to have numerous consequences. For example, maintenance and repair policies should receive a higher priority as the costs of replacement capital become more apparent. The charging system should also encourage a clearer assessment of the relative costs of using capital and labour, and a more thorough consideration of their appropriate mix in service provision.

But the introduction of capital charging has also caused problems. Probably the most notable one is the impact that a system of full capital charging will have on the cost of providing services at inner city locations, especially in London. If hospitals such as Guy's and St Thomas's are expected to meet the full market rental values of their sites, their costs will be substantially above those of hospitals in suburban or provincial locations. Purchasers seeking to maximise the volume of services obtainable from a given budget face a powerful incentive to buy them from less expensive hospitals. As a result, there can be expected to be a run-down of central city hospitals as services are located at less expensive areas (Department of Health, 1993).

However, the government has made it clear that it expects a wide range of designated services to be made available locally in all districts. For this reason, it is unlikely to allow capital charges and other market-based costs totally to determine location decisions. To meet this aim, a series of measures have been introduced to cushion the impact of capital charges at high cost sites.

Clearly, the government wants to ensure that local access to services is maintained. However, in pursuing this perfectly reasonable aim, it is faced with an unavoidable trade-off between policy objectives: that is, it wishes to use market forces to promote efficiency and yet the need to meet an essentially equity aim of local access means that it must place limits on the market process. In principle, a cost-benefit approach could be used to specify equity aims and the level of subsidy payments necessary to achieve them through alternative strategies. In practice, however, the actual balance between efficiency and equity objectives is likely to be determined by the less precise political process. This usually owes more to the 'who shouts loudest' principle than rational decision-making techniques.

Patient choice

Lack of responsiveness to consumers' preferences on the part of public sector, monopoly suppliers has been one of the major criticisms levelled at public organisations in recent years. According to Enthoven (1989), in the health sector: 'They are unresponsive to consumer preferences regarding times and places and modalities of treatment. They are guided much more by provider preferences and convenience than consumer preferences. They ration by queues. They lack accountability.'

Often, public monopolies have been contrasted with private firms in competitive markets where responsiveness to consumer demands is a necessary condition of success and/or survival. Ultimately, provider responsiveness derives from consumers' possession of purchasing power, with which they can back up their demands, and their choice between alternative suppliers. This is the essence of consumer sovereignty.

With the aim of increased consumer sovereignty in mind, in the period of debate preceding the publication of the NHS reforms, some commentators argued for the introduction of vouchers in health care (Green, 1988; Whitney, 1988). These would have a nominal cash value and be distributed to everyone so that they could buy health services from providers of their choosing. Services could be purchased directly but, given the uncertainty of demand associated with health care, they would probably be used to purchase health insurance. Many different forms of voucher scheme are possible. Their value could be adjusted in the light of the likely demands of different age groups. Equally, their value could be inversely related to income so that lower income groups receive more support. They could be used solely in the public sector or could be used in both the public and private sectors. However, whatever variant of the proposal is favoured, supporters of a voucher scheme claim that it would guarantee access to health care for all groups, that it would offer patients greater choice, and that it would ensure that suppliers are responsive to patients' preferences.

In fact, although the government's arguments for the NHS reforms attach particular emphasis to choice and responsiveness to patients' needs, it has not chosen to devolve responsibility for the purchase of health care down to the individual consumer. As we have seen, the main budget-holders with responsibility for purchasing services are district health authorities. Whatever the merits of this arrangement in terms of better informed purchasers, enhanced bargaining power resulting from large-scale purchasing, etc., it is difficult to see how it enhances consumer choice.

In the case of GP fundholders, it is possible that more discussion is taking place between individual doctors and their patients about appropriate forms of hospital treatment and the location of possible referrals. This possibility, together with the greater freedom offered for patients to change their registration between GPs, appears to offer some scope for greater patient choice. But these arrangements still cover only a minority of GPs and hospital services. Most patients will have decisions about where they are treated determined for them in contracts taken out by their DHAs.

In discussion of the DHAs' role, a great deal of emphasis has been placed upon the separation of purchaser and provider functions. The opportunity this offers purchasers to access the health care needs of their populations and to act on their behalf by making sure that the required services are actually provided, free from the pressures of providers' vested interests, has been stressed. While there is no doubt that many district purchasing teams are approaching their new tasks with considerable enthusiasm, there are at least four factors which suggest that the expectation of this arrangement should not be over-optimistic, at least in the short run.

First, there is no clear incentive structure designed to encourage DHAs to carry out their responsibilities as custodians of their populations' preferences in the optimal fashion. Despite a wide consensus about the task of assessing needs via better epidemiological information, consumer surveys, etc., progress in this respect is likely to be uneven given the continued reliance on the 'dedication and idealism' identified by Enthoven.

Second, techniques for actually establishing populations' health needs and the services that will meet these needs are not well developed. At the moment, it is only possible to identify and express health needs in a very general and aggregate form; while knowledge about the relationship between many health sector interventions and patients' health status (i.e. the health production function) is sufficiently unclear as to make the task of optimal service specification extremely hazardous.

Third, it would be naive to believe that the considerable provider power presently bound up in existing patterns of service provision will be eroded by the purchaser/provider split to the extent that purchaser preferences will dominate. The prospect of provider capture is particularly pronounced given the fact that directly managed units are still a DHA responsibility and can, therefore, expect to have a close working relationship with them.

Fourth, there is potential conflict between GPs' traditional freedom of referrals of patients to any hospital of their choosing and the restrictions on hospitals to which they may refer, as specified in the service contracts taken out by DHAs. The DoH has made it clear that it expects districts to take account of GPs' preferences regarding referrals when placing service contracts. Moreover, GPs will retain a residual right to refer some patients to non-contract hospitals. It may be that these safeguards are sufficient and that the preferences of patients, GPs and DHAs will all be met. But, equally, some conflicts are already arising. In these circumstances, because it is the DHA which is ultimately responsible for expenditure, it will retain final control over the placing of contracts and, thereby, the pattern of referrals. In some cases, this is bound to limit individual choice.

Service quality

By making hospitals' funding dependent on service contracts obtained from purchasers of health care, the NHS reforms are designed to provide suppliers with an incentive to provide high quality services that are responsive to patients' needs. In short, competition is expected to take place in terms of quality as well as price.

This expectation means that both purchasers and providers are having to develop means of measuring quality and of including quality standards in their service contracts. These include details of the facilities to be made available to their patients, criteria for admission to and discharge from hospital, maximum waiting times for appointments and admissions and, most important of all, measures of the quality of clinical care. Unfortunately, however, at the moment there is little systematic information available upon which measures of the quality of clinical care can be based, especially in the crucial area of the outcomes of treatment. The government intends that this information should be generated through extension of medical audit; that is, the process through which hospital clinicians regularly meet as a group and review their own performance. Annual reports based upon these meetings will provide purchasers with some information about relative standards between hospitals.

As aspects of quality become more clearly defined, it might be expected that competition would indeed increase standards. Certainly, evidence from the United States, where competition between hospitals has been a feature of the market for some time, confirms that non-price competition – in terms of the range of services and facilities offered – is positively related to the degree of competition in local markets (Luft *et al.*, 1986). However, in the US, quality competition has developed in the context of non-cash-limited expenditure on health services. In the UK, Barr *et al.* (1989) have raised the possibility that cost-conscious purchasing agencies, faced with cash-limited budgets, will be under heavy pressure to take out least-cost service contracts. In the event of a cost/quality trade-off, this poses the threat of a reduction in service quality.

To guard against this possibility, there is a clear role for a regulatory agency designed to monitor the quality of services offered by individual hospitals and to ensure that they meet acceptable standards. This could take the form of an NHS inspectorate or an accreditation agency (Brooks, 1989).

Equity in the distribution of health care

The NHS has traditionally attached considerable importance to its equity objectives. In view of this emphasis, concerns have been expressed that the new-style market will lead to a more unequal and hence less equitable distribution of services. It is possible to discern three sets of arguments which make up this case.

The first argument maintains that the adoption of a market-type system will inevitably increase inequality between different income groups. This view derives from the fact that, within a market system, ability to pay is the major determinant of access to goods and services. And, because incomes are distributed unequally, so access to services will also be unequal. However, while this proposition may be true of market systems in general, it will not be necessarily a feature of the new-style health market in the NHS. This is because the purchasing power 'assigned' to each individual, via a cash allocation to their DHA, will not be determined by a market process, but by a formula specified by the DoH. This formula will be able to be adjusted to produce whatever distribution of purchasing power is deemed appropriate. Hence, although a quasi-market system will be used to allocate spending made by DHAs between competing hospitals, it will not be used to determine the initial cash allocation to purchasers. To this extent, fears about inequity are unfounded.

The second argument for fearing a less equitable system points to the danger that self-governing trusts, in their quest to generate maximum income, may be tempted to offer high technology medicine to a national or international clientele while the needs of their local population suffering from chronic sickness are neglected. In fact, the government intends to regulate the market so this cannot happen. It has made it clear that all hospitals must provide a comprehensive range of designated services so that local access is guaranteed. Community-based services, including those for elderly and mentally ill patients, have both been mentioned as examples of these services. It is most unlikely that a self-governing trust will be able to exclude these services from those it offers if there is no adequate alternative in the locality. As such, claims that self-governing hospitals will lead to major gaps in local service provision are probably unfounded.

A third argument about greater inequity, which had already attracted a good deal of attention, relates to the activities of GP fundholders. Critics of the reforms have claimed that greater freedom offered to fundholders has enabled them to obtain better services for their patients (typically shorter waiting times) at the expense of non-fundholder patients. Others argue, however, that while this might have happened in some cases, it is essentially a transitional phase, and that in the long run efficiency gains will be obtained with no necessary reduction in equity (Glennerster *et al.*, 1992).

Conclusion

As it develops, the internal market will mean a major change to the way that resources are allocated in the NHS. At the moment, however, it is difficult to make precise predictions about the way in which the market will perform. On a theoretical basis, this is because the internal market does not correspond to any well-defined model of health finance and delivery. Rather, it is a hybrid deriving from ideological motives tempered by the recognition of political constraints and practical considerations (Maxwell, 1989). As such, it is impossible to provide predictions about behaviour on the basis of standard models of market structure. On an empirical level, there is no past experience of many of the changes presently being put into place that could be used to provide data for forecasting purposes. And, overlying both of these sources of uncertainty, is the fact that the precise form of the market has not yet been finalised. In this last respect, the increasing amount of regulation that the government and the DoH are seeking to impose on the market is particularly noticeable (Robinson, 1992). How the eventual balance between competition and regulation will be struck remains to be seen.

References

Ascher, K. (1987) *The Politics of Privatisation: Contracting out Public Services,* Macmillan, London.

Audit Commission (1990) *A Short Cut to Better Services. Day Surgery in England and Wales,* HMSO, London.

Barr, N., Glennerster, H. and **Le Grand, J.** (1989) *Working for Patients? The Right Approach,* Welfare State Programme, London School of Economics, London.

Baumol, W., Panzar, J. and **Willig, R.** (1988) *Contestable Markets and the Theory of Industrial Structure,* Harcourt Brace Jovanovich, New York.

Brooks, T. (1989) Giving accreditation where it's due, *Health Service Journal,* 264–5.

Committee of Public Accounts (1988) *Use of Operating Theatres in the National Health Service,* HMSO, London.

Culyer, A. and **Posnett, J.** (1990) Hospital behaviour and competition, in A. Culyer, A. Maynard and J. Posnett (eds), *Competition in Health Care,* Macmillan, London.

Davies, C. (1983) *Underused and Surplus Property in the National Health Service,* HMSO, London.

Department of Health (1988) *Health and Personal Social Services Statistics for England,* 1988 edn, HMSO, London.

Department of Health (1989a), *Working for Patients,* HMSO, London.

Department of Health (1989b), *Self-governing Hospitals,* Working for Patients Working Paper No. 1, HMSO, London.

Department of Health (1993), *Making London Better,* HMSO, London.

Enthoven, A. (1985) *Reflections on the Management of the National Health Service,* Nuffield Provincial Hospitals Trust, London.

Enthoven, A. (1989) What can Europeans learn from Americans about financing and organisation of health care?, *Health Care Financing Review,* Annual Supplement, Health Care Financing Administration, Baltimore, Maryland.

Glennerster, H., Matsaganis, M. and **Owens, P.** (1992) *A Foothold for Fundholding,* King's Fund Institute, London.

Green, D. (1988) *Everyone a Private Patient,* Hobart paperback No. 27, Institute of Economic Affairs, London.

Griffiths, R. (1983) *NHS Management Inquiry,* Department of Health and Social Security, London.

Jowell, R., Witherspoon, S. and **Brooks, L.** (eds) (1987) *British Social Attitudes,* Gower, Aldershot.

Luft, H., Robinson, J., Garnick, D. *et al.* (1986) The role of specialised clinical services in competition among hospitals, *Inquiry,* 23, 83–94.

McGuire, A., Henderson, J. and **Mooney, G.** (1988) *The Economics of Health Care,* Routledge and Kegan Paul, London.

Maxwell, R. (1989) Second thoughts on the White Paper, *King's Fund News* (June), King Edward's Hospital Fund for London, London.

National Audit Office (1987) *Use of Operating Theatres in the National Health Service,* HMSO, London.

National Audit Office (1988) *Estate Management in the National Health Service,* HMSO, London.

Packwood, T., Keen, J. and **Buxton, M.** (1992) *Hospitals in Transition,* Open University Press, Buckingham.

Pollitt, C. *et al.* (1988) Reluctant managers: clinicians and budgets in the NHS, *Finance Accountability and Management,* 4:3, 213–33.

Propper, C. and **Maynard, A.** (1990) Whither the private health care sector?, in A. Culyer, A. Maynard and J. Posnett (eds), *Competition in Health Care,* Macmillan, London.

Robinson, R. (1990) *Competition and Health Care: A Comparative Analysis of UK Plans and US Experience,* King's Fund Institute, London.

Robinson, R. (1992) Health policy in 1991, in F. Terry and P. Jackson (eds), *Public Domain*, Chapman & Hall, London.

Wagstaff, A. (1989) Econometric studies in health economics. A survey of the British literature, *Journal of Health Economics*, 8:1, 1–51.

Whitney, R. (1988) *National Health Crisis: A Modern Solution*, Shepheard–Walwyn, London.

Yates, J. (1987) *Why are we waiting? An Analysis of Hospital Waiting Lists*, Oxford University Press, Oxford.

CHAPTER 9

Privatisation in the former centrally planned economies

Timothy Ash, Paul Hare and Anna Canning

Introduction

The collapse of the communist régimes in Eastern Europe and in the states of the former Soviet Union[1] has, with an almost religious zeal, brought about the replacement of the ideology of communism with that of the market and in particular with that of privatisation. That this should occur is hardly surprising, for it can be seen as a natural reaction to the overburdening dominance of the state in almost all spheres of activity within these societies. Of concern, however, has been the very high expectations placed upon privatisation by the governments of the region. Privatisation has thus frequently been viewed as the means to achieve a number of policy objectives. These range from the strictly economic, such as the desire to improve enterprise efficiency and achieve macro-economic stabilisation, to the overtly political, such as the aim to create a new private property-owning class to provide political support for the market economy and for the governments introducing market reforms. Above all it is hoped that privatisation will provide the basis for the rapid transformation of these economies from highly inefficient essentially second- or third-world economies into developed market economies.

The reality of privatisation has however largely failed to live up to these high expectations, and the most notable result of the privatisations which have occurred thus far has been increased social differentiation. In the less developed economies of the region, especially in the states of the former Soviet Union, the relatively slow progress thus far achieved in the preparation of support policies for privatisation, alongside the prevailing economic and political chaos, have created a potentially explosive situation. Ill-prepared privatisation plans, which produce excessive social inequality at a time when price liberalisation is already increasing social hardship, could provide the spark to ignite the fire of social, political and probably of most concern, nationalist unrest.

Initial difficulties in implementing ambitious privatisation plans have led to the emergence of a new realism about privatisation in the former CPEs. As a result, the privatisation plans of even the most developed of former CPEs, namely Hungary, Poland and the CSFR, are being revised downwards significantly.

Nevertheless, fundamental economic reform is essential for the whole region, and well designed privatisation plans which involve rather than isolate the majority of the population could well act as an important catalyst for bringing about the economic and political transformation of these societies. With this in mind, this chapter aims to review the main theoretical problems of privatisation in the former CPEs while drawing on the actual experience with privatisation in the region thus far.

9.1 Why privatise?

Without a doubt the primary objective of privatisation in the former CPEs is the desire to improve the overall economic performance of these economies. The abysmal economic performance of these economies under the previous communist regimes is not now in question. In this respect the reader should be guided to the now classic works on the inefficiency of the former CPEs by Gomulka (1986) and Kornai (1980). Further discussion of this is not appropriate to this chapter, except to observe that by the end of the 1980s these economies were in a state of economic stagnation and decline. While political developments in the former Soviet Union connected with *perestroika* and *glasnost* probably did most to bring about the collapse of the former communist regimes it was the very poor state of their economies that first pushed Gorbachev into contemplating reform. Once political reform, and particularly *glasnost*, had begun, the economic backwardness of the former CPEs became apparent and acted as a major spur to the populations of these economies to demand further economic and political liberalisation. This pressure finally brought about the collapse of these very oppressive regimes.

Much of the literature analysing the poor performance of the former CPEs lays the blame on the debilitating domination of the state over economic activities, alongside the relative absence of private property rights in almost all spheres of production. It is commonly argued that under large-scale state ownership little interest was shown, either by management or workers, in improving the efficiency of production. The state, via its central planning mechanism, required obedience from enterprises to ensure the fulfilment of the overall economic plan for the economy. In return for playing along with the central planning game and meeting planned physical production targets, there was an almost sacrosanct commitment from the central planners that compliant enterprises would remain in operation whatever their level of (in)efficiency. Enterprise losses were therefore almost automatically underwritten by the state and the presence of the bankruptcy sanction, which has provided such a spur for enterprises in western market economies to improve economic efficiency, was all but absent. Equally, there was no threat of takeover to displace inefficient management, either. Enterprises in the former CPEs thus faced what Kornai terms the 'soft budget constraint', so needed to pay little attention to such goals as economic efficiency or profitability in their day-to-day activities.

Privatisation is generally seen as the key element in the plans of the former CPEs to improve enterprise efficiency. Introducing private property rights will, it is hoped, improve the link between the performance of a particular enterprise and the returns to individual owners, managers and workers, and thereby stimulate improved efficiency. In addition the reduced role for the state in enterprise activity, which privatisation entails, should reduce the ability of enterprises to seek state funding to cover their losses. The budget constraint of newly privatised companies should, therefore, be significantly hardened and enterprises forced to contemplate the prospect of bankruptcy if they fail to operate with a certain level of efficiency.

A second and related motivation underlying the current popularity for privatisation in the former CPEs is its contribution to macro-economic stabilisation. The control of inflation and the introduction of currency convertibility are generally regarded as being among the fundamental requirements for successful economic transformation. Inflation destroys confidence in the currency and makes economic decision-making difficult as costs, prices and profits are difficult to predict. Under inflationary conditions uncertainty and risks are increased and hence investment and other long-term economic activity are discouraged. In addition high inflation complicates the privatisation process as it makes the measurement of the value of enterprise assets and of the market potential of enterprises to be privatised almost impossible.

Inflation in many of the former CPEs is high. In the first year of its stabilisation programme, 1990, inflation in Poland was running at a rate of 584.7 per cent for the year as a whole compared to 251.1 per cent in 1989 (Blazyca, 1991, p. 28), before declining in 1991 to 67 per cent.[2] In 1991 in the CSFR inflation rose to 55 per cent[3] and inflation in Yugoslavia increased to 235 per cent.[4] These figures however pale into insignificance when compared to inflation in the states of the former Soviet Union. In Russia for example *Goskomstat,* the State Statistical Committee, conservatively estimated inflation in 1991 at 92 per cent.[5] However, other reliable sources have suggested that inflation in the last few months of 1991 had produced an annual rate of 600 per cent, and following the price liberalisation introduced on 1 January 1991, the price level is estimated to have risen by a further several (six) hundred per cent in January alone (Gorbachev, 1992). In these circumstances of near hyper-inflation, it is easy to see why the control of inflation is assigned such a high priority in the region's reform programmes.

In the early 1990s, excessively high government budget deficits in the former CPEs have contributed significantly to their rapid inflation. Thus in 1991, in the states of the former Soviet Union, the combined budget deficits of union and republican governments may have been as high as 400 billion roubles or 15 to 20 per cent of GDP (Ash and Hare, 1992).[6] In 1992 it was predicted that the budget deficit of the Russian government would fall as a proportion of GDP to 10 per cent.[7] Unfortunately, the absence of bond markets has resulted in such budget deficits being largely monetarised.

In this context, the sale of state assets is seen by many of the former CPEs as a means to replenish state revenues, either by generating revenues from asset sales, or from reducing the burden of subsidies to inefficient state-owned firms. The Russian government in particular views its privatisation programme as a means of raising revenue to help control spiralling budget deficits. In 1992 it was estimated that 92 billion roubles will be raised for state, municipal and local council budgets from the privatisation of enterprise assets. In 1993 this would increase to 350 billion roubles and in 1994 to 470–500 billion roubles.[8] The Hungarian government has also placed significant stress on privatisation as a means of raising revenue. In 1991 the Hungarian State Privatisation Agency received 40 billion Hungarian Forints ($540 million) from the sale of state assets half of which has been allocated to subsidise the state budget and repay the government debt.[9]

Further, it is also hoped that privatisation will gradually reduce the pressure on state budgets to bail out loss-making enterprise. Privatisation, by establishing individual property rights, should ensure that it is not the government but enterprise owners, management and workers who are responsible for the performance of enterprises.[10]

The third motivation driving privatisation in the former CPEs is one of political expediency. Most of the new democratically elected governments in the former CPEs are dominated by political elites strongly supportive of radical, market-orientated reforms. However, it is generally the case that the populations of the former CPEs are less convinced of the benefits to be derived from such radical reform. There is quite rightly a widespread fear of the negative social consequences of introducing market reforms into economies with highly inefficient industries and where large scale restructuring is required. High unemployment and increasing social inequality are already occurring on an unprecedented scale. In the CSFR by February 1992 unemployment had reached 600,000 or 7.6 per cent and estimates suggest that it will reach 950,000 or 13 per cent by the end of 1992. In Poland by the end of 1991 unemployment had already risen to 11.4 per cent,[11] and estimates made by the Polish Central statistical Office suggested that the rate might well reach 17–19 per cent by the end of 1992.[12] In order to push through radical reform and ensure their own political survival many of the new governments see the creation of a new class of property-owners as being a crucial counterbalance to those demanding a reversal or slowing of reform.

In addition, it is now common to hear complaints that economic reform in the former CPEs is being slowed by the spoiling tactics of the 'old guard' of bureaucrats and state enterprise managers who see privatisation as a direct threat to their own privileged position in society. The above phenomenon has been well publicised in the states of the former Soviet Union but it appears the problem also exists in the more developed economies of Hungary, Poland and the CSFR. In the light of this, a further argument used to support privatisation is that since the 'old guard' cannot be removed overnight, their power has to be undermined through the creation of new pressure groups supporting private enterprise and the market economy; and it is privatisation which will allow this process to occur.

There is a third political argument to explain the current popularity of privatisation among the governments of former CPEs. This is that the announcement of privatisation programmes makes a clear political statement to the developed West of these governments' intentions to establish market economies. With such statements of intent, these governments expect to meet the requirements laid down by the developed market economies for obtaining economic assistance (Kiss, 1991). The desire to privatise on the part of these governments may actually diverge quite considerably from this statement of intent which would explain the relatively slow pace of privatisation thus far.

A further argument supporting the need for privatisation in the former CPEs is that privatisation should not be seen in isolation but should be put in the wider context of the need to develop a market economy. Privatisation is thus not only a process of transferring ownership rights from the state to the private sector but involves a deeper evolutionary process which acts to educate the population about the workings of a fully functioning market economy. Already the process of learning can be seen. Thus, as economists from the former CPEs grapple with the problems of privatisation they are realising that other reforms such as price liberalisation and the introduction of financial and capital markets are also required. Gradually, through the desire to privatise, a whole new market economic system is evolving as a result of a process of 'learning by doing'. Privatisation is thus acting as an important catalyst in the whole process of economic, political and social transformation in these economies.

9.2 Special problems of privatisation in the former CPEs

That the initial experience of privatisation should prove so disappointing, while partly a function of the unrealistic expectations encouraged by either politically motivated and/or economically naive political leaders, can also be explained by the very scale of the problem. Thus in the first eight years of privatisation under Mrs Thatcher's Conservative government in the UK, between 1979 and 1987, the proportion of GDP produced by state-owned enterprises was only reduced from 11.5 per cent to 7.5 per cent (Vickers and Yarrow, 1988). But the extent of state ownership is far higher in Eastern Europe, with typically over 70 per cent of employment and GDP being generated in the state sector. The privatisation plans for Hungary, Poland and the CSFR envisage the disposal of one half of state assets, producing about 30–40 per cent of GDP, within three years. Clearly such privatisation plans involve the sale or transfer of assets on a scale unparalleled in the history of privatisation anywhere else in the world. Even in developed market economies, privatisation on such a scale would be a daunting task, but in economies where the basic infrastructure and institutions of a market economy required for implementing privatisation are either absent or in various stages of construction, such rapid privatisation appears as more a dream than a reality. To mention just one issue, the underdevelopment of product and especially the labour and capital markets makes domestic prices highly unreliable hence the evaluation of enterprise assets and profitability in preparation for privatisation becomes extremely difficult.

High risks caused by the lack of information for the potential purchaser of privatised assets are compounded by the very poor state of production in the state sector of the former CPEs. Research by Hare and Hughes (1992) suggests that a substantial percentage of manufacturing production in these economies produces a negative value-added when production and inputs are valued at world market prices, especially after full account is taken of quality differences.[13] In Bulgaria for example over 50 per cent of manufacturing production yields negative value-added, in the CSFR the figure is 34.8 per cent, in Hungary 34.6 per cent and in the former Soviet Union 22.3 per cent. Only Poland fares a little better with a figure of only 8.4 per cent. In effect these measures imply that large sections of industry in the former CPEs are unattractive to potential investors, so retarding the pace of privatisation. Clearly, prior to or in parallel with privatisation, enterprise restructuring has to occur on quite an enormous scale.

The problems outlined above would suggest that privatisation cannot proceed without the implementation of a whole series of other inter-related reforms, including enterprise restructuring, price liberalisation and the development of the institutions of the market. This raises the question as to where privatisation fits into the sequence of reforms. Given the very poor state of many state enterprises, large-scale restructuring will be required to make those enterprises which are to be privatised attractive to potential investors. In the former East Germany (the new Länder in the united Germany), the state privatisation agency, the Treuhandanstalt, has placed the emphasis on the need to restructure enterprises prior to privatisation, despite which it has been able to proceed with privatisation relatively quickly. Even so, by October 1991 the Treuhandanstalt was still the sole owner of 55 per cent and the majority shareholder in a further 16.9 per cent of the 8,000 state firms placed under its control for privatisation (Carlin and Mayer, 1992). But East Germany, with its access to finance and other support from the Federal Republic, is a special case.[14]

Other CPEs, however, are less fortunate and lack of finance means that many see privatisation itself as the only means to bring about rapid enterprise restructuring. Thus transferring enterprises into the private sector means that these enterprises will have to sink or swim without recourse to state subsidies. The market would then determine which enterprises were profitable and should therefore attract investors' capital. The problem is that, although privatisation would in theory solve the problem of evaluating enterprise performance, private investors cannot be expected to invest in privatised, unrestructured enterprises in the first place without having access to reasonably reliable information regarding their potential future performance.

Ideally, privatisation should follow price liberalisation as it will only be after the emergence of *appropriate prices* that investors are able to evaluate the economic potential of enterprises to be privatised. Unfortunately the current economic structure in the former CPEs is highly monopolistic.

Consequently, price liberalisation without some form of competition policy would merely serve to increase state enterprise profits without either restructuring their activities or shedding light on their asset value or the real level of their profitability. Privatisation can in itself serve to strengthen competition policy if it is associated with steps to break up the large state monopolies.

For most of the economies in transition, with the exception of the former GDR, there may not be time for a proper sequencing of reforms to occur. As a result, privatisation is likely to take place in an *ad hoc* and piecemeal way with the economy operating for a time as a highly unusual hybrid system.

To make matters worse the knowledge of markets and privatisation by the populations of the former CPEs is limited. It is hardly surprising, given the numerous problems and uncertainties associated with privatisation, that surveys of public opinion in the region generally show a high degree of scepticism about privatisation, and a marked reluctance to participate in the process (via the purchase of shares) (for Poland, see Kozak, 1991; and Breitkopf *et al.*, 1991). In the former Soviet Union an opinion poll conducted in October 1990 suggested that only 8 per cent of respondents were willing to use their savings to purchase privatised assets and most preferred to work for state enterprises (Filatotchev, 1991, p. 493). However attitudes may be changing, as an opinion poll of Soviet urban dwellers published just before the coup of August 1991, suggested a high level of support for privatisation. Over 70 per cent supported the proposition that the transfer to a market would be impossible without private land ownership and small scale private enterprises. In addition over 50 per cent suggested that for a successful transition foreign firms had to be attracted into the country. When asked in which type of enterprise they would most like to work over 70 per cent suggested some form of private firm (Babayeva, 1991). There is, however, quite a large difference between the population realising that private enterprise is a prerequisite for successful transition, wanting to work in private enterprises (where wage rates are generally higher than in state employment), and actually being prepared to involve themselves actively in the privatisation process via the purchase of shares.

The relatively low level of interest in the privatisation process on the part of large sections of the population of the former CPEs can partly be explained by the fact that these economies are basically poor and hence the majority of people have relatively little excess income available to invest in shares. In Poland for example it has been estimated that at the end of 1990 the total available money stocks of the population in domestic and foreign currency amounted to some $12.4 billion or just 21 per cent of the net value of productive public sector assets. Making the bold presumption that the populations of the former CPEs would be prepared to invest a similar proportion of their financial wealth in shares as typically occurs in western market economies (namely about 15 per cent), this suggests that only about $1.86 billion would be available to invest in privatised assets. This is only about 3.5 per cent of the net value of public sector productive assets, far short of the targets set for the rate of privatisation (Breitkopf, 1991).

In any event the macro-economic stabilisation measures introduced in several of these economies have served to reduce sharply the real value of the populations' money balances, which could otherwise have been used to purchase shares in privatised companies. The experience in Hungary thus far is that even those sections of the population with the financial resources to invest shy away from investing in privatised assets preferring to invest in new business ventures instead.

All this suggests that privatisation based upon the sale of shares to the population of the former CPEs is likely to be a protracted process extending over many years.

It is not only the lack of available money incomes which causes concern in relation to privatisation, but also the distribution of income. Currently, those participating in the process are increasingly viewed as having earned their income from either illegal means in the 'grey' or 'black' economies or from having been prominent among the *nomenklatura* of the former communist system. This perception is creating a large amount of resentment towards the privatisation process, providing ammunition to those wishing to obstruct the process.

It was the desire to address these specific problems which stimulated the development of schemes for the free or favourable distribution of shares to workers and citizens. These schemes are discussed further below.

A problem largely absent from the privatisation debates in western market economies is assuming some importance with regard to privatisation in the former CPEs. This is the issue of the ownership of the assets to be privatised (Hodjera, 1991). In the western market economies privatised assets have generally, prior to privatisation, been in the ownership of the state. However, in the former CPEs much property is under collective or communal ownership. In the former Soviet Union there are some 26,000 collective farms which are currently in the process of being transformed into private companies and individual private farms by order of a decree of President Yeltsin.[15]

Problems arise in the division of collective property and assets such as farm machinery between cooperative members. In Hungary this has produced much debate on the form of the new law on the transformation of cooperatives. With regard to agricultural cooperatives there is a desire by the government to transform them into private companies or 'real cooperatives'. But unfortunately the new law is so complex and involves so many amendments that it is feared it will deter cooperative members from leaving the cooperatives and starting private businesses. In the meantime the uncertainty about the future of cooperatives is doing much to undermine their efficiency. Agricultural cooperatives in particular are spending considerable time defining their new organisational and ownership structure, which is having a serious impact on their production activities (Felix, 1991).

In the former CPEs there is an additional ownership issue which did not arise in western privatisation programmes. This concerns the restitution of property confiscated from private owners by the former communist regimes. In most of the Eastern and Central European economies it is generally recognised that former owners of land and property should receive compensation. The problem is to decide who should be entitled to compensation and in what form this compensation should be paid. It is also important to devise a restitution policy which meets the popular demand to put right past injustices, while not unduly impeding the privatisation process itself.

Clearly the restitution or compensation of land and property to members of the former nobility in these economies would be unpopular and unworkable. But it is far from easy to deal with the smaller property-holders, for in most cases at least 40 years have passed since confiscation. Establishing claims to property is therefore frequently difficult as many of the ownership records have been destroyed or are missing. In the case of land many of the relevant boundaries have since been changed and it is physically very difficult to establish the precise location of parcels of land now incorporated into large state and collective farms. For housing there is the tricky issue of how to deal with the present occupants, and for commercial or industrial assets, it is almost impossible to identify or value something equivalent to what existed at the time of confiscation.

With regard to the means of compensation, the return of the actual assets confiscated to their former owners is therefore often impracticable. Even where assets do exist in their former state their direct transfer back to former owners is often difficult and depends upon the current ownership position. The transfer of assets currently occupied by a collective or cooperative ownership structure clearly presents a difficult political problem. In most cases the decision has been taken to compensate former owners either in the form of other assets or in the form of a monetary compensation payment.

In the severely depressed state of these economies financing claims for compensation from former owners is a problem in itself, especially as controlling state expenditure is seen as a precondition for imposing economic stabilisation. Hungary has gone some way to solving this problem by compensating former owners of assets in the form of property bonds to be redeemed against the purchase of shares in newly privatised companies or land. It is estimated that the government will have to issue bonds to the value of $1.4 billion to meet the claims of former owners and their descendants. In the case of land confiscated and transformed into agricultural cooperatives, this is to be auctioned off to the highest bidder with former owners able to use their property bonds in the bidding process. Those former owners who are prepared to farm the land receive 100 per cent compensation for their land up to a maximum value of $2,700 (Okolicsányi, 1991). Poland has adopted a similar scheme and former owners are to be compensated in the form of privatisation bonds to be used to purchase shares in privatised state enterprises. By September 1991 there were some 50,000 outstanding claims for the reprivatisation of real estate and 500 for businesses (Wellisz and Iwanek, 1991).[16]

9.3 The design of privatisation programmes in the former CPEs

As outlined above, the problems which have had to be addressed in the design of privatisation programmes in the former CPEs are somewhat more complex than those associated with privatisation in the Western market economies. This fact goes some way to explain why privatisation has thus far proceeded rather slowly. In addition, while it appears that there are numerous benefits to be gained from privatisation in the former CPEs, such as the improvement in economic efficiency, macro-economic stabilisation and enhanced political support, many of these are not mutually compatible. This has complicated the privatisation process.

For instance, the desire to improve economic efficiency is likely to conflict with that of developing a large political mass of support for the privatisation process. Thus to gain the widest possible support for the privatisation programme requires that shares are distributed as widely as possible among the population. It is unlikely that a direct sale of shares in privatised enterprises to the population could meet this objective given the relatively low money incomes (and low available savings) of the majority of the population in the former CPEs. Thus some form of free or favourable share issue would have to be devised which would, by definition, result in the exchequer earning less money from the privatisation process. Consequently, the privatisation programme would make a smaller contribution towards the control of inflation.

In the CSFR and Poland, the desire to involve the widest possible cross-section of the population in privatisation has been a priority *vis-à-vis* the desire to earn revenue for the state budget. In the CSFR shares in privatised companies are to be distributed to workers on a largely free basis by means of a voucher scheme. All CSFR citizens wishing to participate in the privatisation programme must first register their interest by paying a small fee of approximately $35, after which they are allocated vouchers to the value of 1,000 points to be redeemed against shares in privatised companies. A list of the first group of enterprises to be privatised in this way has been published, with financial information on firms' performance and asset values. Individual voucher holders are to use their vouchers to bid for shares in the enterprises of their choice by means of an auction process. The auction process began on 16 March 1992.

In the Russian privatisation programme, instead of vouchers citizens are to be allocated 'privatisation accounts' which are to be actual monetary credits in bank accounts; these will only be redeemable against purchases of shares in privatised enterprises.[17]

The free or favourable distribution of shares to the population also has the potential advantage of bringing about a relatively rapid rate of privatisation. On the other hand, privatisation based on the sale of assets would be a lengthy process, perhaps occurring over decades rather than the relatively short time periods envisaged by the present governments. If it is the case that privately owned enterprises operate more efficiently than state-owned enterprises, then surely the primary objective should be to dispose of assets relatively quickly. In this case the desire to sell state assets clearly conflicts with that of improving the efficiency of enterprise performance.[18]

In addition the free disposal of shares in state assets is also frequently supported on the grounds that this method is the most equitable means of bringing about privatisation. There is a widely held view in the former CPEs that privatisation involves the sale of property already belonging to the people represented by the state. After all, how can property which people already own be sold to them? This view is quite widely held in the states of the former Soviet Union, particularly with regards to land, and it appears to be hindering the privatisation process. This does highlight a particular problem in Russia, where prior to collectivisation land was traditionally farmed communally via the village commune or *mir*. Attempts to promote privatisation are likely to come up against quite strong support for traditional communal property ownership. In another state of the former Soviet Union, Kazakhstan, the privatisation of land has been rejected by the government on the similar grounds that private land ownership conflicts with the Kazakh tradition of nomadic herding.

A wide distribution of free shares in privatised assets would apparently go some way to circumvent this problem, but one wonders how equitable this would be in practice. In Russia housing is currently being privatised by means of the free or favourable disposal of property to the sitting tenants. It is obvious, however, that those currently living in prized locations like the centre of Moscow are being given an implicit rental windfall as compared to those living in less favourable locations.

In a similar vein the argument most frequently used against the CSFR voucher scheme is that information on the performance of enterprises to be privatised is quite complex and the information available to individuals will vary. Some individuals are likely to have 'inside information' on particular enterprises and therefore will be at an advantage relative to others in deciding in which enterprises to redeem their vouchers. This argument, while formally correct, surely overstates the likely inequities from the voucher scheme. The scheme must be more equitable than the sale of shares in privatised companies to the highest bidders which, because of existing income inequalities, is likely to isolate large sections of the population from the privatisation programme. In the voucher scheme, at least the poorer sections of society are given some chance to participate in the programme and if they make the wrong choices regarding the purchase of shares then the likelihood is that they will accept the personal responsibility themselves. In addition similar problems of unequal information would be present in any privatisation scheme whether through the sale of shares or a voucher type scheme.

Privatisation programmes which envisage the free distribution of shares do however have the advantage that, in theory at least, they should also produce a redistribution of income from richer to poor individuals. Thus, once vouchers are redeemed against shares in privatised companies (or trusts) the poor will presumably wish to sell their shares to richer individuals. In this sense the free distribution of shares to the population, if accompanied by poorer individuals reselling shares to the rich, will temporarily reduce the need for state welfare programmes and thus reduce budget expenditure and state budget deficits.

However, it is likely that the poorer sections of society in the former CPEs will not participate even in schemes involving the free distribution of shares. One reason for this is that the poor are less well educated, and may simply be confused by the complexity of privatisation schemes. This problem will be worse in the case of 'opt-in' schemes such as in the CSFR where individuals must first register their interest in participating in the scheme. Thus as of November 1991 only 100,000 people had registered for the scheme and only one-third of these had registered an interest in participating (Carlin and Mayer, 1992). By the end of December 1991, however, some 400,000 people had bought vouchers with the final deadline for their purchase initially being the end of January 1992.[19] This low initial interest in the voucher scheme appeared to be due to the lack of information and of understanding of how the scheme and for that matter of how share markets operate. In order to overcome these problems the CSFR government stepped up advertising of the voucher scheme, a policy which appears to have been successful as by March 1992 some 8.4 million people had registered for the voucher scheme or 60 per cent of the adult population. Given the high response to the scheme individual citizens were likely to receive a smaller allocation of the $9 billion of state assets to be privatised.

The free distribution of shares has also been criticised on the grounds that it would dilute attempts to improve enterprise efficiency. With shares widely dispersed, exercising effective ownership control over enterprise management might be difficult and hence there would not be enough pressure on managers from shareholders to manage efficiently. Unlike in Western market economies, where large institutional investors are represented on company boards and can therefore pressure management to improve performance, the free dispersion of shares would result in shareholders individually being too small to exert sufficient pressure on managers.

In order to reduce the problem of the asymmetry of information and so as to simplify the privatisation process, most of the former CPEs including Romania and now even Albania are developing investment trusts to act as holding companies or mutual trusts for shares in privatised state assets. In Poland these are called 'National Wealth Management Funds' and in Romania 'Private Ownership Trusts'. The system envisages that the shares of privatised enterprises will be allocated between a number of these trusts. Citizens are then able to purchase shares or redeem vouchers against shares in these trusts. The trusts are responsible for managing the share portfolios which they have been allocated by governments and are able to buy and sell shares in privatised enterprises. Likewise, at a later stage citizens will be able to buy and sell shares in the managed trusts. It will be the responsibility of the management of the trusts to manage their portfolios with the interests of their shareholders in mind.

In the CSFR some 480 of these assets funds had been authorised by March 1992 but only 237 had registered with the Ministry of Finance, a requirement for the funds to operate. Citizens can entrust their vouchers to these funds which then bid for shares in privatised assets using these vouchers. In the CSFR some concern has been expressed over the lack of regulation surrounding the operation of these trusts. One of the reasons given for the rapid last minute rush to register for the voucher scheme was that many of the privatisation funds have offered to redeem vouchers for up to ten times their nominal face value. There appears to be little basis for these offers and it is likely that many citizens would be disappointed one year later.[20]

224

Initially, the share portfolios of individual trusts will be quite similar. Citizens purchasing shares in these trusts or redeeming vouchers in them will also begin from a more equitable point. Given the relatively small number of trusts (except in the CSFR, as just indicated) it will be quite easy for citizens to compare the performances of each trust by their share prices and the level of dividends paid. It will also be in the interest of the trust managers to put pressure on enterprises within their share portfolios to operate efficiently as their own performances will be directly linked to that of these enterprises. Trusts would thus appear to overcome the problem of the lack of ownership control being exerted on enterprise management in the free share scheme. Trusts, because of their size relative to enterprises, will be able to pressure enterprises into maintaining a certain level of efficiency. To aid this process it is envisaged that many trusts will be managed by Western companies but with the overall control of the trusts resting with boards of directors composed of members from the host nations.

Hungary has preferred not to follow the example of Poland and the CSFR with a free disposal of shares through a voucher scheme. Instead, to promote as wide a participation in the privatisation process as possible Hungary has introduced a number of credit schemes through which citizens can borrow money to purchase shares in privatised enterprises. The so-called E-Credit scheme has however proved to be somewhat disappointing thus far. By December 1991 only 776 such loans had been taken out. It appears that citizens have been relatively unwilling to take up loans given the degree of economic uncertainty in the economy. In addition banks which offered these loans required a relatively large amount of collateral as security from lenders in such schemes, which has tended to put off potential applicants.[21]

While opinion polls reveal an unwillingness on the part of workers to participate in the privatisation process in general, there appears to be more interest by workers to participate in the privatisation of their own enterprise (Kozak, 1991). In order to build on this to increase participation in the privatisation process, many of the former CPEs are actively encouraging 'worker buy outs'. For example, in the privatisation programme of the Russian Federation announced at the end of 1991 there were a number of incentive schemes to encourage worker participation. Tenders by collectives of workers from enterprises to be privatised were to receive priority in the sale of those enterprises. In addition where enterprises are to be privatised by means of a share issue workers can receive a free allocation of shares up to a maximum of 25 per cent of the capital value of the enterprise. Workers also have the right to purchase an additional 10 per cent of the capital value of the enterprise in the form of shares at a one-third discount. Instalment schemes are being introduced to improve the ability of workers to participate in such schemes.[22] As a further example of how the Russian government is encouraging worker participation in the privatisation process, representatives of workers' councils are included in the privatisation committees established to produce privatisation plans for individual enterprises. The workers' councils have the ability to veto privatisation plans, which gives workers an ability to disrupt the privatisation process if they should so desire.

The question of worker participation in the privatisation process again brings forward the problem of the conflicting objectives of privatisation. While large-scale worker participation in privatisation is desirable on the grounds of increasing overall participation in the process, it is likely to conflict with the objective of improving enterprise efficiency. In particular worker-managed firms and employee share ownership plans (ESOPs) are widely regarded as being less efficient than other types of private ownership because there is an incentive on the part of the workforce to have objectives other than the long run profitability of the enterprise. Thus workers in these enterprises might prefer to avoid taking difficult decisions such as making workers redundant as this could threaten their own positions within the firm as workers. In addition workers are likely to try to maximise current consumption in the form of higher wages and shy away from investment which would increase the long-run returns to the enterprise (Winiecka, 1991). The experience of worker self-management in Yugoslavia tends to support this hypothesis of worker self-managed firms being less efficient (Estrin, 1983).

Worker 'buy-outs' or the preferential distribution of shares to workers can also be questioned on the grounds of equity. It is fairly obvious that share discounts are more valuable to workers in more profitable enterprises than for those in less profitable industries. Those fortunate enough to work in such profitable enterprises may therefore be given a rental windfall bearing no relation to their own contribution to the profitability of the enterprise. Likewise citizens other than the workers in the enterprises are excluded from the privatisation process and hence are discriminated against despite the fact that the current profitability of the enterprise might well be a function of previous large-scale capital investment made from the state budget and hence from taxes levied on the population at large.

Foreign participation in the privatisation process could present one means to overcome the lack of domestic funds and so serve to accelerate the whole process of privatisation. The attitude towards foreign investment has however been mixed. On the one side there is a strong desire to encourage foreign involvement if this produces an influx of capital, technology and an improvement in management. On the negative side there is a commonly held fear among many in the former CPEs that foreign business will simply buy up, at knock-down prices, large sections of these economies. There is some justification for this as with exchange rates in the former CPEs typically very weak the prices of privatised assets appear very low for Western investors. As an example in Russia with the current exchange rate of 80 roubles to the dollar foreign investors could purchase 60 per cent of all enterprises in the food industry for under $500 million, 60 per cent of enterprises in the light industrial sector for less than $150 million and 70 per cent of enterprises in the construction industry for less than $150 million.[23] To overcome this problem the Russian government has introduced a separate exchange rate of 10 roubles to the dollar for foreign investors wishing to purchase assets in privatised enterprises. Foreign investment is also excluded from certain 'strategic' sectors of the economy.

Typically foreign investment in the former CPEs has been encouraged through the use of tax breaks and the priority sale of some of the better enterprises in package deals to foreign investors. As an example of this priority sale, in 1989 General Electric purchased a 75 per cent stake in Tungsram, one of the relatively few profitable Hungarian enterprises. General Electric's motivation for the purchase was to increase its market share in the European market, which as a result of the deal increased from 2 to 9 per cent (Kiss, 1991, p. 11). The sale of state assets to Western companies has been a key part of the privatisation programme of the Treuhandanstalt in East Germany.

Generally, however, the experience thus far with inward foreign investment in the former CPEs has been rather disappointing with foreign investors appearing to hold back from making large-scale investment. Hungary, which has received a large part of all inward foreign investment in Eastern Europe because of its more developed economic and political situation, received only $1 billion in foreign investment in 1990, although this was double the level received in 1989. This took the share of foreign capital in the economy to just 3 per cent. Of concern though is the fact that only 15 individual foreign investments in Hungary amounted to more than $10 million, with most amounting to less than $1 million. The tendency in Hungary at least has been for much of the inward foreign investment to be dominated by Hungarian expatriates investing in family retail and service enterprises (Kiss, 1991, p. 10).

Hungary plans to increase the share of foreign ownership in its economy to 25–30 per cent within three to four years (Apathy, 1991). Figures for the contribution of foreign investment to the privatisation programme in 1991 do seem a little more hopeful, with 80 per cent of the revenue earned from privatisation coming from foreign investment. This still, however, amounts to only just over $500 million, although total foreign investment in Hungary increased to a respectable $1.4 billion dollars in 1991.

Of the foreign investment which has been made thus far in Eastern Europe, it has frequently been the case that the Western companies have demanded a high price from the governments of the former CPEs. The recent announcement by Mercedes Benz is a case in point. Mercedes expressed a willingness to acquire a 31 per cent and 20 per cent share respectively in two of the CSFR's main manufacturers of trucks, Avia and Liaz, but only on the understanding that the CSFR government provided the company with tax holidays, agreed to the removal of tariffs on the import of spare parts for the company, provided state subsidies for investment, and agreed to the introduction of a 40 per cent tariff on all imports of utility vehicles into the CSFR so as to protect Mercedes Benz's investment. In a similar vein, in 1991, as a condition for Volkswagen taking a stake in Skoda the CSFR government was forced to concede to Volkswagen demands for the imposition of an import tariff on cars entering the CSFR market so as to protect VW's investment. Increasing import tariffs puts the CSFR in conflict with its EC Association agreement.[24] In Poland Fiat, General Motors and Volkswagen have pressurised the government into allowing these companies to import 10,000 vehicles apiece duty free in exchange for an agreement to invest $50 million in the

Polish automobile industry. As a result of the Polish government's compliance Fiat has agreed to purchase a 51 per cent stake in the FSM factory in Bielsko-Biala and GM has expressed an interest in acquiring a 70 per cent stake in the Warsaw FSO factory.[25]

Given the reluctance of many foreign investors to participate in the privatisation of even the best East European enterprises without being provided with incentives it seems highly unlikely that this will provide an option for *en masse* privatisation. The fact that many state enterprises in the former CPEs are highly inefficient and loss-making tends to support this claim. In any event it seems likely that the widescale sale of state assets to foreigners would create a great deal of resentment especially in times of increasing national awareness. Governments in the former CPEs can therefore be expected to continue to control the amount of foreign participation in privatisation.

9.4 Privatisation in practice: a case study of Poland

Poland was one of the first of the former CPEs to begin the process of introducing market reform. The seeds of reform can be traced back to the communist Jaruzelski regime which began to liberalise the economy from the early 1980s onwards in an attempt to contain the rise of the Solidarity movement. But the elections of 1989 brought to power a Solidarity-dominated government strongly committed to market reform and privatisation was seen as a pivotal part of these reforms. Poland has now had a period of over ten years of reform. In this respect Poland, along with Hungary, is not typical of the other former CPEs. Despite the talk of 'shock therapy' it would be more appropriate to describe the Polish reform process as one of a gradual adjustment period followed by a rapid acceleration in the pace of economic reform. Other former CPEs were, at the end of the 1980s, thrust into the hot water of economic reform without being allowed to test the water as the Poles and Hungarians had done. However, despite the crucial differences in reform experience of Poland, many of the former CPEs are using the Polish experience of economic reform and in particular of privatisation as a model to follow. This makes Poland a particularly suitable case study for privatisation in the former CPEs.

Privatisation had already begun in Poland under the former communist regime from about 1986 onwards with the emergence of *nomenklatura* privatisation. The State Enterprise Law of 1981 allowed state-owned enterprises to enter into contracts with private partners. The management of the state enterprises frequently formed their own private companies and then entered into agreements with their parent state enterprises. The capital contribution of the state enterprise to the partnership typically consisted of physical assets which were often deliberately undervalued to the advantage of the management of both the state and private firm as these were the same individuals. This form of corrupt privatisation did much to discredit the privatisation process in Poland. As Wellisz and Iwanek (1991) point out, this explains the otherwise rather strange phenomenon whereby the Solidarity leadership initially opposed privatisation in favour of collective ownership and democratic planning, while the communist government was more supportive of privatisation.

It was not until the election of the first non-communist government in 1989 that Poland began to develop a comprehensive privatisation strategy. The overall objective was to implement privatisation as quickly as possible to enable rapid restructuring to occur. To facilitate this a Ministry for Ownership Transformation (MOT) was created to oversee the entire privatisation process. After some heated debate, the final version of the Law on Privatisation presented to the Sejm (Parliament) on 13 July 1990 was something of a hybrid. In trying to satisfy the often conflicting demands on privatisation it allowed for a multiplicity of forms of privatisation from the sale of shares, the free distribution of shares to the population (via vouchers), and employee ownership. Three privatisation paths can be identified for state enterprises:

(a) Small Privatisation
In most of the former CPEs the privatisation of small-scale service enterprises, such as shops and restaurants, is often the easiest part of a privatisation programme and allows for the achievement of rapid results relatively quickly. This is helped by the often more favourable public reaction to this form of privatisation. Public opinion polls have shown that 90 per cent of the respondents favour this form of privatisation and 40 per cent express a willingness to participate themselves (Wellisz and Iwanek, 1991). 'Small' privatisation is thus commonly the first to be implemented. Poland has not been the exception in this regard, as by the end of 1990 70 per cent of all retail outlets had been transferred to the private sector. The sale has been administered by local councils as the Law on Privatisation decreed that from May 1990 the ownership of assets in the service and distribution sector, such as shops, restaurants and building services, should be transferred to local authorities. Although the sale of these assets was not permitted until after October 1990 most shops are in fact rented or leased (Grosfeld and Hare, 1991). Blazyca (1991, p. 42) suggests that local authorities have been enticed away from the sale of assets by the high leaseholds that can be obtained from rentals. Local councils are to decide on whether employees should be given preference.

The small privatisation has not however been without its problems. Where premises have been sold, the type of business activity has often changed. Thus, there has been a tendency to change from the provision of basic foodstuffs to luxury imported goods where profit margins are higher. The result has been a shortage of retail outlets meeting the basic provisions of the population and there have been numerous demonstrations by local inhabitants and employees over this problem. The problem has, however, been alleviated somewhat by the emergence of a flourishing street-market culture.

(b) Privatisation through capitalisation
The second means of privatisation adopted in Poland is that of the flotation of shares in joint stock companies. The first stage of this process involves the commercialisation of a state enterprise prior to privatisation. This entails the transformation of the state enterprise into a joint stock company

under the ownership of the Treasury. Net revenues from the privatisation would thus accrue to the Treasury. Once commercialised, enterprises have some two years in which to be privatised. Commercialisation can be initiated by the MOT or by the management and employees of the enterprise. Where the commercialisation is requested from within the enterprise the MOT has the right of veto where it believes the enterprise is in such a poor financial state as to threaten the success of the privatisation. By the end of September 1991 some 214 state enterprises had become commercialised and were awaiting privatisation (Szomburg, 1991).

The sale of commercialised enterprises can proceed in three ways: a sale by tender, a public share offer, or a negotiated sale.

It is the duty of the MOT to determine the timing and means of sale for each enterprise. Workers are given the option of purchasing 20 per cent of the shares in a flotation at a 50 per cent discount.

To set the so-called 'large' privatisation process in motion at the end of November 1990 the MOT announced a list of seven state enterprises which were to be sold through a share flotation. These enterprises were specially selected as being of particularly sound financial status, although subsequently two of these were stood down from a share flotation, one being sold to the employees and in the other valuation problems delayed its privatisation. Western consultants were actively involved in the flotation, providing economic analysis of the enterprises concerned and preparing prospectuses. The public flotation lasted for three weeks from 30 November 1990 and was (modestly) oversubscribed for all the firms concerned. Employees were also offered 20 per cent of the shares at a 50 per cent discount. In total the flotation raised some $35 million. The privatisation has been criticised on the grounds that the transactions costs involved were high at approximately 13 per cent of the value of the enterprises (Wellisz and Iwanek, 1991). Much of this expenditure consisted of payments to foreign consultants and on advertising. In addition the fact that the flotation was oversubscribed can partly be explained by the fact that in an attempt to make the flotation successful the offer price of shares was set on the low side (cf. the corresponding UK experience).

While the costs of these sales were high this model of privatisation has generally been seen as a success as important lessons were learnt from the process. A further large state enterprise was privatised in this way in May 1991, six more were prepared for privatisation in the summer of 1991 and 20 or so over the winter of 1991–2. Of the initial five privatised, however, one was said to be on the point of bankruptcy and another two were said to be in serious financial trouble soon after privatisation.

(c) Privatisation through liquidation

Bankrupt enterprises can apply to the MOT to be privatised by means of liquidation. The assets of the enterprise are then either sold off by means of an auction or leased out, most commonly to corporations. Privatisation through liquidation has also been seen as a back door means to develop worker ownership, as the privatisation legislation requires that corporations leasing assets from the liquidated enterprise have to include among their stockholders employees of the former enterprise. It has in fact proved to be the most popular means of privatisation, especially for small to medium enterprises employing less than 400 workers. Thus, by the end of September 1991 some 667 enterprises had been privatised by means of liquidation, most being small or medium-sized (Szomburg, 1991).

In February 1991 the privatisation programme drawn up by the MOT was approved by the Sejm. This proposed an acceleration in the privatisation process with the above relatively conventional methods of privatisation being supplemented by the mass privatisation of the largest 500 Polish enterprises: these accounted for 40 per cent of state enterprise employment and 65 per cent of the total value of output.[26] This was to be achieved by means of conventional sales through share flotations, an outright sale to individual investors and a large-scale free distribution of shares through a voucher scheme. The privatisation of a further 2,500 industrial and 3,000 other small and medium-sized enterprises is to be by means of buy-outs, sales and liquidation.

There has been considerable discussion as to how the voucher scheme would operate. The final version of the mass privatisation programme was published in June 1991 and suggests that instead of vouchers every Polish citizen aged over 18 will be allocated a single share in one of a number of managed trusts. These trusts will then be allocated shares from privatised enterprises with 33 per cent of the shares in each privatised enterprise being allocated to a leading fund and 27 per cent of the shares being subdivided between the other funds. The state is to retain a further 30 per cent of shares for disposal at a later date and 10 per cent of shares are reserved for employees. It is hoped that privatisation via the managed trusts will be simplified. Citizens will not then be faced by a vast informational problem in purchasing shares or redeeming vouchers against shares in privatised enterprises. In addition the allocation to individual trusts of a large allocation of shares in each privatised enterprise ensures that ownership control will be exercised on enterprise management, encouraging their efficient performance.

Poland is now actively seeking to encourage inward foreign investment to speed up its privatisation process. On 4 July 1991 the Polish government introduced a new foreign investment law, which allowed for the full repatriation of profits and abolished the need for foreign firms to obtain permits if they wished to invest in Polish companies, except in the case of investment in certain strategic sectors of the economy. In addition foreign investors are now able to wholly own Polish companies, although the three-year tax break which had existed since 1988 for companies with foreign investors was removed.[27]

Conclusions

There is little doubt as to the importance of privatisation to the economic and political transformation of the former CPEs. Privatisation can, as described above, deliver a number of policy objectives, although often these are not mutually compatible.

In many respects privatisation is seen as the weather vane for signalling the success of reform, which is rather unfortunate as privatisation is but one part, albeit perhaps the most important, of an entire package of reforms which needs to be implemented for these economies to negotiate successfully the transition to developed market economies. Privatisation can be only partially successful unless it is accompanied by a whole series of supporting micro-level reforms such as the reform of the banking and legal systems (and in particular the establishment of the law of contract as an integral part of the business ethos), tax reform and the development of competition policy. The relatively disappointing progress of privatisation thus far must surely be attributed to the failure, or rather inability, of the new governments in the former CPEs to implement this 'package' of reforms.

The reality however is that this package of accompanying reforms cannot be introduced overnight. Reform of the entire economic, legal and political system is required, and this will take time, even if the structures are modelled on those in Western market economies. Reform and change of any kind is disruptive and needs some adaptation to local conditions. Thus privatisation, and for that matter the entire reform process in the former CPEs, has to be developed to meet specific conditions in individual countries.

Following the logic through to its conclusion suggests that privatisation will be a lengthy process. Yet this presents a problem, since it implies that for some time yet the majority of large industrial enterprises will remain in the state sector. If overall enterprise efficiency is to be improved then measures need to be introduced to tackle the problem of inefficiency in these state-owned enterprises. As Vickers and Yarrow (1988) suggest, privatisation, and therefore ownership, is not the crucial determinant of enterprise efficiency, but competition is. Measures thus need to be introduced to increase competition in general in Eastern Europe. An obvious initial step which must be taken is the removal of the 'soft budget constraint' for enterprises. Thus, enterprises, be they in the state or private sector, must realise that if they are unable to operate profitably they will face the prospect of bankruptcy. The threat of closure must therefore act to stimulate improved performance. This not only implies a new enterprise mentality but also a new role for the state, which must pull itself back from intervening in enterprise activities. The state has to learn how to say no to inefficient enterprises (and workers) requesting financial support to prevent bankruptcy.

Many existing state enterprises in the former CPEs have the advantage of being in a monopolistic or close to monopolistic market position and hence have relatively little motivation to act efficiently. Anti-monopoly legislation has to be introduced. One means of overcoming the monopoly problem would be to increase market access for foreign competitors. Already market access has been greatly improved in the former CPEs. The evidence suggests that this is already having the desired effect as there are increasing demands by domestic firms, unable to compete with foreign companies, to impose import restrictions. If domestic firms are to be taught how to compete and produce efficiently then these demands must be resisted. It is disappointing that in some markets, notably in agriculture, many East European governments are increasing barriers to trade.

In summary, privatisation in the former CPEs has generally failed to live up to the expectations set for it. Those expectations were, however, too ambitious by far given the undeveloped nature of market institutions in these economies. Privatisation should be seen as a longer-term process and as but one part of a wider market reform strategy. Already popular disillusionment with the early privatisation process has forced the new Polish government to put a large part of its privatisation programme on hold. The whole future of the programme now appears somewhat uncertain, although the IMF is encouraging the Polish government to push ahead with rapid privatisation. In the CSFR the results of the voucher scheme were not immediately apparent. Even Hungary has had to scale down the pace of its privatisation programme until market institutions are developed further.

Some of the research for this chapter was carried out with the help of an ESRC under the East-West Programme, for which the authors are grateful.

Notes

1. Hereafter referred to as the former Centrally Planned Economies, i.e. former CPEs.
2. East European Statistics Service, East West Publications, No. 188, 24 January 1992, p. 1.
3. *News from Prague*, 12/1991, p. 1.
4. Figures produced by the Yugoslavian Federal Institute of Statistics but excluding Croatia.
5. *Ekonomika i Zhizn'*, No. 4, January 1992, pp. 4–5.
6. Increasing budget deficits in the former Soviet Union in 1991 were primarily the result of the collapse of the tax base. In the old central planning mechanism taxes were collected from state enterprises through the ministerial hierarchy. However with the collapse of the economic system the authority of ministries has now largely evaporated and with it their ability to collect taxes. New private enterprises are developing but the tax authorities often find it difficult to monitor the activities of these new enterprises which have frequently grown out of the black economy. The state budget crisis in many of the former CPEs has been compounded because of the impact of government macro-economic stabilisation programmes which have generally cut economic activity and hence also government tax revenues, as well as increasing unemployment and therefore the expenditure of the state on social welfare programmes. New tax reforms are currently in the process of being introduced in all the former CPEs but until the tax system is fully in place government revenues are likely to continue to be squeezed.
7. *Financial Times*, 13 March 1992, p. 2
8. 'Basic programme for the privatisation of state and municipal enterprises in the Russian Federation in 1992' signed by Boris Yeltsin on 3 July 1991, *Ekonomika i Zhizn'*, No. 2, January 1992, pp. 18–20. In February 1992 the free market exchange rate for the rouble was approximately 80 roubles to the dollar.
9. *Heti Világgazgaság*, Vol. XIII, No. 51–2, 1991, p. 11.

10. However, the state may well have to write off the debts of currently loss-making enterprises to make them attractive to potential investors. Other loss-making enterprises which no longer obtain state subsidies and are currently unattractive to potential investors will presumably be forced to close in which case the state will have to fund unemployment and possibly redundancy payments. The restructuring of loss-making enterprises which privatisation requires is thus likely to continue to act as a severe drain on state budgets in the short to medium term so helping to increase inflationary pressures.

11. *RFE/RL Research Report,* Vol. 1, No. 7, 14 February 1992, p. 63.

12. *East Europe & USSR Agriculture and Food Monthly,* No. 113, February 1992, p. 15.

13. That is these enterprises produce a value of output which is less than the value of inputs used to produce that output.

14. Thus it is estimated that making GDR enterprises viable for privatisation has involved the Treuhandanstalt writing off 75 per cent of their debts.

15. See the resolution of the government of the Russian Federation, 'concerning orders for the reorganisation of collective and state farms', signed 29 December 1991, *Sel'skaya Zhizn',* 7 January 1992, p. 1.

16. In the states of the CIS this problem is less serious. Few former owners of land are currently alive, as in most cases property was confiscated over 50 years ago. In the Baltic states, however, the problem of compensating former owners is assuming some importance.

17. There is some concern that monetarising privatisation credits in this way will cause the money supply and hence inflation to be increased. Monies from these 'privatisation accounts' used to purchase shares are to flow into the accounts of those organs deemed to have owned the former assets. These bodies, such as local councils, are expected to use these resources firstly to cover budget deficits and only then to fund additional spending on such things as welfare programmes.

18. The issue is actually more complicated, since free distribution alone may not ensure that effective new management structures emerge from the privatisation process. Hence devising proper management structures, and reforming the ways in which enterprises are linked to the financial system, must also be part of successful privatisation programmes.

19. *RFE/RL Research Report,* Vol. 1, No. 3, 1992, p. 46.

20. *Central European,* February 1992, p. 12.

21. *Heti Világgazgaság,* Vol. XIII, No. 51–52, p. 57.

22. 'Basic programme for the privatisation of state and municipal enterprises in the Russian Federation in 1992', signed by Boris Yeltsin on 3 July 1991, *Ekonomika i Zhizn',* No. 2, January 1992, pp. 18–20.

23. Figures derived from 'Basic programme for the privatisation of state and municipal enterprises in the Russian Federation in 1992', signed by Boris Yeltsin on 3 July 1991, *Ekonomika i Zhizn',* No. 2, January 1992, pp. 18–20.

24. *East-West,* No. 518, 16 January 1992, pp. 5–7.

25. *RFE/RL Research Report,* Vol. 1, No. 5, 31 January 1992, p. 51.

26. However, practical problems of privatising such a large number of enterprises have resulted in the number of enterprises being scaled down to just 200.

27. Although companies which issued invoices prior to 4 July 1991 continue to enjoy the tax holiday. The Ministry of Finance can also offer tax breaks for foreign investors investing more than 2 million ECU or investing in regions suffering from particularly high unemployment.

References

Apathy, E. (1991) Hungary: a case study of the IBUSZ privatisation, ed. by Paul G. Hare, (for OECD).

Ash, T. N. and Hare, P. G. (1992) 'Economic Reform Proposals in the Soviet Union', chapter in C. Lin (ed.) *Limits to Transitions in Post-Soviet-type Systems.*

Babayeva, L. (1991) Privatisation: not against the grain, *Moscow News*, No. 31, August 4–11, p. 10.

Blazyca, G. (1991) Poland's next five years: the dash for capitalism, The Economist Intelligence Unit, Special Report No. 2110.

Breitkopf, M., Górski, M. and Jaszczynski, D. (1991) Privatisation in Poland, Friedrich-Ebert-Foundation, Economic and Social Policy Series, No. 6, Warsaw.

Carlin, W. and Mayer, C. (1992) Restructuring enterprises in Eastern Europe, paper presented for the 13th panel meeting of Economic Policy, Paris, 2–3 April, mimeo.

Charemza, W. (1991) Market failure and stagflation: some aspects of privatisation in Poland, University of Leicester Department of Economics Discussion Paper No. 163.

Estrin, S. (1983) *Self-Management: Economic Theory and Yugoslav Practice,* Cambridge: Cambridge University Press.

Felix, P. (1991) Reform of Agricultural Cooperatives, *Heti Világgazgaság,* vol. XIII, no. 49, December 7, p. 79.

Filatotchev, I. V. (1991) Privatisation in the USSR: economic and social problems, *Communist Economies and Economic Transformation*, vol. 3, no. 4, pp. 481–98.

Gomulka, S. (1986) *Growth, Innovation and Reform in Eastern Europe,* London: Harvester Press.

Gorbachev, B. (1992) Inflation greedily eats up savings, the population is resentful but endures the pain, *Ekonomika i Zhizn'*, no. 3, January p. 14.

Grosfeld, I. and Hare, P. (1991) Privatisation in Hungary, Poland and Czechslovakia, Centre for Economic Performance, Discussion Paper No. 31.

Hare, P. and Hughes, G. (1992) Industrial policy and restructuring in Eastern Europe, *Oxford Review of Economic Policy.*

Hodjera, Z. (1991) Privatisation in Eastern Europe: problems and issues, *Communist Economies and Economic Transformation*, vol. 3, no. 3, pp. 269–81.

Kiss, J. (1991) Privatisation in Hungary – wishful thinking or economic way-out?, paper prepared for the conference: 'International Privatisation: Strategies and Practices', University of St Andrew's, Scotland, 12–14 September.

Kornai, J. (1980) *Economics of shortage,* Amsterdam: North-Holland.

Kozak, M. (1991) Privatisation in Poland, *Communist Economies and Economic Transformation,* vol. 3, no. 2, pp. 155–67.

Okolicsányi, K., (1991) Compensation law finally approved, *Radio Liberty Report on Eastern Europe,* vol. 2, no. 36, pp. 22–5.

Szomburg, J., (1991) Poland: a country study, ed. by P. G. Hare (for OECD).

Vickers, J. and **Yarrow, G.** (1988) *Privatization: An Economic Analysis,* MIT Press, London.

Wellisz, S. and **Iwanek, M.** (1991) The privatisation of the Polish economy, paper presented at the conference, 'Moving to a Market Economy: Economic Reform in Eastern Europe and the Soviet Union', The Jerome Levy Economics Institute, Bard College, New York, October 25–26.

Winiecka, J. (1991) Theoretical underpinnings of the privatisation of state-owned enterprises in post-Soviet-type economies, *Communist Economies and Economic Transformation,* vol. 3, no. 4, pp. 397–416.

CHAPTER 10

Privatisation in less developed countries

Catherine Price

Introduction

Much of this volume examines aspects of the British privatisation programme, a reasonably coherent and integrated policy, even if it owed its genesis more to expedient financial and political forces than to a well thought-out philosophy. Privatisation in less developed countries (LDCs) is significantly different in several essentials. The policy is generally imported (often with Western aid) rather than home-grown; and there are as many varieties of experience of privatisation as there are countries and economies to whom the term 'less developed' applies; they usually experience much more rapid structural change and capital markets are much more narrow and underdeveloped. Moreover many of the factors which apply to more developed economies (MDCs) are writ large for less developed countries because of both market and government failure. Hence a distinct chapter on these countries is appropriate because the experience is very different from that in the UK, but these characteristics also pose some difficulties. The line between over-generalisation, and an incoherent list of various experiences is a delicate one to follow. Rather than an exhaustive list of privatisation programmes this chapter will mention specific examples within an overall framework, and refer interested readers to more comprehensive surveys.

The chapter first outlines the general features of developing countries. Specific aspects are then examined: first, the degree of market and government failure inherent in such economies, the macro-economic dimension of the problem, the significance of different forms of privatisation and their sequencing, and the identification of gainers and losers in the political context of the policy. Finally an assessment of the programme is suggested.

10.1 Privatisation and LDC characteristics

The similarities between LDCs should not obscure their differences, particularly in this context, the role that the state has played in development. Bouin and Michalet (1991) have identified three degrees of state involvement in LDCs: state dominated, state promoted or serving special interests. In the former, the state was seen as controlling the 'commanding heights' of industry, and taking an active role in any sectors considered strategic for either political or economic reasons. (The 1967 Arusha declaration for Tanzanian development is perhaps the best known statement of this philosophy.) Micro-economic considerations such as relation between costs and prices were not of prime importance. State ownership of enterprises is widespread, and often includes industries expropriated from former colonial powers. Such nationalised industries are seen as an integral part of the government's economic development plan, which is itself often highly centralised. State-promoted economies however see private industry as having a much more crucial role in the economy, with the state's purpose being to encourage such enterprise, using nationalised industries to guide but not dominate the economy. Governments where the state is seen as serving special interests (Malaysia with its New Economic Policy promoting the interests of the Malays is an overt example) are likely to use state industry in selective ways to meet such ends.

In all these countries, the public sector and nationalised industries in particular have experienced a large growth in the decades up to 1980. The reasons vary though the objectives, to achieve economic independence and freedom from foreign domination, are often similar. Both the state itself and nationalised industries were expected to play a significant role in economic development. On independence, many countries took over the administration of industries from the departing colonial power. Leaders of the newly independent states were often members of the ex-colonial administration with a predisposition for central administration. For many African and Asian countries independence in the 1960s meant growth and development of public enterprise. Expropriation was part of the desire both to control vital (often export) industries and to indigenise the economy. In southern and Latin America independence had usually come earlier, but state involvement increased during the 1930s and '40s when traditional links with North America and Europe were weakened and supply shortages arose. Governments encouraged state industries to fill the gap created by the missing imports.

Import substitution was further encouraged in the 1960s and early '70s, when developing countries dependent on primary commodity exports and manufactured inputs experienced a steady worsening of their terms of trade. Import substituting industrialisation (ISI) was identified as the solution, in which countries moved away from dependence on world markets by expanding the public sector to produce both intermediate and capital goods and final consumer products. Much of this programme was actively supported by the World Bank, and many such programmes flourished in the 1970s. Conditions were particularly favourable: the terms of trade moved temporarily in favour of the primary producers (led by oil in 1973), increasing export earnings; and the rise in oil prices and the recession in 'northern' countries released considerable 'petro-dollars' available for borrowing on easy terms. Thus the public sector in most developing countries expanded considerably, from 7 per cent of GDP in 1970 to 10 per cent in 1980 (Cook and Kirkpatrick, 1988), often with lax financial discipline. In developing countries as a whole public enterprise represented nearly 30 per cent of total investment (compared with 10 per cent in industrialised countries) and 11 per cent of value added (compared with 8 per cent for developed countries). However this 11 per cent average represents a range of 7 to 76 per cent, illustrating the diversity concerned (Adhikari and Kirkpatrick, 1990). The ratio of proportion of investment to output is much higher in LDCs, illustrating the sector's inefficiency. These figures seem even worse when account is taken of the greater diversity, i.e. not just inherently capital-intensive industries, of public enterprises in LDCs.

Public sector industries initially acquired or developed were traditionally concentrated in the public utilities and natural resource sectors, with an increasing stake in manufacturing as ISI policies were pursued. The infant industry argument for protecting them was invoked to capture the effects of dynamic externalities. These reflected the objectives of nationalisation in these countries to counteract the imperfect capital markets, thought to be unduly risk-averse, and to control industries with significant linkage effects. Both the efficacy of capital markets and the prospects for growth were thought to suffer from inadequate savings, and public enterprises were seen as a means for generating surpluses to counteract these tendencies. (This particular objective seems somewhat ironic in view of the deficits which most such sectors had generated 20 years later.) Socialism and interventionist economic management were seen as appropriate responses to the need for development in view of such market failures.

The form of public enterprise which LDCs developed was itself somewhat more varied than in the UK. Government ownership was often partial, though control was not necessarily affected. A particular form of public body, parastatal organisations, are unique to LDCs, acting as agricultural agencies and intermediaries between farmers and consumers or exporters. They are a logical unit in economies with poor infrastructure in roads, communications and information. But they have often been abused, making large losses through inefficiencies (sometimes an inevitable result of the prevailing circumstances). Such organisations came under double attack for their contribution to the budget deficit and for distorting prices and incentives within crucial markets.

The bubble of public sector expansion was bound to burst (at least with the benefit of hindsight). The crisis came almost universally in the early 1980s. The terms of trade suddenly worsened, exacerbated for non-oil exporting countries by the exogenous second oil price shock of 1978, causing drastic deterioration in the balance of payments. Demand was slow to respond since consumers were protected by artificially low exchange rates, and economies experienced shortages in vital imports rather than (or as well as) price rises. Real interest rates rose, increasing the burden of servicing, culminating in Mexico's default on overseas debt in 1982. After this international banks became very cautious about lending or even rescheduling outstanding debt. Many countries, from middle income

Latin American countries to impoverished African states were in severe difficulties. These external problems were accompanied by rampant inflation and large public sector debts. Import substituting industrialisation had failed, and its results were in marked contrast to the policy of newly industrialising countries such as Korea and Singapore to base development on the economic tradition of comparative advantage. Such countries had succeeded in competing in world markets after initial protectionism (especially in home markets).

International agencies and western governments were called upon to assist, not least in their own interests. The UK privatisation programme was still in its infancy, but the election of Margaret Thatcher and Ronald Reagan marked a political shift to the right and a new economic orthodoxy. The IMF and the World Bank started to expound a fresh export: the new market rationality. Missions were sent to countries considering privatisation to extol its virtues (and of course the services of experts from countries more experienced in implementing such a programme). These were sometimes camouflaged as seminars, but none the less betrayed a rather naive belief that the UK programme (say) could easily be transplanted to countries like Brazil. The problems in LDCs were not the same as in MDCs (nor even the same in different developing countries) and appropriate solutions were as varied as the circumstances.

Less developed countries may also differ from MDCs in the various objectives which they hope privatisation will serve. This is obvious in the case of governments serving special interests (often racial or ethnic), but this is merely an extreme case. Managerial and economic efficiency are clearly important in any economy, but may be subservient to distributional implications in countries where income distribution is very disparate and absolute poverty is rife. Moreover managerial efficiency may be more a means to the end of reducing the burden on the exchequer in countries where privatisation has been adopted (or imposed) as a result of external crisis. Macro-economic objectives are likely to loom larger as discussion later in this chapter shows. There are obvious parallels with Eastern Europe.

Privatisation in developing countries can be categorised by references to the original framework and models presented in the opening chapter. Here three aspects of privatisation were distinguished: denationalisation or divestiture, liberalisation, and contracting out. The same options apply in developing countries, where privatisation is even more of a catch-all phrase. The balance between forms of privatisation varies both between more and less developed countries and within the LDC category. Like privatisation in Eastern Europe (see Chapter 9 by Ash, Hare and Canning) privatisation (in all its manifestations) is but one of a series of economic reforms, where sequencing is all important but limited by local constraints.

In Chapter 1 several models of privatisation were outlined. Beesley and Littlechild (1989), in their first categorisation of privatisation and appropriate targets (in the UK context) identified as significant both the supply and demand characteristics of the market. Such models have been extended and developed for other economies where the balance of difficulties is different. Bos (1991) viewed the divestiture decision as one of degree rather than 'all or nothing', and focused on the extent of privatisation, i.e. transfer of assets from public to private owners, concluding that in normative terms sales were often less than the optimum. This is particularly relevant to LDCs where partial sales are a more likely solution than in the UK. Jones *et al.* (1990) also concentrated on divestiture, using cost-benefit analysis to highlight particular issues such as market structure in determining whether privatisation would increase welfare. Although this was equally applicable to MDCs the methodology was developed as a project for the World Bank and is therefore particularly appropriate to LDCs. Ott and Hartley (1991) on the other hand concentrate more on the internal than the external changes in firms. Of course many of the changes in external environment are significant primarily because they produce new incentives and behaviour in internal arrangements. However the concentration on internal alterations *per se* is particularly important for developing countries, both because of a greater perceived need and because the external environment may be more hostile. Thus the general framework is a helpful basis for assessing the experience of developing countries, though the interpretation may incorporate different emphases.

10.2   *Market and government failure*

Generalisation is dangerous even within a country, but particularly over a group of countries as diverse as Brazil, Tanzania, Malaysia and Bangladesh. However we have seen that there are some common experiences, both in terms of internal factors and external pressure. As a group these countries, by definition 'less developed' are more likely to experience market failure than are developed countries. The size of the (effective) market is smaller, incomes are lower and the economies are not only at an earlier stage of their development but have also for the most part experienced heavy protectionism during the 20 years until the early 1980s. The economies are often heavily dependent on a few exports, usually of primary products, and have experienced severe external shocks in the last decade. Indeed the destabilisation caused by these shocks often spawned their privatisation programmes. However their experience of government control and protection has not been without its problems, and excessive bureaucracy and corruption is common. Thus both market and government failure are likely to be greater than in, say, the UK.

Moreover environmental factors, another form of market failure, are also likely to be significant, both in absolute terms and because of increasing international concern. This is especially serious for countries hoping to industrialise and develop in a world committed to reduction of global warming and carbon dioxide emissions. In particular any move to limit emissions to existing levels on a country by country basis will prejudice the industrialisation plans of those whose present development (and emissions) are at a comparatively low level. These problems are even more poignant in view of developing countries' experiences of hosting the environmentally damaging industries of Western investors, often with significant danger to local populations.

Criticisms levelled at public industries were familiar: they were managerially inefficient and made inappropriate factor choices. Surveys of nationalised industries in developing countries have failed to establish this conclusively (Chan and Singh, 1992), but some evidence indicates that such perceptions are justified (Millward, 1988) and many run at a huge deficit. However it is important to note that the conflict of interests inherent in the UK nationalised industries (outlined in Chapter 3 in this volume) applied with even greater force to these countries. In particular distributional objectives in economies insufficiently developed to achieve them through more conventional means were very important, both for political and economic stability. This was often exacerbated by ill-defined property rights. Even where the state was interested in general development rather than specific interest groups, raising the income of the very poor was often seen as a (Keynesian) way of raising aggregate demand for macro-economic purposes, as well as for direct alleviation of poverty.

Similarly raising prices for necessities in the interests of allocative efficiency is much more difficult where there is no system of income support to cushion effects for the worst affected. Many of these problems had become institutionalised and compounded. For example the tradition of holding down public sector wages in an attempt to combat inflation, whose adverse effects were observed in the UK, became much more injurious in countries where inflation was rampant. Here public servants could no longer earn a living wage in their official employment, and were forced to take second private sector jobs, or, where pressures were transmitted through shortages rather than price rises, to take time from work to acquire necessities. This had an inevitable effect on the standard of public service and created an obvious private market for such employees to satisfy demands (perhaps for connection to an electricity supply) which they were unable (and eventually unwilling) to do in their official work time. Thus the unofficial economy took over from official services, exacerbating the inefficiencies. One positive by-product was that many participants were in fact quite used to operating in a private (albeit unofficial) market when privatisation was forced upon them.

Objectives for nationalised industries incorporated objectives such as income distribution, economic growth and industrialisation as well as a variety of special interests. This is important both in the context of nationalised industries and their privatisation. For it means that the objectives of nationalised industries in LDCs are even more confused than in MDCs, and there is likely to be even greater interference and application of incompatible objectives by governments. This is exacerbated in one-party states where minister, party and state seem inseparable, with public enterprises asked to satisfy the needs of all, as well as financial and market objectives. Nationalised industries may not even be clear who is the responsible minister to whom they are accountable (Rutabanzibwa, 1993). Thus these industries were virtually doomed to cause dissatisfaction, and their privatised successors entered a confused and difficult market. Governments will retain many of their objectives, for example for income distribution. But the very nature of the LDCs reduces the options available to achieve these (there will be no established system for reallocation via income taxes in an economy with a large subsistence or unofficial sector). Thus however unsatisfactory nationalised industries have been for addressing their myriad (and often contradictory objectives) their transfer to the private sector deprives governments of a significant policy tool if such industries are to be truly liberalised.

Even if the government eschews any non-commercial objectives for these industries, the economic environment into which they are released is, by definition, undeveloped. Statutory protection and conflicting ends can be removed, but market failure is likely to be significant, not only in the public utilities, where economies of scale cause complications world wide, but in other markets also. Transport and communications difficulties and low purchasing power limit the available market size. Moreover providing consumer protection through regulation, an accepted requirement in cases of market failure in the UK, poses difficulties for just the same reasons. Information on quality and price is sparse, and enforcement is especially problematic in countries which have evolved elaborate informal markets in response to years of price and exchange controls. Thus the scope for well regulated private industries is limited, and fears of monopoly or foreign exploitation may be justified.

10.3   *Macro-economic and distributional factors*

These, like most other complications, loom larger for LDCs than for MDCs. Privatisation is likely to be part of a programme aimed at budgetary and exchange rate stabilisation. The former is particularly important because of the transmission mechanism from deficit to inflation. Absence of other forms of borrowing forces monetisation of the debt, a significant cause of high inflation and price instability. Public enterprises are often seen as the chief culprits in causing these problems. Our discussion suggests that this is rather simplistic, since as in most countries the industries have been subject to incoherent and often contradictory objectives which make success very difficult to define, let alone achieve. Though public enterprises have rarely been the chief cause of the problem, they have certainly been instruments, and are often depicted as the scapegoats.

To reduce the public sector deficit nationalised industries must either reduce deficits (increase profits) or be transferred to the private sector at a price greater than the present value of future earnings (positive or negative) or be closed down. The latter course will be unacceptable in strategic sectors, and the first two both suppose some restructuring either before or after divestiture. Governments may be tempted to realise present assets as a solution to current problems without acknowledging the forgone (potential) profit once the industry is in private hands. There may also be other fiscal implications, for example for benefits or taxation proceeds, though this is more likely to be significant in middle income countries where such systems are less rudimentary than in the least developed economies.

The macro-economic environment in LDCs was very different from that prevailing in the UK when privatisation was initiated. The Conservatives' stringent view of the public sector borrowing requirement was a matter of choice rather than necessity. In LDCs an external crisis had arisen through pressure on foreign exchange, exogenously caused through deterioration in the terms of trade, and programmes of reform were often forced on governments by foreign agencies. This generally focused on both the size and the nature of the public sector deficit, previously met from increased money supply because the bond and equity markets were so narrow and underdeveloped. The new discipline required this practice to cease, which immediately caused examination of its nature.

A substantial part was due to public enterprise deficits (Adhikari and Kirkpatrick, 1990). Nationalised industries became the focus of the problem, though other public sector expenditure was also scrutinised. Provision of basic health and education services were threatened, an additional motive for governments to reduce nationalised industries' debts where possible in order to protect services still provided at a very minimal level.

The programme represents a complete volte-face in terms of political, economic and, more specifically, development ideology, particularly for those countries pursuing a state-dominated strategy. Whereas in the past international development agencies and bilateral donors had assisted in at least state-led development, this was now anathema. Many of the LDCs felt that their development was the subject of whims in the northern world, even where the economic logic was recognised. This caused some initial resistance to such programmes of privatisation, though the climate has improved somewhat, both with time and the willingness of aid donors to adapt strategies and timing to particular circumstances. There have also been internal conflicts in implementing reforms. The passage of time has enabled LDCs to adapt to some of these difficulties, though sometimes at the cost of the programme's credibility.

The change in development philosophy towards increased reliance on markets was enthusiastically embraced and proselytised by the World Bank and IMF, and their programmes were designed accordingly. These generally included drastic realignment of the exchange rate, reduction in protectionism and liberalisation of internal markets. Privatisation formed part of this process, and became a byword for the new ideology. This was no temporary rebalancing of economies in difficulty, but a drastic alteration in the way their development was enabled. Two important consequences for the present discussion ensued: the importance of the label of privatisation; and, more substantively, the significance of sequencing of the reforms. Here the parallel with Eastern European reforms is close and obvious.

10.4 Forms and sequencing of privatisation

Privatisation is generally applied to a much wider range of policies in LDCs than in MDCs. This is partly because the rhetoric of the new economic orthodoxy requires it (any action which can be so labelled is likely to win favour and aid) and partly because, as we have seen, circumstances differ both from those in the UK and between countries. However the basic classification of privatisation into denationalisation, liberalisation and contracting-out remains helpful. In this context contracting out may include franchising of whole industries, or their substantive internal reorganisation.

Denationalisation lay at the heart of the initial UK privatisation programme, reflecting *inter alia* the government priority for raising money for the exchequer. This was comparatively easy in a country where capital markets are well developed and it was possible to involve a large number of small investors. Indeed such involvement was portrayed as a significant goal, people's capitalism, though this may have been a thinly disguised wish to create a large proportion of the electorate with a vested interest in the health of the privatised industries and the re-election of a Conservative government. Britain enjoyed other advantages in its privatisation programme. Assets and accounts of the nationalised industries were generally well documented and agreed and the parliamentary process of debate and divestiture clear if not unchallenged. Even so it took more than 12 months to prepare a company for privatisation and enact the necessary legislation. In complex industries like water and electricity, where original proposals were withdrawn and redrafted in the light of discussion, the process took several years to complete.

Most developed countries have few of these advantages. The low level of local savings which was one of the justifications for creating nationalised industries (which it was hoped would contribute to exchequer surplus rather than deficits) renders the potential for involving local investors very small. Capital markets are often non-existent, rudimentary, or dominated by few local investors and many foreign actors. Thus flotation on a stock exchange in the British manner is not generally feasible.

Divestiture therefore has to take some other form. It may be a private sale, probably by tender, in which interested organisations are invited to bid for the industry, stating not only financial but other terms on which they would (undertake to) run it. Bidders usually include foreign investors, willing to take over firms in industries with which they are familiar but in new territories. This reverses the process of indigenisation which led to nationalisation and expropriation in the 1960s and 70s. It may also lead to undesirable concentration of production in a particular region, increasing monopoly power of the foreign investor. If domestic companies bid, the problems of market concentration are likely to be even greater since many developing economy markets are in any case very small, and oligopolists will be keen to extend their market control. Here arises a direct contradiction with liberalisation, the second strand of privatisation.

In the UK divestiture was generally 'all or nothing'; the industry was restructured so that management answered to private shareholders rather than the government, even if all the shares were not immediately sold (many were offered in tranches, though with more than 50 per cent being offered initially). Capital market restrictions in developing economies may make a partial sale more appropriate. However this raises problems of whether effective privatisation has really occurred, viz. whether there is an alteration in management attitude (Bouin and Michalet, 1991). Unless the government really cedes control to a different group there is unlikely to be much effect except for the (no doubt welcome) injection of capital from private investors. There may be little interest in such investment in a loss-making enterprise which continues under government control; potential profits, even if recognised by prospective investors, will not be realised while the old regime remains. Despite these difficulties partial or gradual privatisation is common in developing countries as a first stage in the process. The problem illustrates the more general issue of credibility and the ability of governments to precommit in bargaining with potential investors.

The difficulty of selling loss-making enterprises, the main focus of attention in LDCs, is particularly acute. Where losses are due to market protectionism which will be removed (for example by devaluation) some industries may automatically become more profitable. In this case they do not pose a problem for the budget deficit; indeed there is a danger of selling them for less than their true worth, worsening the long-term fiscal outlook. The true loss-makers, inappropriate or inefficiently run, are not an attractive prospect for local or international buyers, as the Malaysian government found when it offered the railway system for sale at a nominal one ringitt. This example illustrates both the opportunities and difficulties of such sales. If no conditions were attached the investment would be attractive for asset-stripping; but where the government wants operations to continue it must either accept that these are likely to be on different terms or provide a subsidy which continues to be a drain on the exchequer. Only if liberalisation and management reform alone can transform the industry is a sale likely to be in the national interest. These are just the factors highlighted by the 'Jones' cost-benefit model of divestiture.

Liberalisation poses even more difficulties for less developed countries. The original justification for widespread public ownership was extensive market failure, both at micro and macro level, as we have seen in the previous section. Such failure is not dissolved by the recognition of government failure which is an intrinsic part of the drive for privatisation. Market failure has two aspects: the familiar problems of natural or other monopoly, externalities and information poverty, all of which are much greater in countries with poor infrastructure and low income, unequally distributed; and the consequent difficulty for governments to achieve objectives through usual market mechanisms. Here the order in which reforms are enacted has a crucial influence on their effectiveness. Such sequencing can be considered at three levels: whether privatisation proceeds or follows broader economic reforms (e.g. liberalisation of the exchange rate or agricultural markets); the order in which industries are privatised; and whether such industries should be reformed before privatisation or sold 'intact'. For example, as Booth (1991) demonstrates for Tanzania, liberalising prices to increase incentives to farmers is worse than useless if it precedes changes which enable them to increase output. Such policies merely cause hardship by allowing the price of food to rise without any consequent increase in supply. Privatisation must therefore be seen as a small (but significant) part of a much broader and very radical reform.

Such sequencing is not a new difficulty in development policy: where transport is undeveloped there is no point in providing trucks before roads, but roads will be unused if there are no suitable vehicles. Much of the problem stems from a comparative static approach in which countries identify a desirable state and try to replicate its characteristics without examining the dynamic process of arriving there. Such dynamic forces are particularly significant in a change as radical as the current programmes of restructuring.

The most significant ordering is between structural adjustment and economic liberalisation: privatisation comes into both categories through its interpretation as either ownership, and probably more significantly management, change and as liberalisation of particular markets. The problem arises where real quantity constraints impede the otherwise desirable adjustments which they induce. Liberalising the exchange rate so that the domestic prices of imports rise is of no help if domestic supplies cannot expand to fill at least part of the supply gap. Similarly improved incentives for exports are not useful if export earnings cannot be transformed into raw materials or consumption goods because of transport difficulties. These problems will all be exacerbated by information gaps, and the programme itself may cause sufficient confusion to further cloud the issue. Where such difficulties threaten political stability potential problems are even greater. It is of course much easier to define these problems than their solutions, but the difficulties experienced by many countries in the implementation of their programmes owe much to these factors. This is not an argument for abandoning the reforms, which in most cases seem to offer the only feasible means of progress, but for exercising patience in their timing and caution in their sequencing.

International aid and lending agencies are significant players in the privatisation game, and will have their own objectives which determine the constraints under which local governments operate. Just as the World Bank (IBRD) and International Monetary Fund (IMF) played a vital role in enabling the public sector to develop, they are also crucial in the reversal of this process. The IBRD and IMF provided more than passive discipline to countries where their help was needed. In the two decades before 1980 they had been active proponents of state intervention in the development process. This did not lie easily with the theory of public policy which suggested that markets should operate except where market failure made this inappropriate and which predominated in the 1980s.

Here the balance between market and government failure is particularly fine. Just as government intervention proved an inadequate response to market difficulties in the 1960s, so markets known to be monopolistic or have other significant failure will provide unsatisfactory alternatives to the present perceived government failure. To some extent this problem is recognised through the ordering of the privatisation process. The much greater extent of public enterprise in LDCs offers opportunities other than in the traditional natural monopolies for early privatisation. Many countries start by privatising small businesses (for example tourist operations) which can compete with both other domestic and foreign companies. This follows the example in the UK where initial divestiture was of companies which were in government ownership for a variety of reasons, and generally operated in reasonably competitive markets.

Indeed British proponents of privatisation recommend for political purposes that privatisation should start with the 'easy' cases, i.e. those for which markets are reasonably strong and which will be generally popular. This reduces any resistance to the programme, particularly if investors benefit and consumers do not suffer. The issue of privatising the traditional natural monopoly utilities has not yet arisen, as programmes have proceeded rather more slowly than expected, and by concentrating first on the smaller enterprises. Delaying these privatisations also postpones the difficult question of regulation. The argument for retaining utilities is that they form part of a strategic sector which needs to remain in state ownership. This discussion tends to be somewhat circular, since the strategic sector is generally defined as industries which cannot be privatised.

Exceptions among the traditional utilities are telecommunications and electricity. Several countries (including Chile, Jamaica, Malaysia and Mexico) have sold telecoms industries at a relatively early stage. Telecommunications benefits from increasing competitiveness and cost reduction through technological change, and a general understanding and willingness to invest by overseas investors. Moreover it is not usually seen as a vital factor in the development process. Electricity competition is being introduced mostly at generation level where economies of scale do not predominate, rather than distribution level; the process of purchase from the generators can itself provide a competitive environment (for example in Turkey). Again this follows the UK pattern, though there are increasing doubts as to the efficacy of such competition there.

Because of difficulty with natural monopolies, privatisation usually starts with relatively small firms, as we have seen, and proves reasonably popular at this level. (No doubt governments lavish care and resources on these front-runners for the sake of their own reputations.) Where the financial sector is largely publicly owned this has also often been involved in early privatisation moves (for example Korea), and transport is a popular target. Agriculture is often little directly affected, but may see significant changes through reform of marketing boards and parastatals, and is often drastically affected by price liberalisation.

In view of the difficulties inherent in both divestiture and liberalisation, much of the privatisation activity has concentrated on internal reorganisation as emphasised in the Ott and Hartley model (1991). Privatisation is here taken to mean that management acts in the same manner as that of a private company, with both commercial objectives and financial accountability. If this can be imposed there may be gains in managerial and economic efficiency, while the enterprise is retained in government control and the limits of the market to impose these disciplines effectively are recognised. Reduction of deficits will of course help the government's fiscal situation, though there will be few immediate gains from capitalising the value of the industry.

Reorganisation may be a necessary accompaniment rather than an alternative to divestiture. In this case it may be reorganised prior to sale, to improve its attractiveness to investors, or sold in its current (sorry) state, leaving buyers to bid on the basis of potential rather than realised profits and enact the necessary reforms themselves. Opinion differs as to the appropriate sequence, in this as in many other reforms. If the government accepts that the firm should be sold without 'strings', so the only considerations are commercial, it should determine merely which provide greater yield, balancing the costs of prior reform against the lost revenue if potential gains are not fully reflected in the sale price. However this requires great prescience about the effectiveness of such reforms, which are often very difficult to enact with a reluctant management. (One advantage which the British government had was the ability to 'pay-off' the management through pay rises and share offers, so that they cooperated in the privatisation process; this was vital both for speed and efficacy.) It is probably better to leave an industry to the mercies of its new private owners if reforms are to be fully effective, otherwise the government merely creates yet another rod for its own back in its attempts to institute reforms.

If reorganisation occurs without divestiture the government must solve the inherent problem of discipline for management. This will be difficult if, as in many countries, such positions are closely related to political influence and granted as part of a non-commercial bargain. Reform requires the alteration of the entire political process and its incumbent difficulties. But without sanctions reform cannot be effective. The government can clearly remove any obvious anomalies arising from conflicting or inappropriate objectives (political difficulties so imposed may be partly deflected by reference to pressures from external agencies); but it may not be able to extract itself from the web of political obligations with which the public sector has become involved. This is a mark of how much greater government failure has been in LDCs than in MDCs, where such influence is disapproved of and generally avoided. It also demonstrates the relative youth of the political process in many LDCs.

One way to untangle this dilemma may be to franchise the operations of the industries, thus employing managers on new terms, even if the personnel themselves remain the same. Such franchise may indeed be to a management group formed from the industry, but the terms on which they operate can change, and may well be explicit for the first time. However some external scrutiny may be required to ensure that governments do not yield to pressure to reinstate the status quo, or some other unsatisfactory arrangement. Again the lack of information about existing and potential operations will be a handicap in such an explicit contract, but the provision and checking of additional data may themselves form part of the contract. This route is one being explored in many developing countries with the support of international agencies.

One compromise with both legal and economic ramifications is that of joint ventures. These are based on foreign capital and technological knowledge partnered by local access to markets and information. They may be formed either by the government selling some equity to a foreign operator (usually a multinational corporation) in an existing enterprise, or by a specific agreement to set up new operations. In either case the extent of the agreement needs to be carefully defined, causing some familiar difficulties of definition where information is scarce or unequal between the partners. Nevertheless this route is being increasingly explored as a means to retain local involvement while attracting much needed foreign capital and technical expertise.

The distinction between public and private companies has been assumed in this discussion, but the classification of some operations is less clear cut. These include those of non-government organisations, both domestic and foreign, who often undertake activities which in other countries would be part of the private market. They often originated in charitable trusts or aid agencies who have initiated undertakings which become self-financing, such as agricultural or craft projects. Where these are not subsidised they can be considered part of the private sector, and may be a significant part of local economies.

10.5   Political factors

All governments must identify the winners and losers from privatisation, as from any other policy and we have seen in the previous section how political factors may affect the process of privatisation. This is not merely because of their responsibility for anticipating the effects on the population, but to ensure political support. Here again the advice of British enthusiasts is telling. The labour force, one of the chief potential losers from privatisation because of the benefits it gains from public ownership, needs to be reassured about the consequences. Employment conditions and pensions rights may be secured on existing terms (as occurred in Malaysia). Such bargains run counter to increased managerial efficiency if the latter is to be obtained by reducing the wage bill; but such compromises in the short term may be justified by the longer-term freedom to alter the size of the workforce and employ new recruits on different terms. A strategy like this may reassure individual employees, who can be further enticed by the promise of shares in the firm, but trade unions will still see their power weakened by a reduction in the total number of the industry's employees. Ensuring union cooperation may therefore be more difficult than for their individual members, but undermining support from their constituency would considerably weaken them.

How far the government honours such agreements may however be open to question. Just as changing economic regulation alters the implicit bargain between shareholders and government *ex post* (see Price, Chapter 3) so bargains with employees may also be broken. An example in the UK concerned the Ravenscraig steel works in Scotland, a part of British Steel; at privatisation employment was assured until 1995. However attempts were made to close it in 1990, when only public uproar ensured government support, and closure was finalised in 1992. The British government may have had an advantage in making such agreements which its successors will not enjoy if there is a history of ignoring such assurances.

The losers from privatisation in developing countries will be not only employees but also contractors who have turned the lax conditions in nationalised industries to their own advantage. The latter will see not only fewer opportunities for profits, but the need to invest in a new network of contacts if management personnel alter. Emphasis on changed management in developing countries is very different from that in the UK where managers stayed largely the same (indeed continuity was vital for the smooth transition) and changes were assumed to emanate from the profit motive introduced by private ownership. Obstruction from management could be a major handicap in both preparing and selling enterprises, where incumbent interests (and their contractors) see the process as damaging. Some sweetener may be required, as with other employees, to make an opening for market forces.

Consumers may also lose in the short term if depressed prices are liberated. In the longer term the introduction of competition and cost-reducing mechanisms should be to their benefit, but the transitional problems may be acute, particularly where there is extreme poverty and no safety net. Humanitarian concerns are likely to be exacerbated by political anxieties where hardship is acute among the urban poor, and such transitional problems may require temporary help from aid agencies. There is an obvious danger of impeding the development of local markets through such intervention, or of continuing the help for an inappropriately long time (the familiar problem of protecting infant industries which refuse to grow up). Here again sensitivity to local conditions in determining sequencing is vital.

The identification of the winners depends on the objectives of the reforms, the structure of the economy and the time scale involved. In the sense that the reforms are instigated in the best interests of the country, all citizens are winners. This is the familiar cake analogy: the reforms can enable the cake to grow larger even if some people have smaller slices in the short term. But there will be some immediate beneficiaries. These mainly will be families which have been traditionally influential in the economy, some ethnic groups in the case of states serving or protecting special interests, and the middle classes (who might be defined as those who manage to operate any system to their own advantage). These groups will be valuable allies for the government, but care must be taken that the benefits (compared with the experience of losers) do not harbour class or ethnic jealousy which may be politically destabilising. (Booth's study of one area of Tanzania found that fears of ethnic favouritism, either to the old European settlers or newer Asian and Arab immigrants, had been exaggerated, but changes had generated a new class resentment against a mixed race middle class which included Africans.)

The emphasis on profitability and financial measures undermines the previous social objectives of government, which must now be met directly through an often undeveloped fiscal system, rather than informally through subsidies and special deals. This will cause some resentment, which will be most effectively dissipated by the success of the reforms enabling not only greater access to products, but increased purchasing power to all, including beneficiaries from the previous regime.

Assessment

The variety and extent of privatisation programmes is as great as the range of countries included under this heading and their own patterns of state ownership. The late 1980s and early 1990s have been difficult years for all economies, and progress has almost everywhere been slower than had at first been hoped. Political changes have not been consistent, though there is a general move towards governments who are prepared to implement market solutions, despite some backlash. Many governments, concentrating on the legal transfer of enterprises with inadequate information, have become bogged down in the process and made disappointing progress.

However this has not led to abandonment of schemes, and programmes continue with varying paces and at different stages. The most successful divestitures have been of 'modern' industries which have attracted foreign investment, for example Telecoms and MAS in Malaysia. These provide an injection of overseas capital and management discipline, often without wresting control from indigenous hands. (Indeed the transfer of Malaysian industries to Bumiputera holding companies emphasised the government's priorities.) The continuation of local management may dissipate the advantages of changed ownership, but the concept and practice of private capital seem to achieve some success themselves, especially in industries which are operating in a similar mode and markets to those of the MDCs.

In countries where the stage of development or political factors make such definite progress difficult, most concentration has been on other aspects of the reform programme, with initial attempts to liberalise prices as a prelude to rectifying financial problems in public enterprises and parastatals. The most important task here is to ensure that prices reflect resource values when subsidies and import controls are removed and exchange rates adjusted to more realistic levels. Sequencing here is as important as in other parts of the liberalisation programme, since supply must be able to respond to these price messages, but these reforms should clearly precede any necessary restructuring of public bodies.

Delay in the privatisation programme may be due to a sensible reassessment of priorities and realities in local circumstances. International agencies, having established the principle of privatisation through the energy with which they initially forced the acceptance of such programmes now seem to take a more relaxed attitude to the policy; this is welcome when the variety of countries poses different issues and suggests varied solutions in the appropriate extent and ordering of reform. Of course there is a danger that momentum so lost will never be regained, but a more cautious approach is more likely to yield long-term benefits if it can be sustained and gain political acceptance from within the countries concerned.

With such variety of circumstances and programmes the initial models of privatisation provide a valuable framework. Bos's concept of 'optimal' public ownership in light of the conflicts between allocative and managerial efficiency is particularly significant for developing countries where local stock markets and available money for investment are inadequate for flotation. A gradual programme of private involvement can be devised, with reassurances to both the public and private investors. This has the danger of initiating no real change in management practices, and is likely to be effective only if a programme of complete reform is defined and has credibility with management. In this context the initial force of these programmes may be helpful in convincing participants not only of their value but of their inevitability. Partial privatisation is achieved either by selling part of a publicly owned enterprise or by setting up a new one as a joint stock company, defining a specific legal framework for the operations. Both methods are being applied.

Here the model which Ott and Hartley present, showing the importance of internal management reforms in the context both of ownership and liberalised markets is significant. The package of reforms in developing countries often concentrates initially on liberalising both external and internal prices. Economists would welcome liberalisation as the most effective way to achieve both allocative and managerial efficiency; other policies are likely to be poor substitutes for such market forces. Any frustration at slow progress to formal divestiture should therefore be curbed in recognition of the prior importance of more significant changes.

Policy changes reflect a complete change in development philosophy, from a state-centred to a market-centred approach, and have consequently redefined the relation and boundary between the public and private sectors. As in the UK, where privatisation began, this is largely a reaction to perceived government failure in organising the public sector to the benefit of the economy at large (rather than any particular interest group). There is a danger that the public sector baby will everywhere be thrown out with the bath water, and that in discovering government failure states and agencies forget that market failure is also rampant. The consequences of inappropriate balance (in either direction) are much more serious in poor countries which are vulnerable to more than a cold when their developed partners sneeze. The model presented by Jones, Tandon and Vogelsang (1990) has the merit of concentrating the analysis on the particular circumstances of the country concerned. It uses a cost-benefit technique which is familiar to developing countries (indeed this application was evolved for the IBRD), though like all such analyses it is necessarily partial, relying on assumptions about other variables in the economy. Nevertheless its focus on the particular issues facing each divestiture is a welcome change from generalised rhetoric.

The challenge of privatisation world wide is to find the appropriate balance between public and private sectors while providing necessary safety nets which do not distort the very incentives which are the main benefits of market forces. Where political destabilisation, civil war, famine and impoverishment are real dangers that balance is likely to be different and may take longer to reach.

References

Adhikari, R. and **Kirkpatrick, C.** (1990) Public enterprise in less developed countries in J. Heath (ed.) *Public Enterprise at the Crossroads*, Routledge.

Index